4 1344 00015

MathWorks 10 Workbook

Lillian Osborne High School

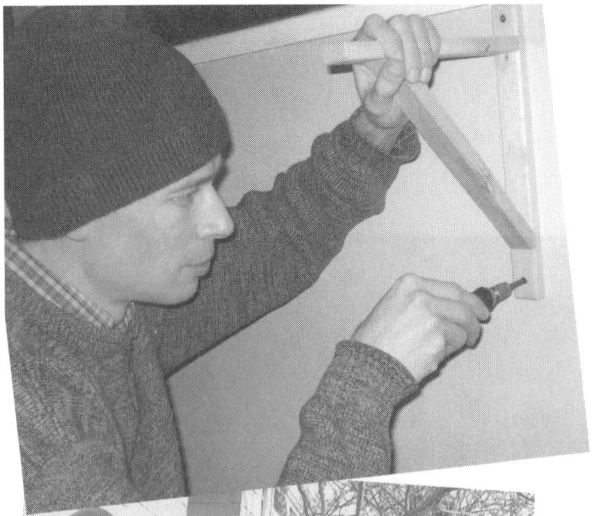
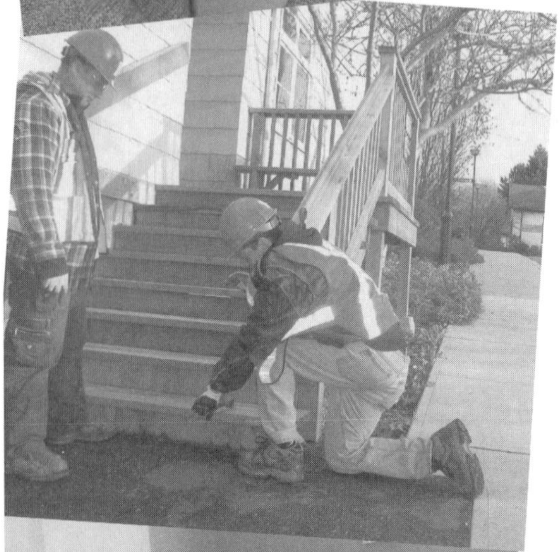
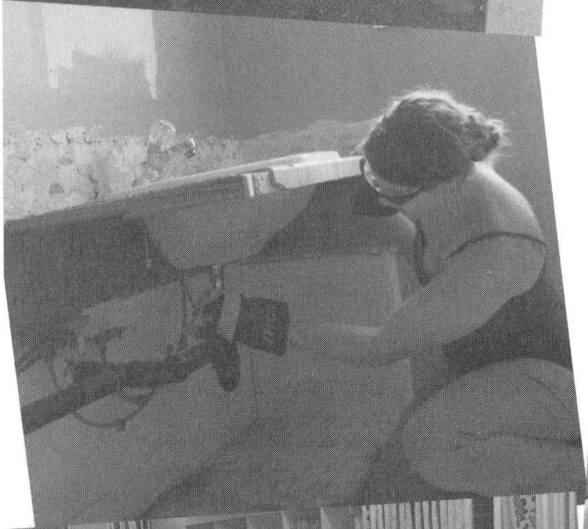
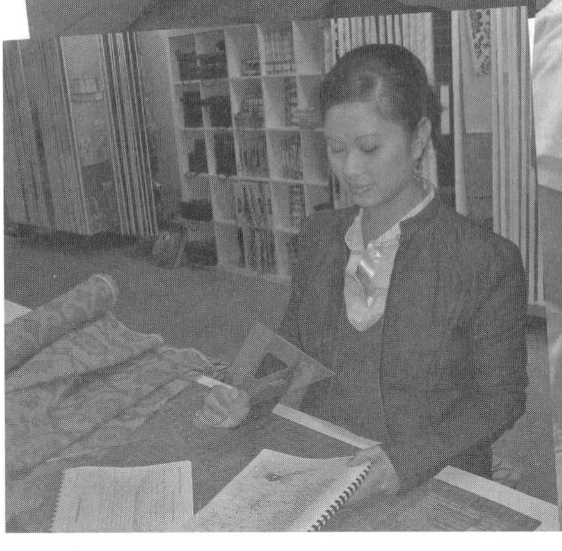
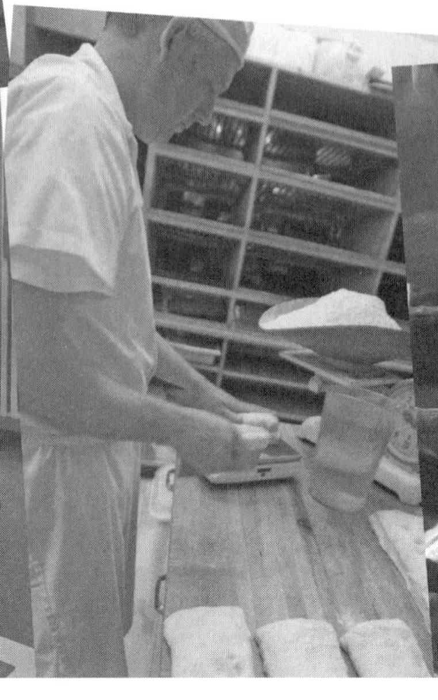
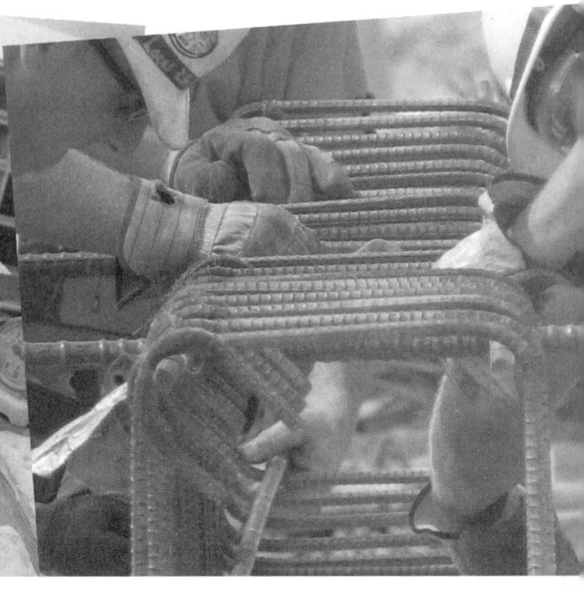

MathWorks 10
Workbook

Pacific Educational Press
Vancouver, Canada

Copyright Pacific Educational Press 2010

ISBN 978-1-89576-694-3

Published by Pacific Educational Press
Faculty of Education, University of British Columbia
411 – 2389 Health Sciences Mall
Vancouver, BC V6T 1Z3
Telephone: 604-822-5385
Fax: 604-822-6603
Email: pep.sales@ubc.ca
Website: http://pacificedpress.ca

All rights reserved. Pacific Educational Press is a member of Access Copyright. No part of this publication may be reproduced, stored in a retrieval system, or transmitted in any form or by any means, electronic, mechanical, photocopying, recording, or otherwise without the prior written permission of the publisher or a licence from Access Copyright. For a copyright licence, visit www.accesscopyright.ca or call toll-free 1-800-893-5777.

3   4   5   6   7   15   14   13   12

Writer
Katharine Borgen, Vancouver School Board and University of British Columbia

Consultants
Katharine Borgen, PhD, Vancouver School Board and University of British Columbia
Jordie Yow, Mathematics Reviewer

Design, Illustration, and Layout
Sharlene Eugenio
Five Seventeen

Editing
Catherine Edwards
David Gargaro
Leah Giesbrecht
Nadine Pedersen
Katrina Petrik

Photographs
Cover photo courtesy Colin Pickell;
Men fixing stairs: Leah Giesbrecht;
Woman measuring fabric: Sharlene Eugenio;
Surveyor: Jacqueline Chandler/ Public domain/ Wikimedia Commons/ FEMA-42251;
Man mowing lawn: Selmer Van Alten/ www.flickr.com;
Veterinarian: Veronica Pierce/ Public domain/ Wikimedia Commons/ VIRIN 050722-F-3177P-047;
Chapter 1: ©Jean-marie Guyon | Dreamstime.com;
Chapter 2: Courtesy U.S. Army Element Assembled Chemical Weapons Alternatives;
Chapter 3: Courtesy Ashlea Earl-Robinson;
Chapter 4: Morgan M. Wayling;
Chapter 5: Photo by Gary Schotel, Quesnel, BC;
Chapter 6: Leah Giesbrecht;
Chapter 7: Leah Giesbrecht.

Printed and bound in Canada.

Contents

How to Use this Book   7

1 Unit Pricing and Currency Exchange   9

    1.1 Proportional Reasoning   9
    1.2 Unit Price   26
    1.3 Setting a Price   36
    1.4 On Sale!   49
    1.5 Currency Exchange Rates   59
    Chapter Test   70

2 Earning an Income   74

    2.1 Wages and Salaries   74
    2.2 Alternative Ways to Earn Money   87
    2.3 Additional Earnings   97
    2.4 Deductions and Net Pay   106
    Chapter Test   114

3 Length, Area, and Volume   118

    3.1 Systems of Measurement   118
    3.2 Converting Measurements   131
    3.3 Surface Area   142
    3.4 Volume   158
    Chapter Test   169

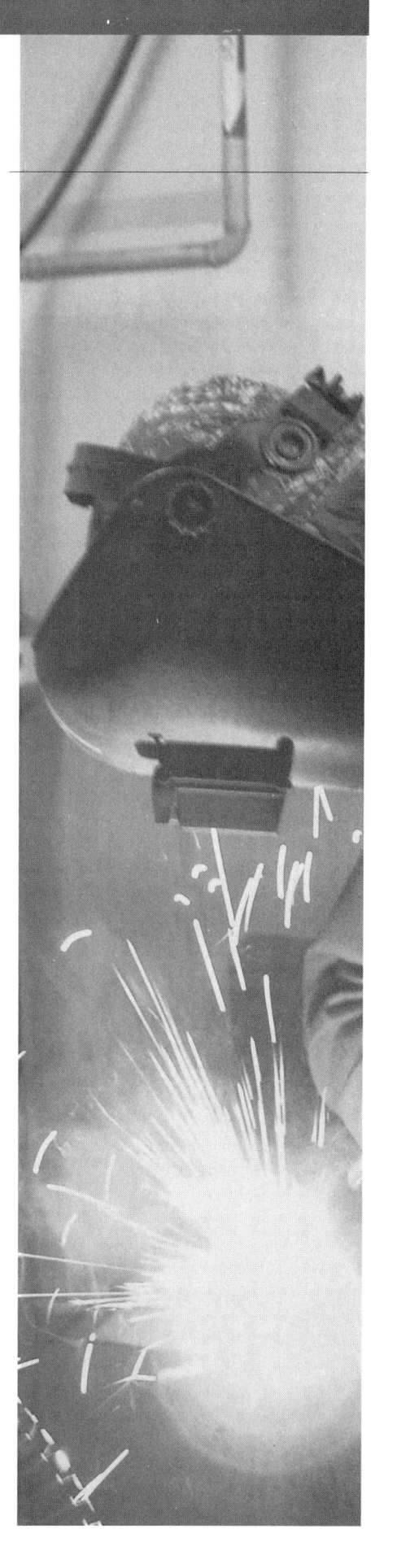

Contents continued

4 Mass, Temperature, and Volume — 175

- **4.1** Temperature Conversions — 175
- **4.2** Mass in the Imperial System — 183
- **4.3** Mass in the Système International — 195
- **4.4** Making Conversions — 203
- Chapter Test — 210

5 Angles and Parallel Lines — 214

- **5.1** Measuring, Drawing, and Estimating Angles — 214
- **5.2** Angle Bisectors and Perpendicular Lines — 225
- **5.3** Non-Parallel Lines and Transversals — 231
- **5.4** Parallel Lines and Transversals — 239
- Chapter Test — 248

6 Similarity of Figures — 253

- **6.1** Similar Polygons — 253
- **6.2** Determining if Two Polygons Are Similar — 265
- **6.3** Drawing Similar Polygons — 271
- **6.4** Similar Triangles — 277
- Chapter Test — 284

7 Trigonometry of Right Triangles — 288

- **7.1** The Pythagorean Theorem — 288
- **7.2** The Sine Ratio — 297
- **7.3** The Cosine Ratio — 308
- **7.4** The Tangent Ratio — 318
- **7.5** Finding Angles and Solving Right Triangles — 324
- Chapter Test — 336

Glossary — 340

Answer Key — 342

How to Use This Book

This workbook is a companion to *MathWorks 10* student resource, the authorized resource for the WNCP course, Apprenticeship and Workplace Mathematics. The *MathWorks 10 Workbook* is a valuable learning tool when used in conjunction with the student resource, or on its own. It emphasizes mathematical skill-building through worked examples and practice problems.

Here, you will learn and use the practical mathematics required in the workplace. Whether you plan to enroll in college, learn a trade, or enter the workforce after graduating from secondary school, the mathematical skills in this workbook will support you at work and in your daily life.

The *MathWorks 10 Workbook* contains seven chapters. Chapters are divided into sections, each focussing on a key mathematical concept. Each chapter includes the following features.

Review

Each chapter opens with a review of mathematical processes and terms you will need to understand to complete the chapter's lessons. Practice questions are included.

Example

Each example includes a problem and its solution. The problem is solved step by step. Written descriptions of each mathematical operation used to solve the problem are included.

New Skills

The chapter's core mathematical concepts are introduced here. This section often includes real-world examples of where and how the concepts are used.

Build Your Skills

This is a set of mathematical problems for you to solve. It appears after each new concept is introduced and will let you practise the concepts you have just learned about. Build Your Skills questions often focus on workplace applications of mathematical concepts.

Practise Your New Skills

The section's key concepts are presented as review problems at the end of each chapter section.

Chapter Test

At the end of each chapter, a chapter test is provided for review and assessment of learning.

Definitions

New mathematical terms are defined in the sidebar columns. They are also included in the glossary at the back of the book.

Answer Key

An answer key to this workbook's questions is located at the back of the book.

Glossary

Definitions for mathematical terms are provided here. To increase understanding, some glossary definitions include illustrations.

Chapter 1

Unit Pricing and Currency Exchange

Canadian wheat is processed into flour and sold nationally, where most of it becomes baked goods. Canada also exports about 20 million tonnes of its wheat and grain each year.

Proportional Reasoning 1.1

REVIEW: WORKING WITH FRACTIONS

In this section, you will use fractions to solve for unknown values.

Example 1

Simplify $\frac{18}{27}$.

SOLUTION

factor: one of two or more numbers that, when multiplied together, form a product. For example, 1, 2, 3, and 6 are factors of the product 6 because:

$1 \times 6 = 6$

$2 \times 3 = 6$

$3 \times 2 = 6$

$6 \times 1 = 6$

To simplify a fraction, state the fraction in its lowest terms. To find the lowest terms, divide the numerator and the denominator by their largest common **factor**.

$\frac{18}{27}$ ← numerator
← denominator

Identify the factors of 18 and 27.

$18 = \{1, 2, 3, 6, 9, 18\}$

$27 = \{1, 3, 9, 27\}$

The largest factor common to both 18 and 27 is 9. Divide both the numerator and the denominator by 9.

$$\frac{18}{27} = \frac{18 \div 9}{27 \div 9}$$

$$\frac{18 \div 9}{27 \div 9} = \frac{2}{3}$$

$$\frac{18}{27} = \frac{2}{3}$$

ALTERNATIVE SOLUTION

The fractions $\frac{18}{27}$, $\frac{6}{9}$, and $\frac{2}{3}$ are equivalent fractions because they represent the same amount.

Using the largest common factor when simplifying fractions takes the least number of steps, but you can use any common factor.

$$\frac{18}{27} = \frac{18 \div 3}{27 \div 3}$$ Simplify, using the factor 3.

$$\frac{18 \div 3}{27 \div 3} = \frac{6}{9}$$

$$\frac{18}{27} = \frac{6}{9}$$

$$\frac{6}{9} = \frac{6 \div 3}{9 \div 3}$$ Simplify further, again using the factor 3.

$$\frac{6 \div 3}{9 \div 3} = \frac{2}{3}$$

$$\frac{6}{9} = \frac{2}{3}$$

BUILD YOUR SKILLS

1. Simplify these fractions to their lowest terms.

    a) $\frac{4}{16} = \frac{1}{4}$

    b) $\frac{3 \div 3}{12 \div 3} = \frac{1}{4}$

    c) $\frac{25}{75} = \frac{1}{3}$

    d) $\frac{15}{21} = \frac{5}{7}$

    e) $\frac{8}{18} = \frac{4}{9}$

    f) $\frac{45}{100} = \frac{9}{20}$

    g) $\frac{20}{50} = \frac{2}{5}$

    h) $\frac{3}{21} = \frac{1}{7}$

    i) $\frac{7}{56} = \frac{1}{8}$

Handwritten work:

1) $\frac{6}{7} + \frac{8}{7} \to \frac{6}{7} \times \frac{1}{1} = \frac{6}{7}$

2) $\frac{12}{5} - \frac{1}{10} = \frac{4 \times 12}{4 \times 5} - \frac{1 \times 2}{10 \times 2} = \frac{48}{20} - \frac{2}{20} = \frac{46}{20} = \frac{23}{10}$

3) $-\frac{1}{3} \times \frac{4}{5} = \frac{-4}{15}$

4) $\frac{4}{3} \div \frac{3}{2} \to \frac{4}{3} \cdot \frac{2}{3} = \frac{8}{9}$

Example 2

Solve for *x* in this equation containing fractions.

$$\frac{x}{16} = \frac{5}{24}$$

SOLUTION

To solve an equation, the same operation must be applied to both sides of the equation.

Begin by multiplying both sides of the equation by the same number so that you can clear it of fractions (by eliminating the denominators). This will allow you to isolate *x*.

The simplest multiplier is the lowest common denominator of the two fractions.

Identify the **multiples** of 16 and 24.

16 = {16, 32, 48, 64, 80, ...}

24 = {24, 48, 72, 96, ...}

multiple: the product of a number and any other number. For example, 2, 4, 6, and 8 are some multiples of 2 because:

$2 \times 1 = 2$

$2 \times 2 = 4$

$2 \times 3 = 6$

$2 \times 4 = 8$

The lowest common multiple between 16 and 24 is 48, so begin solving the equation by multiplying both fractions by 48.

$$\frac{x}{16} = \frac{5}{24}$$

$$48 \times \frac{x}{16} = \frac{5}{24} \times 48 \qquad \text{Multiply by 48.}$$

$$\frac{48x}{16} = \frac{240}{24} \qquad \text{Simplify.}$$

$$3x = 10$$

$$\frac{3x}{3} = \frac{10}{3} \qquad \text{Divide by 3 to isolate } x.$$

$$x = \frac{10}{3} \text{ or } 3\frac{1}{3}$$

ALTERNATIVE SOLUTION

You did not need to use 48 as your multiplier. Any common multiple will work, and people often choose to multiply by the product of the denominators.

In this question, the product would be 16 multiplied by 24. You will get the same answer in the end, but you will work with larger numbers.

$$\frac{x}{16} = \frac{5}{24}$$

$$(24 \times 16) \times \frac{x}{16} = \frac{5}{24} \times (16 \times 24) \qquad \text{Multiply both sides by the product of the denominators.}$$

$$384 \times \frac{x}{16} = \frac{5}{24} \times 384 \qquad \text{Simplify.}$$

$$\frac{384x}{16} = \frac{1920}{24}$$

$$24x = 80$$

$$\frac{24x}{24} = \frac{80}{24} \qquad \text{Divide both sides by 24 to isolate } x.$$

$$x = \frac{80}{24}$$

$$x = \frac{80 \div 8}{24 \div 8} \qquad \text{Simplify, using the factor 8.}$$

$$x = \frac{10}{3} \text{ or } 3\frac{1}{3} \text{ or } 3.\overline{3}$$

> If x is not a whole number, it is best to leave the answer as a fraction or in mixed numeral form rather than as a decimal because the decimal answer would often have to be rounded.

BUILD YOUR SKILLS

2. Solve for x.

a) $\frac{x}{10} = \frac{40}{50}$

$\frac{40 \cdot 10}{50} = \frac{400}{50} = 8$

b) $\frac{12}{16} = \frac{18}{x}$

$\frac{18 \cdot 16}{12} = \frac{288}{12} = 24$

c) $\frac{56}{64} = \frac{x}{8}$

$\frac{56 \cdot 8}{64} = \frac{448}{64} = 7$

d) $\frac{18}{27} = \frac{36}{x}$

$\frac{36 \cdot 27}{18} = \frac{972}{18} = 54$

e) $\frac{x}{2056} = \frac{3}{4}$

$\frac{2056 \cdot 3}{4} = \frac{6168}{4} = 1542$

f) $\frac{3}{12} = \frac{15}{x}$

$\frac{15 \cdot 12}{3} = \frac{180}{3} = 60$

g) $\frac{3}{5} = \frac{x}{460}$

$\frac{3 \cdot 460}{5} = \frac{1380}{5} = 276$

h) $\frac{25}{x} = \frac{40}{200}$

$\frac{25 \cdot 200}{40} = \frac{5000}{40} = 125$

NEW SKILLS: WORKING WITH RATIO AND PROPORTION

ratio: a comparison between two numbers measured in the same units

When a carpenter bonds two pieces of wood with epoxy resin, she must first mix the epoxy with a hardener. She mixes these materials in a **ratio** of 10 to 1, where there are 10 parts of epoxy to 1 part of hardener. This ratio can be written as 10:1 or as a fraction, $\frac{10}{1}$.

If the carpenter wanted to use 150 parts of epoxy, she would need 15 parts of hardener. This would give her a ratio of 150 to 15 between the amount of epoxy and the amount of hardener. You can write this as 150:15 or as $\frac{150}{15}$.

The ratio $\frac{150}{15}$ can be simplified to $\frac{10}{1}$.

$$\frac{150}{15} = \frac{150 \div 15}{15 \div 15}$$

$$\frac{150 \div 15}{15 \div 15} = \frac{10}{1}$$

$$\frac{150}{15} = \frac{10}{1}$$

It is common to express ratios as fractions when doing calculations.

proportion: a fractional statement of equality between two ratios

When you state that two ratios are equal, as they are in the following equation, you have written a **proportion**.

$$\frac{150}{15} = \frac{10}{1}$$

For more information, see page 12 of *MathWorks 10*.

Example 3

Charles works as a cook in a restaurant. His chicken soup recipe contains:

- 11 cups of seasoned broth
- 5 cups of diced vegetables
- 3 cups of rice
- 3 cups of chopped chicken

He wants to make the recipe at home for his parents. To reduce the recipe yield, he needs to know what the ratios are between the quantities of ingredients.

a) What is the ratio of vegetables to chicken?

b) What is the ratio of broth to vegetables?

c) What is the ratio of chicken to rice?

d) What is the ratio of the chicken to the total ingredients in the recipe?

SOLUTION

a) Since there are 5 cups of vegetables and 3 cups of chicken, the ratio of vegetables to chicken is 5:3 or $\frac{5}{3}$.

b) Since there are 11 cups of broth and 5 cups of vegetables, the ratio of broth to vegetables is 11:5 or $\frac{11}{5}$.

c) There are 3 cups of chicken and 3 cups of rice, so the ratio of chicken to rice is 3:3 or $\frac{3}{3}$. This can be simplified to 1:1 or $\frac{1}{1}$.

d) There are 3 cups of chicken in the recipe, and a total of 22 cups of ingredients. The ratio of chicken to the total amount of ingredients is 3:22 or $\frac{3}{22}$.

> A ratio can have a numerator larger than the denominator. Because a ratio compares two numbers, do not rewrite it as a mixed fraction.

> Although $\frac{1}{1}$ is usually written as the number 1, keep it as a fraction when it is a ratio comparing two numbers.

BUILD YOUR SKILLS

3. For a silk screening project, Jan mixes a shade of orange ink. She uses a ratio of red ink to yellow ink of 2:3 and yellow ink to white ink of 3:1.

    a) How many mL of yellow ink would she need if she used 500 mL of white ink?

    b) How many mL of red ink would she need if she used 750 mL of yellow ink?

4. On a bicycle with more than one gear, the ratio between the number of teeth on the front gear and the number of teeth on the back gear determines how easy it is to pedal. If the front gear has 30 teeth and the back gear has 10 teeth, what is the ratio of front teeth to back teeth?

5. Some conveyor belts have two pulleys. If one pulley has a diameter of 45 cm and another has a diameter of 20 cm, what is the ratio of the smaller diameter to the larger diameter?

6. Bank tellers use ratios when converting currencies. If $1.00 CAD equals approximately 1.13 Australian dollars, what is the ratio of Canadian dollars to Australian dollars?

7. What is the ratio of 250 mL of grape juice concentrate to 1 L of water? (Hint: Convert both measurements to the same units. There are 1000 mL in 1 L.)

8. A mechanic mixes oil with gas to lubricate the cylinders in a motorcycle engine. He uses 1 part oil and 32 parts gas. What is the ratio of oil to gas?

Example 4

Tom and Susan make $180.00 from holding a garage sale. Because Tom contributed fewer items to the sale, the money is to be divided between Tom and Susan in the ratio of 1:2. How much money will each person receive?

SOLUTION

Since the ratio is 1:2, this means that for every $1.00 Tom receives, Susan receives $2.00. Stated another way, this means that for every $3.00 earned, Tom gets $1.00 and Susan gets $2.00.

Therefore, Tom receives $\frac{1}{3}$ of the money and Susan receives $\frac{2}{3}$ of it.

$\frac{1}{3} \times 180 = 60$

$\frac{2}{3} \times 180 = 120$

Tom gets $60.00 and Susan gets $120.00.

BUILD YOUR SKILLS

9. The ratio of flour to shortening in a recipe for piecrust is 2:1. If a baker makes 30 cups of piecrust, how many cups of flour and shortening does he use?

20:10

Because 20+10=30
2+1=3
30÷3=10

10. A compound of two chemicals is mixed in the ratio of 3:10. If there are 45 litres of the compound, how much of each chemical is in the mixture?

11. Cheryl is an automotive repair technician. She mixes paint and thinner to apply to a bus. The instructions say to mix paint with thinner in the ratio of 5:3. If Cheryl needs 24 L of paint/thinner mixture, how much of each will she use?

NEW SKILLS: WORKING WITH RATE

A **rate** is a ratio comparing two numbers measured in different units.

Some examples of rates are:

- $1.69/100 g or $\frac{\$1.69}{100 \text{ g}}$ for the cost of ham at the deli
- 80 km/h or $\frac{80 \text{ km}}{1 \text{ h}}$ for how fast a car travels
- $38.00/4 h or $\frac{\$38.00}{4 \text{ h}}$ for how much you earn at work

For more information, see page 17 of *MathWorks 10*.

rate: a comparison between two numbers measured with different units

Example 5

The amount of fuel consumed by a vehicle when it is driven 100 km is referred to as the rate of fuel consumption. Write a rate statement that indicates that a car uses 6.3 litres of gas for every 100 km driven.

SOLUTION

6.3 L:100 km, $\frac{6.3 \text{ L}}{100 \text{ km}}$, or 6.3 L/100 km

BUILD YOUR SKILLS

12. Write a rate statement that indicates that you earned $65.00 interest on your investment in the last 3 months.

13. Write a rate statement that indicates how much you earn in an 8-hour day if you are paid $9.25 for each hour you work.

    $9.25/hr
    $74/8hr

14. Write a rate statement that indicates that 1 cm on a map represents 2500 km in real distance.

Example 6

If you earn $150.00 in 12 hours, how much will you earn if you work 40 hours?

SOLUTION

$$\frac{\$150.00}{12 \text{ h}} = \frac{\$x}{40 \text{ h}}$$

$$\frac{150}{12} = \frac{x}{40} \qquad \text{In your calculation, omit the units.}$$

$$(12 \times 40) \times \frac{150}{12} = \frac{x}{40} \times (40 \times 12) \qquad \text{Multiply both sides of the equation by the product of the denominators.}$$

$$480 \times \frac{150}{12} = x \times 480 \qquad \text{Simplify.}$$

$$40 \times 150 = x \times 12$$

$$6000 = 12x$$

$$\frac{6000}{12} = \frac{12x}{12} \qquad \text{Divide both sides by 12 to isolate } x.$$

$$\frac{6000}{12} = x$$

$$500 = x$$

You will earn $500.00 in 40 hours.

BUILD YOUR SKILLS

15. If a type of salami at the deli costs $1.59 per 100 g, how much will you pay for 350 g?

16. As a janitor, Janine makes a cleaning solution by mixing 30 g of concentrated powdered cleanser into 2 L of water. How much powder will she need for 5 L of water?

17. An office has decided to track how much paper it uses to reduce waste. At the end of each month, the secretary records the total number of sheets used and their mass. If paper has a mass of 4.9 kg for every 500 sheets, what is the mass of 700 sheets of paper?

PRACTISE YOUR NEW SKILLS

1. Find the unknown value in each of the following proportions. Give answers to the nearest tenth of a unit (to one decimal place).

   While calculating, omit the units.

   a) $\dfrac{24}{18} = \dfrac{x}{12}$

   $\dfrac{24 \cdot 12}{18} = \dfrac{288}{18} = 16$

   b) $\dfrac{168 \text{ km}}{2 \text{ h}} = \dfrac{548 \text{ km}}{x \text{ h}}$

   $\dfrac{2h \cdot 548 \text{ km}}{168 \text{ km}} = \dfrac{1096 \text{ km/h}}{168 \text{ km}} = 6.5 \text{ km/h}$

c) $\dfrac{40}{28} = \dfrac{60}{x}$

d) $\dfrac{6 \text{ pizza slices}}{2 \text{ people}} = \dfrac{x \text{ pizza slices}}{21 \text{ people}}$

$\dfrac{6 \text{ ps} \cdot 21 \text{ ppl}}{2 \text{ ppl}} = \dfrac{126 \text{ ps/ppl}}{2 \text{ ppl}} =$

63 ps/ppl

e) $\dfrac{87 \text{ blankets}}{x \text{ bundles}} = \dfrac{24 \text{ blankets}}{8 \text{ bundles}}$

f) $\dfrac{12}{25} = \dfrac{25}{x}$

$\dfrac{25 \cdot 25}{12} = \dfrac{625}{12} = 52$

g) $\dfrac{7}{15} = \dfrac{x}{1}$

h) $\dfrac{12}{45} = \dfrac{16}{x}$

2. A hairdresser mixes brunette hair colouring for a client using 20 mL hair colour, 40 mL colour developer, 15 mL conditioner, and 3 mL thickener. Find the following ratios and simplify them to their lowest terms. Express your answers as fractions.

a) The ratio of hair colour to thickener.

20 : 3

b) The ratio of thickener to conditioner.

   3:15

c) The ratio of colour developer to hair colour.

   40:20

d) If this treatment costs the customer $68.00 and the cost of labour and materials used is $14.20, what is the ratio of customer price to actual cost?

   $68.00 ÷ $14.20 = $4.78

3. If the ratio of yellow pigment to blue pigment in a shade of green paint is 2:3, how many drops of yellow pigment will be needed if 12 drops of blue are used?

4. If 5 cm on a map represents 2.5 km of actual ground, how many centimetres would 15 km of actual ground be on the map?

15 km ÷ 2.5 km = 6 cm

5. If a can of paint will cover 48 m² of wall space, how many cans will you need to paint 220 m²?

6. The ratio of teeth on a pair of driving gears is 13:6, with the larger gear having more teeth. If the larger gear has 52 teeth, how many does the smaller gear have?

6 goes in to 13 2.5 times

$\frac{52}{2.5} = 20.8$

52:21

7. If Stephie can type 75 words per minute, how long will it take her to type an 800-word term paper? Is the solution a rate or a ratio? Explain your answer.

8. If the ratio of flour to sugar in a recipe is 3:2, how much flour would you need if you used 1.5 cups of sugar?

9. If a machine can produce 85 parts in 40 minutes, how many parts can it produce in 8 hours?

85/40 min

$\frac{85}{40} = 2.125$

$2.125 \cdot 60 = 127.5$

$127.5 \cdot 8 = \boxed{1020}$

1.2 Unit Price

NEW SKILLS: WORKING WITH UNIT PRICE

unit price: the cost of one unit; a rate expressed as a fraction in which the denominator is 1

When items are sold in quantities of more than 1, the **unit price** indicates how much 1 of the items would cost. For example, if you buy a package of 3 pencils, the unit price is the price of 1 pencil.

For more information, see page 23 of *MathWorks 10*.

Example 1

If a carton of one dozen eggs costs $3.29, how much are you paying for 1 egg?

SOLUTION

Solve using a proportion. Let x represent the cost of 1 egg.

$$\frac{\$3.29}{12 \text{ eggs}} = \frac{x}{1 \text{ egg}}$$

$$\frac{3.29}{12} = \frac{x}{1} \quad \text{Omit the units in the calculation.}$$

$$12 \times \frac{3.29}{12} = \frac{x}{1} \times 12 \quad \text{Multiply both sides of the equation by 12.}$$

$$3.29 = 12x \quad \text{Simplify.}$$

$$\frac{3.29}{12} = \frac{12x}{12} \quad \text{Divide both sides by 12 to isolate } x.$$

$$\frac{3.29}{12} = x$$

$$0.27 \approx x$$

One egg costs approximately $0.27.

Chapter 1 Unit Pricing and Currency Exchange 27

BUILD YOUR SKILLS

1. If 12 apples cost $10.20, how much does one apple cost?

   $$\frac{\$10.20}{12 \text{ apples}} = \frac{x}{1}$$

   $$\frac{\$10.20 \cdot 1}{12 \text{ apples}} = \frac{\$10.20}{12} = .85$$

   1 apple costs $.85

2. Lindsay is the kitchen manager of an Ethiopian café. She purchases a case of 1000 paper coffee cups for $94.83. How much does one cup cost?

3. Frank is a locksmith who owns his own business. He buys a case of 144 bulk brass padlocks for $244.97. He sells each lock for $5.50.

   a) How much does each lock cost Frank?

   $5.50 - 1.70 = 3.8$

   b) How much profit does Frank make when he sells one lock?

   $$\frac{\$5.50}{\$3.23} = \$1.70$$

Example 2

> People often think that larger-sized packages cost less per unit, but this is not always so.

Often unit price is used to compare costs.

A 48-oz can of tomatoes costs $2.99. An 18-oz can costs $1.19. Which is a better buy?

SOLUTION

Calculate the cost of 1 oz of tomatoes for each size of can.

Calculate the cost of 1 oz from the 48-oz can.

$2.99 ÷ 48 ≈ $0.062   Divide the total cost by the total number of ounces.

1 oz of tomatoes costs approximately $0.06.

Calculate the cost of 1 oz from the 18-oz can.

$1.19 ÷ 18 ≈ $0.066   Divide the total cost by the total number of ounces.

1 oz of tomatoes costs approximately $0.07.

It costs more for one ounce of tomatoes from the 18-oz can, so the 48-oz can is the better buy.

BUILD YOUR SKILLS

4. *La Boutique du Livre* is a francophone bookstore in St. Boniface, MB. It sells notebooks in packages of 12 for $15.48. Another bookstore sells the same notebooks in packages of 15 for $19.65. Which is the better price?

5. Which is the better buy: 6 muffins for $7.59, or one dozen muffins for $14.99?

$$\frac{6 \text{ muffins}}{\$7.59} = \frac{1 \text{ muf}}{x}$$

$$\frac{\$7.59 \cdot 1\text{muf}}{6\text{muf}} = \frac{\$7.59}{6} = \$1.26$$

$$\frac{12 \text{ muf}}{\$14.99} = \frac{1 \text{ muf}}{x}$$

$$\frac{\$14.99 \cdot 1\text{muf}}{12} = \frac{\$14.99}{12} = \$1.25$$

1 dozen is the better buy

6. Johnny can buy two 8-foot pieces of 2″ by 4″ lumber at $2.60 each, or three 6-foot pieces for $1.92 each. Which is the better buy per foot?

Example 3

Shirin is the manager of a fabric store and is training a new employee. Shirin wants to make an easy reference chart that lists the prices of different lengths of a fabric. One metre of the fabric costs $8.42. Fill in the rest of the chart.

FABRIC COST BY LENGTH	
Length of fabric	Cost of fabric
0.5 m	
1 m	$8.42
1.75 m	

SOLUTION

You can solve this using proportions. First find the cost of 0.5 m.

$$\frac{\$8.42}{1 \text{ m}} = \frac{\$x}{0.5 \text{ m}}$$

$$\frac{8.42}{1} = \frac{x}{0.5} \quad \text{Omit the units during calculations.}$$

$$0.5 \times 8.42 = \frac{x}{0.5} \times 0.5 \quad \text{Multiply both sides of the equation by the product of the denominator, 0.5.}$$

$$0.5 \times 8.42 = x \quad \text{Simplify.}$$

$$4.21 = x$$

The cost of 0.5 m of fabric is $4.21.

Then find the cost of 1.75 m.

$$\frac{8.42}{1} = \frac{x}{1.75}$$

$$1.75 \times 8.42 = \frac{x}{1.75} \times 1.75$$

$$1.75 \times 8.42 = x$$

$$14.74 = x$$

FABRIC COST BY LENGTH	
Length of fabric	Cost of fabric
0.5 m	$4.21
1 m	$8.42
1.75 m	$14.74

ALTERNATIVE SOLUTION

You can use unit rates rather than proportions.

1 m costs $8.42. Use this unit cost to calculate the cost of the other lengths

$8.42 × 0.5 = $4.21

$8.42 × 1.75 = $14.74

BUILD YOUR SKILLS

7. Sasha is a landscape gardener. He sees that a 200-foot roll of string trimmer line costs $18.75. A 150-foot roll of line costs $15.21.

   a) Which roll of line is the least expensive per foot?

   $$\frac{200 ft}{\$18.75} = \frac{1 ft}{x} \quad \frac{\$18.75 \cdot 1}{200} = \frac{\$18.75}{200} = .093$$

   $$\frac{150 ft}{15.21} = \frac{1 ft}{x} \quad \frac{15.21 \cdot 1 ft}{150} = \frac{15.21}{150} = .10$$

   b) What is the difference in price, per foot?

   The difference is $0.01

8. If $2\frac{1}{2}$ kg of tomatoes cost $8.25, how much will you pay for 7 kg?

9. If Wayne bought 5 litres of gas for his lawnmower for $5.45, how much would he have to pay to fill his car with 48 litres of gas?

PRACTISE YOUR NEW SKILLS

1. During the summer, Dean works as a cashier in a store near Saskatchewan's Greenwater Lake Provincial Park. The store sells a case of 12 bottles of water for $8.50 and individual bottles of the same brand of water for $1.55.

   a) Approximately how much does each bottle of water in the case of 12 cost?

   $$\frac{\$8.50}{12} = \frac{x}{1}$$

   $$\frac{\$8.50 \cdot 1}{12} \qquad \frac{\$8.50}{12} = \$.71$$

   b) How much would a customer save by buying a case of water, rather than 12 individual bottles?

   $$\$1.55 - \$.71 = \$.84$$

2. Maureen purchased enough carpet to cover a rectangular room measuring 7 metres by 12 metres. The carpet costs $8.15 per square metre.

   a) How much carpet did Maureen buy?

   b) How much did the carpet cost?

3. Tyler is a self-employed sheet metal worker. He purchases 25 sheets of aluminum that measure 4 feet by 8 feet. The cost is $4000.00 before tax and shipping.

   a) How much does 1 sheet cost?

   $$\frac{\$4000}{25} = \frac{x}{1} \qquad \frac{\$4000 \cdot 1}{25} = \frac{\$4000}{25} = \$160$$

   each sheet costs $160

   b) What is the price per square foot?

4. A painting business buys 3-inch wide paintbrushes from a supplier in cases of 6. One case costs $31.29.

   a) How much do two brushes cost?

   b) If a customer buys two or more cases, the supplier reduces the price of the case by 10 percent. How much would 3 cases of paintbrushes cost? How much would each brush cost?

5. Which is the better buy: 8 ounces of Brie cheese for $4.95 or 12 ounces for $7.49?

$$\frac{8oz}{\$4.95} = \frac{1oz}{x}$$

$$\frac{\$4.95 \cdot 1oz}{8oz} = \frac{\$4.95}{8} = \$.62$$

$$\frac{12oz}{\$7.49} = \frac{1oz}{x}$$

$$\frac{\$7.49 \cdot 1oz}{12oz} = \frac{\$7.49}{12} = \$0.62$$

They are both equal price

6. Debbie is a cook in a restaurant that is open 6 days a week. She is responsible for recording and monitoring the amount of money she spends on food. In the summer, she uses an average of 9 loaves of bread per day.

a) On average, how many loaves of bread does Debbie use each week?

b) If bread costs $1.25 per loaf to buy from a wholesale distributor, how much money should Debbie budget to purchase it, for the month of June? Assume that there are just 4 weeks in June.

7. The cost of a 355-mL can of juice is $1.25 in a vending machine. A 1.89-L carton of the same juice costs $3.89 at the grocery store. How much would you save per mL if you bought juice from the grocery store instead of the vending machine? (Hint: 1 L equals 1000 mL.)

8. Patricio is ordering cartons of detergent for resale in his store. He can order a carton of 12 for $34.68 plus $5.45 for delivery, or a carton of 18 for $51.30 plus $6.25 for delivery. Which is a better buy, and by how much per unit?

1.3 Setting a Price

REVIEW: WORKING WITH PERCENTS AND DECIMALS

In this section, you will calculate percentages and convert between percents and decimals.

Example 1

Convert 65% to a decimal.

percentage: a ratio with a denominator of 100; percent (%) means "out of 100"

SOLUTION

To convert a **percentage** to a decimal, first convert it to a fraction with a denominator of 100, then divide the numerator by the denominator.

65% means 65 out of 100, or, stated as a fraction, $\frac{65}{100}$.

Divide 65 by 100 to express 65% as a decimal.

$65 \div 100 = 0.65$

65% is equal to 0.65.

Dividing by 100 gives the same result as moving the decimal two places to the left. Many people use this as a shortcut.

BUILD YOUR SKILLS

1. Convert the following percentages to decimals.

   a) 78%   .78

   b) 93%   .93

   c) 125%   1.25

   d) 324%   3.24

   e) 0.5%   .005

   f) 0.38%   .0038

   g) 1.2%   .012

   h) 100%   1

Example 2

Calculate 20% of 45.

SOLUTION

To find a percentage of a number, you can use proportional reasoning.

Let x represent 20% of 45. Use proportional reasoning to solve for x.

$$\frac{20}{100} = \frac{x}{45}$$

$$4500\left(\frac{20}{100}\right) = \left(\frac{x}{45}\right)4500 \quad \text{Multiply both sides of the equation by the product of the denominators.}$$

$$45 \times 20 = 100x \quad \text{Simplify.}$$

$$900 = 100x$$

$$\frac{900}{100} = \frac{100x}{100} \quad \text{Divide both sides by 100 to isolate } x.$$

$$9 = x$$

20% of 45 is 9.

ALTERNATIVE SOLUTION

First convert 20% to a decimal.

$$20 \div 100 = 0.20$$

Then calculate 20% of 45 by multiplying 0.20 by 45.

$$x = 0.20 \times 45$$

$$x = 9$$

Chapter 1 Unit Pricing and Currency Exchange 39

BUILD YOUR SKILLS

2. Calculate the following percentages.

If the percentage is larger than 100, then your answer will be larger than the number you started with.

a) 15% of 300

$$\frac{x}{300} = \frac{15\%}{100} \quad 100x = 15 \cdot 300 \quad 100x = \frac{4500}{100} = x = 45$$

b) 45% of 1500

$$\frac{x}{1500} = \frac{45\%}{100} = 100x = 45 \cdot 1500 \quad 100x = \frac{67500}{100} = x = 675$$

c) 140% of 70

$$\frac{x}{70} = \frac{140\%}{100} = 100x = 140 \cdot 70 \quad 100x = \frac{9800}{100} = x = 98$$

d) 175% of 24

$$\frac{x}{24} = \frac{175\%}{100} \quad 100x = 175 \cdot 24 \quad 100x = \frac{4200}{100} = x = 42$$

e) 7.8% of 50

$$\frac{7.8\%}{100} = .078 \cdot 50 = 3.9$$

f) 0.3% of 175

$$\frac{0.3\%}{100} = .003 \cdot 175 = .525$$

g) 200% of 56

$$\frac{200\%}{100} = 2 \cdot 56 = 112$$

h) 135% of 25

$$\frac{135\%}{100} = 1.35 \cdot 25 = 33.75$$

Example 3

What percent is 5 of 20?

SOLUTION

To calculate what percent one number is of another means that you need to determine what number out of 100 is equivalent to your ratio.

You can use proportional reasoning to solve the question.

$$\frac{x}{100} = \frac{5}{20}$$

$$100 \times \frac{x}{100} = \frac{5}{20} \times 100 \quad \text{Multiply both sides of the equation by 100.}$$

$$x = 5 \times 5 \quad \text{Simplify.}$$

$$x = 25$$

5 is 25% of 20.

ALTERNATIVE SOLUTION

5 of 20 is the same as $\frac{5}{20}$. You can find the percent by dividing 5 by 20.

$$5 \div 20 = 0.25$$

This is 25 hundredths, or 25%.

BUILD YOUR SKILLS

3. Calculate what percentage the first number is of the second (to the nearest tenth of a percent).

   a) 65 of 325

   b) 135 of 405

   $$\frac{135}{405} = \frac{x}{100} \qquad 135 \cdot 100 = 405x$$
   $$\frac{13500}{405} = \frac{405x}{405}$$
   $$x = 33.\overline{33}$$

   c) 68 of 42

   d) 13 of 65

   $$\frac{13}{65} = \frac{x}{100} \qquad 13 \cdot 100 = 65x$$
   $$\frac{1300}{65} = \frac{65x}{65}$$
   $$x = 20$$

   e) 1 of 12

   f) 625 of 50

   $$\frac{625}{50} = \frac{x}{100} \qquad 625 \cdot 100 = 50x$$
   $$\frac{62500}{50} = \frac{50x}{50}$$
   $$x = 1250$$

NEW SKILLS: WORKING WITH MARKUPS AND TAXES

When a person owns a business, she usually buys merchandise at a wholesale price. She then sells it at a higher price, called a retail price, to make a profit. The retail price is often determined by adding a certain percentage of the wholesale price to the wholesale price. The amount added is referred to as the **markup**.

Sales taxes are usually added to the retail price. There are three kinds of taxes that you may need to consider when purchasing items: Goods and Services Tax (GST), Provincial Sales Tax (PST), and Harmonized Sales Tax (HST).

For more information, see page 28 of *MathWorks 10*.

markup: the difference between the amount a dealer sells a product for (retail price) and the amount he or she paid for it (wholesale price)

Example 4

Melanie owns a clothing store. Her standard markup is 85%. She bought a coat from the wholesaler at $125.00.

a) What would the markup be?

b) How much would Melanie charge her customer for the coat?

SOLUTION

a) Change 85% to a decimal.

$$85 \div 100 = 0.85$$

Multiply the wholesale price by the markup.

$$\$125.00 \times 0.85 = \$106.25$$

The markup is $106.25.

b) Melanie would charge her customer the wholesale price plus the markup.

$$\$125.00 + \$106.25 = \$231.25$$

With a markup of 85%, Marnie would charge her customer $231.25.

BUILD YOUR SKILLS

4. The markup on a bicycle in a sporting goods store is 125%. The bicycle's wholesale price is $450.00. What is the markup in dollars?

Chapter 1 Unit Pricing and Currency Exchange 43

5. Marco buys a certain brand of shampoo from a supplier at $7.25 per bottle. He sells it to his customers at a markup of 25%. What would the markup be?

6. A *hanbok* is a formal, traditional outfit of Korean clothing. At a markup of 60%, what would be the retail price for a child's *hanbok* with a wholesale price of $117.45?

7. What should Max charge for a package of paper plates in his store if he bought them for $9.00 and wants to make a 75% profit?

$$\frac{75\%}{100\%} = \frac{x}{9} = \frac{75 \cdot 9}{100} = \frac{675}{100} = 6.75$$

$$\$9 + \$6.75 = \$15.75$$

Example 5

Quentin wants to buy a pair of steel-toed boots listed at $179.95. How much will the boots cost if 5% GST and 6% PST are charged?

SOLUTION

Calculate the GST by changing 5% to a decimal and multiplying by the retail price.

$$5 \div 100 = 0.05$$

$$0.05 \times \$179.95 = \$9.00$$

Calculate the PST by changing 6% to a decimal and multiplying by the retail price.

$$6 \div 100 = 0.06$$

$$0.06 \times \$179.95 = \$10.80$$

The final price is calculated by adding the tax amounts to the retail price.

$$\$179.95 + \$9.00 + \$10.80 = \$199.75$$

Quentin will have to pay $199.75.

ALTERNATIVE SOLUTION 1

5% + 6% = 11%	Add the two taxes together.
11 ÷ 100 = 0.11	Change to a decimal.
0.11 × $179.95 = $19.79	Multiply to find 11% of the retail price.
$179.95 + $19.79 = $199.74	Add the total tax to the retail price.

This is different than the first solution because rounding occurs at a different spot.

ALTERNATIVE SOLUTION 2

You can think about the retail price as 100% of the cost. If you add the two sales taxes (5% plus 6% equals 11%) to this, the total cost is 111%.

Convert 111% to a decimal and multiply this by the initial cost.

$$111 \div 100 = 1.11$$
$$\$179.95 \times 1.11 = \$199.74$$

While it is convenient for you to use the methods in Alternative Solutions 1 or 2, the store would have to use the first method because they must keep track of how much GST and PST they collect.

BUILD YOUR SKILLS

8. What would you have to pay for a jacket that is listed at $99.95 if you live in Nunavut, where the only tax is 5% GST?

9. Find the total cost of a washing machine that is being sold for $944.98 in Saskatchewan, where PST is 6% and GST is 5%.

10. Calculate the HST (12%) on a return flight from Cranbrook, BC to Vancouver, BC that costs $372.00.

    $$\frac{12\%}{100\%} = \frac{x}{\$372.00} = \frac{12 \cdot \$372}{100} = \frac{4464}{100} = \$44.64$$

    $$372 + 44.64 = 416.64$$

11. Saskatchewan charges 5% GST and 6% PST. How much GST and PST would Krista pay on a can of paint priced at $45.89?

12. If the markup is 125% on a certain brand of jeans that have a wholesale price of $30.00, what will the consumer pay, if GST and PST are each 5%?

13. The markup on a restaurant meal is 250%. A meal costs $7.25 to produce. How much will the customer be charged, after markup and 5% GST are applied?

PRACTISE YOUR NEW SKILLS

1. Calculate the following percentages.

a) 5% of 72

$$\frac{x}{72} = \frac{5\%}{100} \quad 100x = 5 \cdot 72$$
$$100x = 360 = 3.6$$

b) 275% of 8

$$\frac{x}{8} = \frac{275\%}{100} \quad 100x = 275\% \cdot 8$$
$$100x = 2200 = 22$$

c) 152% of 200

$$\frac{x}{200} = \frac{152\%}{100} \quad 100x = 152 \cdot 200$$
$$100x = \frac{30400}{100} = 304$$

d) $6\frac{3}{4}$% of 700

$$\frac{x}{700} = \frac{6.75\%}{100}$$
$$100x = 6.75\% \cdot 700$$
$$100x = \frac{4725}{100} = 47.25$$

2. An electrician buys his material at the local hardware store, then charges his customer 20% more. The material for a given project is $253.75 at the hardware store.

   a) What is the markup?

   b) How much does he charge the customer for the material?

3. Maria is a florist in a small boutique. If Maria paid her supplier $8.50/doz for roses and sold them for $19.95, what was the percent markup?

   $19.95 − $8.50 = $11.45

4. Garth buys snow tires from a dealer in Thunder Bay, ON. The tires cost $79.00 each. To make a profit, he must mark them up 40%. How much must a customer pay for 4 tires if there is a 12% HST on the final sale?

$$\frac{40\%}{100\%} = \frac{x}{79.00} = \frac{40 \cdot 79}{100} = \frac{3160}{100} = 31.60$$

$$\frac{12}{100} = \frac{x}{31.60} = \frac{12 \cdot 31.60}{100} = \frac{379.20}{100} = 3.79$$

$$379.20 + 3.79 = 382.99$$

5. Because the cost of ingredients has gone up, Maurice has decided to increase the cost of meals in his restaurant by 12%. How much will he now charge for a grilled salmon fillet that used to cost $17.95?

$$\frac{12}{100} = \frac{x}{17.95} = \frac{12 \cdot 17.95}{100} = \frac{215.40}{100} = 2.15$$

$$17.95 + 2.15 = 20.10$$

6. The wholesale cost of a certain brand of T-shirts is $132.00/dozen. To cover costs and make a profit, Lorena marks them up by 75%. If GST is 5% and PST is 7%, what will a customer have to pay for 1 T-shirt?

7. An MP3 player that Harry wants to buy sells for $89.95 in BC where there is 12% HST. When he is on holiday in Alberta (where there is only the 5% GST), Harry sees the same MP3 player for $94.89. Which is a better buy and by how much?

On Sale! 1.4

NEW SKILLS: SALE PRICES

When you go shopping, you see signs that advertise **promotions**, such as "For Sale," "Up to 50% Off," and "Discounted Prices," that mean you will pay less than the price on the tag.

For more information, see page 34 of *MathWorks 10*.

promotion: an activity that increases awareness of a product or attracts customers

Example 1

Samantha wants to buy a new TV. The model she likes costs $675.95, but the clerk tells her that it is going on sale next week at 20% off. If Samantha waits one week, how much will she save on the price of the TV?

SOLUTION

The discount is 20%, so find 20% of $675.95 by multiplication.

Convert 20% to a decimal.

20 ÷ 100 = 0.20

Multiply 0.20 by the original price.

0.20 × $675.95 = $135.19

The original price will be discounted by this amount, so Samantha would save $135.19.

BUILD YOUR SKILLS

1. How much will Jordon save on the price of a computer listed at $989.98 if it is discounted by 30%?

2. The Midtown Bakery sells Chinese specialties such as pineapple buns and lotus seed buns. Day-old goods at the bakery are sold at a discount of 60%. If the original price of a loaf of sweet bread was $2.98, how much would you save by buying a day-old loaf?

3. If the sale price is 25% off, what will you save if you buy a sofa regularly priced at $999.97?

Example 2

Michelle is a member of the Xat'sull First Nation and is fluent in the Shuswap language. She works as a language instructor and gift shop cashier at the Xat'sull Heritage Village, near Williams Lake, BC.

The gift shop is selling off summer inventory. What will be the cost of a carving that was priced at $149.95 if the sale sign says "Reduced by 60%"?

SOLUTION

Calculate 60% of $149.95 to determine the savings.

First, convert 60% to a decimal.

60 ÷ 100 = 0.60

Multiply the original price by 0.60.

0.60 × $149.95 = $89.97

The original price will be reduced by this amount, so subtract $89.97 from $149.95.

$149.95 − $89.97 = $59.98

The cost of the carving will be $59.98.

ALTERNATIVE SOLUTION

If the price of the carving is reduced by 60%, that means that the customer will pay only 40% of the cost (100% minus 60% is 40%).

Convert 40% to a decimal.

40 ÷ 100 = 0.40

Multiply the original price by 0.40.

0.40 × $149.95 = $59.98

The carving will cost $59.98.

BUILD YOUR SKILLS

4. Sarbjit charges $24.95 for a haircut in her beauty salon, but gives students a 30% reduction on Thursday evenings. How much would you have to pay to have your hair cut on a Thursday evening?

5. Margariet manages a second-hand clothing store in Flin Flon, Manitoba. The store advertises that if you buy 3 items, you will get 15% off the most expensive item, 20% off the second most expensive, and 30% off the cheapest item. You choose three items costing $10.00, $25.00, and $12.00. How much will you pay for the three items?

6. Normally Chiu charges $75.00 to paint a room. However, if he paints 3 or more rooms for you, he gives you a 15% discount. How much will he charge if he paints 4 rooms for you?

Example 3

Lisa specializes in selling products from the Philippines, including rattan, bamboo, and palm baskets. Medium-sized bamboo baskets are regularly priced at $19.98. They are on sale, advertised as "Buy one, get the second at half price." What is the discount rate, as a percent?

SOLUTION

Calculate the regular cost of 2 baskets.

$19.98 × 2 = $39.96

In buying 2 baskets, you save half the price of 1 basket.

$\frac{1}{2}$($19.99) = $9.99

Calculate the percent savings by dividing the discount by the regular price, and multiplying by 100.

$\frac{\$9.99}{\$39.96} \times 100\% = 25\%$

The discount rate is 25%.

BUILD YOUR SKILLS

7. What is the percentage markdown if a $175.00 item sells for $150.00?

8. In a store opening promotion, Fred advertises T-shirts: "Buy 4 get 1 free." If the cost of 1 T-shirt is $15.97, what is the discount rate, as a percent?

9. Cameron is buying new computers for his office. Each computer costs $789.00. He is told that if he buys 5 computers, he can get a 6th one free. What will be his percent saving compared to buying all 6 at the regular price?

10. Shelly works as an optician in Whitehorse, YT. Her store is selling last year's glasses frames at a savings of 30%. What will you pay for frames that were originally priced at $149.00 if 5% GST is charged?

> GST and PST are paid on the selling price, not the original price.

11. Nicole wants to buy a coat originally priced at $249.95. It is on sale at 25% off. How much will she pay if 5% GST and 5% PST are charged?

12. Yasmin owns a kitchen and bath fitting store. She is selling a kitchen sink at a reduction of 40% because of a scratch in the finish. The original price was $249.95.

   a) Determine the total savings to the customer, including 5% GST and a PST of 8%.

   b) Calculate the percentage of savings.

PRACTISE YOUR NEW SKILLS

1. In Abbotsford, BC, Mack works as a used car salesman. He offers a 15% reduction to repeat customers. If the price marked on a car is $9879.00, how much will it be reduced for a repeat customer?

$$\frac{15\%}{100\%} = \frac{x}{\$9879} = \frac{15 \cdot 9879}{100} = \frac{148185}{100}$$

$$= \$1481.85$$

2. A fishing rod originally priced at $49.98 is reduced by 30%.

   a) How much is the discount?

   b) What will the cost be before tax?

3. Senior citizens are offered a 20% discount on their lunch on Tuesdays in Hay River's local diner. How much will Rita and Dick, both senior citizens, save if they order the teriyaki chicken salad at $14.98 and the pork cutlets at $17.98? (Ignore taxes.)

$$\frac{20}{100} = \frac{x}{14.98} = \frac{20 \cdot 14.98}{100}$$

$$= \frac{299.60}{100} = \$3.00$$

They both save a total of $6.60

$$\frac{20}{100} = \frac{x}{17.98} = \frac{20 \cdot 17.98}{100}$$

$$= \frac{359.60}{100} = 3.60$$

4. A can of paint costs $59.95. There is a 20% price reduction for contractors. How much will the contractor save if he buys 5 cans?

5. A furniture store offers a "Closing Out Sale: Everything 80% Off."

   a) How much will you pay for a bedroom suite that originally cost $2989.97 if GST is 5% and PST is 7%?

   $$\frac{5}{100} = \frac{x}{\$2989.97} = \frac{5 \cdot 2989.97}{100} = \frac{14949.85}{100} = 149.50$$

   $$\frac{7}{100} = \frac{x}{2989.97} = \frac{7 \cdot 2989.97}{100} = \frac{20929.79}{100} = 209.30$$

   b) What are your total savings on this purchase?

   $$\frac{80}{100} = \frac{x}{358.80} = \frac{80 \cdot 358.80}{100} = \frac{28704}{100} = 287.04$$

   $$\begin{array}{r} 209.30 \\ + 149.50 \\ \hline 358.80 \end{array}$$

6. Robert sells bicycles, skateboards, and snowboards at his sporting goods store. A bicycle that was originally priced at $785.00 sold for $553.00. What percent markdown did Robert offer?

7. The wholesale cost of a *tawa*, a griddle used to cook Indian flatbread, is $53.00. A merchant marks it up 65%. At the end of the season, he sells the remaining stock at 60% off.

   a) What was his original asking price?

   $\dfrac{65}{100} = \dfrac{x}{53} = \dfrac{65 \cdot 53}{100} = \dfrac{3445}{100} = 34.45$

   $53 + 34.45 = 87.45$

   b) At the original price, how much would a customer pay with 5% GST and 5% PST?

   c) What was the end-of-season sale price?

   d) How much would a customer pay when it was on sale, including 5% GST and 5% PST?

   e) What would the total savings be if it were bought on sale?

   f) What would be the percentage savings?

Currency Exchange Rates 1.5

NEW SKILLS: EXCHANGE RATES

Different countries use different monetary units and/or different currencies. It is important when travelling to consider **exchange rates**, or the value of one monetary unit compared to another.

For more information, see page 41 of *MathWorks 10*.

exchange rate: the price of one country's currency in terms of another country's currency

Example 1

Lucas is a glazier who operates a window installation business. He regularly travels to the United States to buy supplies. Before travelling, he converts $500.00 CAD into American dollars for personal expenses. If one Canadian dollar is worth 0.94192 of an American dollar, how many American dollars will Lucas receive in exchange for $500.00 CAD?

SOLUTION

Use unit pricing.

$1.00 CAD = $0.94192 USD

$500.00 CAD = $0.94192 USD × 500

$500.00 CAD = $470.96 USD

Lucas will receive $470.96 USD.

Using approximation when working with exchange rates is useful if you want to quickly convert between currencies. You can think of the exchange rate in Example 1 as meaning that for every Canadian dollar, you will lose approximately 6 cents when converting to American dollars.

BUILD YOUR SKILLS

1. Ray purchased $500.00 CAD worth of parts from Hungary for use in his garage. If the exchange rate is one Canadian dollar to 180.0779 Hungarian forints (Ft), how many forints will you receive for $500.00 CAD?

2. If one Canadian dollars is worth 0.5911 British pounds sterling (£), calculate how many pounds sterling you would get for $200.00 CAD.

3. Madeline is attending a trade show in Denmark. She runs short of spending money and must convert $100.00 CAD into Danish kroner (kr). The exchange rate is 5.3541 Danish krone for one Canadian dollar. How many kroner will she receive?

Example 2

One Thai baht is worth 0.023541 of a Canadian dollar. How many bahts would a tourist in Thailand receive for $200.00 CAD?

SOLUTION

    1.00 baht = $0.023541 CAD

200 ÷ 0.023541 = 8495.82

For $200.00 CAD, a tourist in Thailand would receive 8495.82 bahts.

BUILD YOUR SKILLS

4. If the exchange rate for converting a Canadian dollar to the euro is 0.7180 on a particular day, how many euros would you get for $300.00 CAD?

5. The exchange rate for converting a Canadian dollar to the Swiss franc (SFr) is 1.0542. How many Swiss francs will you get for $400.00 CAD?

6. Canada imports steel, iron, and organic and inorganic chemicals from Trinidad and Tobago. The exchange rate for converting the Canadian to the Trinidad and Tobago dollar is 6.1805. How many Trinidad and Tobago dollars will you get for $200.00 CAD?

7. Using the following exchange rates, calculate how much foreign currency you would receive for $200.00 CAD.

   a) $1.00 CAD is worth 1.72904 Brazilian reals

   b) $1.00 CAD is worth 8.71137 Moroccan dirhams

   c) $1.00 CAD is worth 7.72277 Ukrainian hryvnia

   d) $1.00 CAD is worth 3.19889 Polish zloty

8. Calculate the value in Canadian dollars of an item that costs $449.75 Singapore dollars. Assume the exchange rate for one Canadian dollar is 0.75529.

9. Henry returns home to Whale Cove, Nunavut, after a trip to Europe. On his travels he purchased a jacket for 125.98 euros. Calculate the value of Henry's jacket in Canadian dollars. Assume that a euro is worth 1.3987 of a Canadian dollar.

10. The exchange rate between the South African rand and the Canadian dollar is 0.138469 (1 rand equals $0.138469 CAD). What is the cost in Canadian dollars of an item priced at 639.00 rand?

> Exchanging money is not quite as simple as the transactions here show. Although the calculations will be the same, you have to consider bank buying rate and bank selling rate when exchanging currency. When the bank buys foreign currency from you, they pay you less than they charge when they sell it to you.

Example 3

Anne works for an automotive parts distributor and visits Switzerland to source new products. On a given day, the bank selling rate of the Swiss franc compared to the Canadian dollar is 1.0501 and the buying rate is 1.0213.

a) How many Swiss francs would Anne receive for $400.00 CAD?

b) If Anne sold them back to the bank, how much would she receive?

c) What would her net loss be?

SOLUTION

a) The bank will sell Swiss francs to Anne, so use the selling rate. 1 Swiss franc is worth $1.0501 CAD.

$$\frac{1 \text{ SFr}}{\$1.0501} = \frac{x}{\$400.00}$$

$$\frac{1}{1.0501} = \frac{x}{400.00} \quad \text{Omit the units.}$$

$$(400.00 \times 1.0501) \times \frac{1}{1.0501} = \frac{x}{400.00} \times (1.0501 \times 400.00) \quad \text{Multiply both sides of the equation by the product of the denominators.}$$

$$400.00 = 1.0501x \quad \text{Simplify.}$$

$$\frac{400.00}{1.0501} = x \quad \text{Divide both sides by 1.0501 to isolate } x.$$

$$380.92 = x$$

Anne would receive 380.92 Swiss francs.

ALTERNATIVE SOLUTION

a) 1 Swiss franc is worth $1.0501 CAD.

$1.00 is therefore worth $\frac{1}{1.0501}$ Swiss francs. Multiply this by 400 to calculate what $400.00 CAD is worth.

$$400.00 \times \frac{1}{1.0501} = 380.92 \text{ Swiss francs}$$

b) The bank buys the Swiss francs back at a rate of 1.0213 Swiss francs per $1.00 CAD.

$$\frac{1 \text{ SFr}}{\$1.0213} = \frac{380.92 \text{ SFr}}{x}$$

$$\frac{1}{1.0213} = \frac{380.92}{x} \quad \text{Omit the units.}$$

$$(1.0213 \times x) \times \frac{1}{1.0213} = \frac{380.92}{x} \times (x \times 1.0213) \quad \text{Multiply both sides of the equation by the product of the denominators.}$$

$$x = 380.92 \times 1.0213 \quad \text{Simplify.}$$

$$x = 389.03$$

Anne would receive $389.03 CAD.

ALTERNATIVE SOLUTION

b) 1 Swiss franc is worth $1.0213 CAD.

Multiply 380.92 Swiss francs by 1.0213 to find the value in Canadian dollars.

380.92 × 1.0213 = $389.03 CAD

> Unit rates often work best for exchanging currency.

c) Anne's net loss would be $400.00 minus what she received back.

$400.00 − $389.03 = $10.97

Anne would lose $10.97 in the transaction.

> When customers exchange money at a bank or other institution, the bank will usually only deal with paper money, not coins.

BUILD YOUR SKILLS

11. If the exchange rate of a country compared to the Canadian dollar is 0.00519, will you get more or less of their currency units when you exchange money?

12. Dianne works as a bank teller in Canmore, AB. A customer wishes to buy 250 British pounds at a rate of 1.5379 $CAD. How many Canadian dollars would the British pounds cost?

13. If the selling rate of a euro (€) is 1.4768 and the buying rate is 1.4287, how much would you lose if you exchanged $1000.00 CAD for euros and then converted them back to $CAD on the same day?

PRACTISE YOUR NEW SKILLS

1. Using the following information, calculate how much of the foreign currency you would get for $500.00 CAD. Round to the nearest unit.

   a) $1.00 is worth 95.4911 Japanese yen

   $$\frac{1}{95.4911} = \frac{x}{500} = \frac{500 \cdot 95.4911}{1}$$
   $$= 47745.55$$

   b) $1.00 is worth 1.41046 Turkish lira

   $$\frac{1}{1.41046} = \frac{x}{500} = \frac{500 \cdot 1.41046}{1}$$
   $$= 705.23$$

   c) $1.00 is worth 0.680228 euro

   $$\frac{1}{0.680228} = \frac{x}{500}$$
   $$\frac{500 \cdot 0.680228}{1} = 340.114$$

   d) $1.00 is worth 6.43033 Chinese yuan

   $$\frac{1}{6.43033} = \frac{x}{500} =$$
   $$\frac{500 \cdot 6.43033}{1} = 3215.165$$

2. Damien is training to become a customer service representative at a credit union in Saskatoon, SK. Given the following exchange rates compared to the Canadian dollar, calculate how much foreign currency Damien would give to a customer who wished to convert $500.00 CAD.

   a) Mexican peso, 0.0818085

   b) Estonian kroon, 0.0939564

   c) British pound, 1.3376

   d) South Korean won, 0.000922277

   e) Indian rupee, 0.0229526

   f) Russian ruble, 0.0352667

3. Using the rates from question #1, calculate the amount you would get in Canadian dollars if you sold the following.

   a) 8750 Japanese yen

   b) 900 Turkish lira

   c) 250 euros

   d) 3000 Chinese yuan

4. Use the exchange rates from question #2. Calculate how many Canadian dollars you would get for each of the following.

   a) 6750 Mexican pesos

   b) 145 British pounds

   c) 15 000 Indian rupees

   d) 750 Russian rubles

5. If the exchange rate is 0.1736 between the Norwegian krone and the Canadian dollar, what would the price be in Canadian dollars of an item that cost 275 kroner?

6. A hand-woven shawl costs 35 Botswana pula. How much does it cost in Canadian dollars if the exchange rate is 0.1515?

7. If the selling rate of the Omani rial is 2.96845 and the buying rate is 2.86145, how much would you lose if you bought and then sold $800.00 on the same day?

CHAPTER TEST

1. When he works as a landscape gardener, Mark sometimes uses a powdered fertilizer. It must be mixed at a rate of 1 part of powder to 14 parts of water. How much water will Mark use for 3 litres of powder?

2. A car uses 5.5 litres of gas when it travels 100 km.

    a) Express this as a rate of fuel consumption.

    b) How much fuel would be needed for a 400-km trip?

3. Loretta works as a surveyor near Burwash Landing, YT. Her map uses a scale of 2.5 cm:100 km. On her map, two sites she must visit are 7.4 cm apart. What is the actual distance between the two sites?

4. If a package of 12 pens cost $38.98, what is the cost of 1 pen?

5. If the wholesale price of 10 packages of smoked salmon is $99.50, what will the cost be for one package after a markup of 45%?

6. The bakery in Lund, BC is selling day-old buns at a 40% reduction. If the regular price is $4.79/doz, what is the reduced price?

7. A sofa in a furniture store was originally $1899.00. The price was "reduced by 35% for quick sale." When it did not sell, the manager offered another reduction of 20%.

   a) What was the final price of the sofa with 5% GST and 7% PST?

   b) Is this the same as a 55% reduction? Show why or why not.

8. A furniture store in The Pas, Manitoba, advertises: "All weekend, no GST and no PST." If GST and PST are usually 5% each, what is the actual saving as a percent on an item that costs $24.97?

9. After prime planting season was over, a horticulturist sold lilac bushes for $15.00. If the original price was $39.00, what is the percentage markdown?

10. Non-profit agencies get a 12% reduction from Polly's Printers. How much will they save on a printing job that regularly costs $865.00?

11. James works for an industrial lighting company. He travels to Hong Kong to attend a trade show. James sees a fluorescent track lighting unit priced at 1295.31 Hong Kong dollars. What is the cost in Canadian dollars if $1.00 CAD is worth 7.3181 Hong Kong dollars?

12. Marian travels to Spain to visit her mother and father.

   a) $1.00 CAD is worth €0.680228. If Marian converts $450.00 CAD into euros, how many euros does she receive?

   b) During her visit, Marian buys a leather purse for €125.00. What is the cost in Canadian dollars?

Chapter 2

Earning an Income

Many tradespeople such as electricians, welders, carpenters, and plumbers are employed by the construction industry. These men are installing rebar, the steel rods used to reinforce the walls and floors of concrete buildings.

2.1 Wages and Salaries

REVIEW: WORKING WITH MIXED FRACTIONS

A proper fraction is a fraction where the numerator is smaller than the denominator, for example, $\frac{2}{3}$ and $\frac{8}{12}$.

An improper fraction is one in which the numerator is greater than or equal to the denominator, for example, $\frac{3}{2}$ and $\frac{12}{8}$. Improper fractions can be changed to mixed numerals.

A mixed numeral is a number represented as a whole number and a fraction, for example, $2\frac{3}{4}$ and $12\frac{5}{8}$. In most cases, the fraction is simplified to its lowest terms.

Example 1

Change the improper fraction to a mixed numeral, expressed in its simplest form.

$$\frac{188}{12}$$

SOLUTION

To change an improper fraction to a mixed numeral, divide the numerator by the denominator and write the remainder as a fraction of the **divisor**.

$188 \div 12 = 15$, remainder 8

When 188 is divided by 12, the **quotient** is 15 and the remainder is 8. The mixed numeral is $15\frac{8}{12}$. However, the fraction $\frac{8}{12}$ can be further simplified.

$$\frac{8}{12} = \frac{8 \div 4}{12 \div 4}$$

$$\frac{8 \div 4}{12 \div 4} = \frac{2}{3}$$

$$\frac{8}{12} = \frac{2}{3}$$

divisor: in a division operation, the number by which another number is divided; in $a \div b = c$, b is the divisor

quotient: the result of a division; in $a \div b = c$, c is the quotient

The simplified mixed numeral is written as $15\frac{2}{3}$.

ALTERNATIVE SOLUTION

First simplify the improper fraction, then divide the numerator by the denominator.

$$\frac{188}{12} = \frac{188 \div 4}{12 \div 4} \qquad \text{Simplify.}$$

$$\frac{188 \div 4}{12 \div 4} = \frac{47}{3}$$

$$\frac{188}{12} = \frac{47}{3}$$

$47 \div 3 = 15$, remainder 2   Divide.

The quotient is 15 and the remainder is 2, so the mixed numeral is $15\frac{2}{3}$.

76 MathWorks 10 Workbook

BUILD YOUR SKILLS

1. Change the improper fractions to mixed numerals.

   a) $\dfrac{29}{7}$

   $29 \div 7 = 4\tfrac{1}{7}$

   b) $\dfrac{493}{9}$

   $493 \div 9 =$
   $54 \tfrac{7}{9}$

   c) $\dfrac{1005}{29}$

   $34 \tfrac{19}{29}$

   d) $\dfrac{45}{6}$

   $45 \div 6 = 7\tfrac{1}{2}$

   e) $\dfrac{398}{16}$

   $398 \div 16$
   $24 \tfrac{7}{8}$

   f) $\dfrac{1000}{15}$

   $1000 \div 15$
   $= 66 \tfrac{2}{3}$

Example 2

Change the mixed numeral $2\tfrac{3}{4}$ to an improper fraction.

SOLUTION

The mixed numeral can be broken up as follows:

$$2\tfrac{3}{4} = 2 + \tfrac{3}{4}$$

Change 2 to a fraction whose denominator is 4.

$$\tfrac{2}{1} = \tfrac{2 \times 4}{1 \times 4}$$

$$\tfrac{2 \times 4}{1 \times 4} = \tfrac{8}{4}$$

$$\tfrac{2}{1} = \tfrac{8}{4}$$

Now substitute this improper fraction into the expression above.

$$2\tfrac{3}{4} = 2 + \tfrac{3}{4}$$

$$2 + \tfrac{3}{4} = \tfrac{8}{4} + \tfrac{3}{4}$$

$$\tfrac{8}{4} + \tfrac{3}{4} = \tfrac{8+3}{4}$$

$$2\tfrac{3}{4} = \tfrac{11}{4}$$

BUILD YOUR SKILLS

2. Change the mixed numerals to improper fractions.

   a) $5\frac{6}{11}$

   $\frac{58}{11}$ 5·11+6

   b) $4\frac{7}{9}$ $\frac{43}{9}$

   4·9+7

   c) $15\frac{8}{17}$ $\frac{263}{17}$

   15·17+8

   d) $7\frac{5}{8}$

   7·8+5
   $=\frac{61}{8}$

   e) $12\frac{4}{5}$

   12·5+4
   $=\frac{64}{5}$

   f) $10\frac{7}{12}$

   10·12+7
   $=\frac{137}{12}$

NEW SKILLS: WORKING WITH INCOME

A salary, a wage, or an income is the amount of money you receive for work you do. In some jobs, pay is calculated by the hour, while other jobs offer an annual income (paid weekly, biweekly, or monthly).

Gross pay is the amount you make before **deductions**. Deductions will be discussed in section 2.4.

For more details, see page 54 of *MathWorks 10*.

gross pay: the total amount of money earned before deductions; also called gross earnings or gross income

deduction: money taken off your paycheque to pay taxes, union fees, and for other benefits and programs

Example 3

Marcus works as an electrician and earns $24.68/h. If it takes him 15 hours for one job, how much will he earn?

SOLUTION

Multiply his hourly wage by the number of hours he works.

$\frac{\$24.68}{1 \text{ hour}} \times 15 \text{ hours} = \$370.20$

He will earn $370.20 on the job.

BUILD YOUR SKILLS

3. Martha works as a window dresser in her hometown of Victoria, BC. She charges $16.72/h and it takes her 5 hours to finish the window at a local department store. How much will her gross pay be for the job?

   $16.72 · 5 = $83.60

4. Ben works as a carpenter for $20.87/h. How much will he earn in a 40-hour work week?

   $20.87 · 40 = $834.80

5. Harpreet works in the trucking business. He charges $35.75/h to haul materials for a local contractor. Last week he worked the following hours:

   - 6 hours on Monday
   - 8 hours on Tuesday
   - 8 hours on Wednesday
   - 12 hours on Thursday

   What was his gross income for the week?

   6 + 8 + 8 + 12 = 34h

   $35.75 · 34 = $1215.50

Example 4

Last week, Chi worked 34 hours cutting lawns. His gross income was $329.12. What was his hourly wage?

SOLUTION

Divide his gross income by the number of hours he works to calculate his wage per hour.

$$\frac{\$329.12}{34 \text{ hours}} = \frac{\$9.68}{1 \text{ hour}}$$

Chi earns $9.68/h.

BUILD YOUR SKILLS

6. Last year, Liliana earned $45 183.36 working in a Grande Prairie hair salon.

   a) What was her average monthly income?

   $45183.36 ÷ 12 = $3765.28

   b) What was her average weekly income?

   $3765.28 ÷ 4 = $941.32

7. If Janny works a 40-hour work week as a receiving clerk in the Powell River Hospital and earns $552.88 per week, what is her hourly wage?

   $552.88 ÷ 40 = $13.82

8. Emile is a flag person and earned $321.25 last week. If he worked 32.5 hours, what was his hourly salary?

   $321.25 ÷ 32.5 = $9.88

Example 5

Antonio is a cashier in a store that sells Caribbean products, such as ginger syrup, *ackee* (a type of fruit), and *dasheen* (also known as taro, a root vegetable). His time card for one week is shown below.

Time Card: Antonio					
Day	Morning		Afternoon		Total Hours
	IN	OUT	IN	OUT	
Monday	9:00	11:45	12:45	3:00	5.30
Tuesday	8:45	10:45	2:00	5:30	5.30
Wednesday	9:00	12:00	1:00	4:00	6
Thursday	9:30	12:00	1:15	3:45	5
Friday	9:00	11:30	12:15	3:15	5

a) How many hours did he work?

   26.6

b) If he earns $15.85 per hour, how much did he earn that week?

   $15.85 · 26.6 = $421.61

SOLUTION

a) On Monday, Antonio worked $2\frac{3}{4}$ hours in the morning and $2\frac{1}{4}$ hours in the afternoon for a total of 5 hours.

On Tuesday, he worked 2 hours in the morning and $3\frac{1}{2}$ hours in the afternoon for a total of $5\frac{1}{2}$ hours.

On Wednesday, he worked 3 hours in the morning and 3 hours in the afternoon for a total of 6 hours.

On Thursday, he worked $2\frac{1}{2}$ hours in the morning and $2\frac{1}{2}$ hours in the afternoon for a total of 5 hours.

On Friday, he worked $2\frac{1}{2}$ hours in the morning and 3 hours in the afternoon for a total of $5\frac{1}{2}$ hours.

Add these amounts together.

$5 + 5\frac{1}{2} + 6 + 5 + 5\frac{1}{2} = 27$

Antonio worked 27 hours.

b) Multiply the number of hours he worked by his hourly wage.

27 × $15.85 = $430.70

Antonio earned $430.70 that week.

BUILD YOUR SKILLS

9. Monty works after school at a gas station in Swift Current, SK. He earns $9.45/h. How much would he earn if the time card below represents his work week?

Time Card: Monty			
Day			Total Hours
	IN	OUT	
Monday	3:30	6:45	3.15
Tuesday			0
Wednesday	5:00	9:30	4.30
Thursday	5:00	9:30	4.30
Friday	3:30	7:00	4.30

9.45 · 16.05 = $151.67

> Hae-rin often works a split shift, where her work day is split into two time blocks.

10. Hae-rin works as a part-time warehouse technician. She gets paid $12.76/h and keeps her own time card. How much did she earn during the week?

Time Card: Hae-rin					
Day	Morning		Afternoon		Total Hours
	IN	OUT	IN	OUT	
Monday	7:45	9:00	5:00	7:45	
Tuesday			4:00	8:00	
Wednesday	9:00	11:00			
Thursday	9:00	11:00	3:00	5:00	
Friday			3:00	6:00	
Saturday	9:00	12:00			

NEW SKILLS: WORKING WITH OVERTIME PAY

Many full-time jobs have a 40-hour work week, but others may have different regular hours. If you work more than the regular number of hours, it is classified as overtime and you will earn overtime pay for those extra hours. Overtime is often paid at "time and a half"—that is, 1.5 times your regular wage—but can be any other agreed-upon amount.

Example 6

Marcel works for a construction company and earns $15.82/h for a $37\frac{1}{2}$-hour work week. He is paid time and a half for any time that he works in excess of $37\frac{1}{2}$ hours. If he works $42\frac{1}{4}$ hours during one week, how much will he earn?

SOLUTION

Calculate Marcel's overtime wage. It is time and a half, which means 1.5 times his regular wage.

1.5 × $15.82 = $23.73

His overtime salary is $23.73/h.

Calculate how many hours of overtime he worked by subtracting $37\frac{1}{2}$ from $42\frac{1}{4}$. (Hint: Change these values to decimals to make subtracting easier.)

42.25 − 37.5 = 4.75

He worked 4.75 h overtime.

Find his total income by calculating his regular income and then his overtime income. Add the two amounts together.

Regular income:

37.5 × $15.82 = $593.25

Overtime income:

4.75 × $23.73 = $112.72

Total income:

$593.25 + $112.72 = $705.97

Marcel earned $705.97 during the week.

BUILD YOUR SKILLS

11. Pete works in road construction as a grader operator. His regular work week is 40 hours. During the busy season, he often has to work overtime. For overtime hours worked Monday to Friday, he earns time and a half. If he has to work on Saturday, he earns double time and a half. How much will Pete make if he works 45.25 hours during the week and 5.75 hours on Saturday? His regular salary is $15.77/h.

12. Ingrid works as a medical receptionist at a rate of $11.82/h. She regularly works 35 hours per week, but her clinic wants to increase her work week to 42 h. She agrees to do this if they will pay her overtime, at time and a half, for the extra hours. If they agree to pay this amount, what will her weekly pay be?

13. Nathalie works as a playground supervisor for 8 weeks during the summer at a rate of $15.27/h for a 40-hour week. If she averages 3 hours of overtime each week, paid at time and a half, how much will she earn during the summer?

PRACTISE YOUR NEW SKILLS

1. What is your daily income if you earn $10.75/h as a camp counsellor and you work 10 hours per day?

   $10.75/h · 10 hr = $107.50

2. Lauren worked as an assistant at the National Métis Youth Conference. Her job was to provide support to people giving workshops. Lauren worked for $7\frac{1}{2}$ hours at a rate of $12.36/h. How much did she make?

   7.5h · $12.36 = $92.70

3. Juanita has been offered a job that pays $497.35 for a 35-hour work week. A second company offers her a job at $16.75/h, but will only guarantee 30 hours per week. Which job would you advise Juanita to take?

   $497.35 ÷ 35 = $14.21

   $16.75/h · 30 = $502.50

   Less hours w/ more pay would be the better job.

4. Rita's annual income at her part-time job walking dogs is $6758.00. Assuming she works the same amount of time each week, what is her weekly salary?

$6758.00 ÷ 52/w-y = (129.96/w)

5. Abdul's time card is below. If his hourly wage is $9.05, how much did he earn during the week?

Time Card: Abdul					
Day	Morning		Afternoon		Total Hours
	IN	OUT	IN	OUT	
Monday	9:05 3.20	12:15	1:20 4.20	5:00	7.40
Tuesday	9:02 3.15	12:13	1:12 3.27	4:25	6.42
Wednesday	8:58 5.12	12:14	1:05 3.24	4:19	9.36
Thursday	9:02 3.14	12:12	12:58 3.12	4:14	6.26
Friday	8:45 3.20	12:35	1:05 3.20	4:15	6.40

34.84 · $9.05/h =
($315.30)

6. Tandor has begun a job as an animal trainer in the movie industry. His starting wage is $10.53/h for 30 hours per week. If he works more than 30 hours, he is paid 1.25 times his regular salary. How much will he earn if he works 35 hours in one week?

(1.5 written above 1.25)

$10.53/h · 30h = $315.90

$10.53 · 1.5 = $15.80
(overtime pay)

15.80 · 5 = 9
15.80 + 9 = 24.80

315.90
+ 24.80
─────
340.70

Chapter 2 Earning an Income

Alternative Ways to Earn Money   2.2

NEW SKILLS: WORKING WITH INCOME OPTIONS

Not all working people earn wages or a salary. There are other ways to earn income, including piecework, commission, salary plus commission, and contract work.

For more information, see page 64 of *MathWorks 10*.

Example 1

Greg works as a tree planter during the summer and he earns his income through piecework. He is paid $2.50 for each seedling he plants. If he plants 45 seedlings in a day, how much will he earn?

SOLUTION

Multiply $2.50 by 45.

$2.50 × 45 = $112.50

He will earn $112.50 that day.

BUILD YOUR SKILLS

1. Thomasina knits sweaters and sells them in her craft shop. She has been hired to knit sweaters for a team of 4 curlers and their spare. If she charges $75.50 for a large sweater and $69.75 for a medium sweater (because they require different amounts of wool), how much will she earn if she knits 3 large and 2 medium sweaters?

2. Patricia works in the garment industry. She is paid $1.50 for each hem and $2.25 for each waistband. How much does she earn by hemming 12 dresses and attaching 15 waistbands?

3. Jack cleans windows for extra income. He charges $3.00 for a main floor window and $5.00 for a second-storey window. How much will he earn if he cleans the windows on a house that has 7 main floor windows and 6 second-storey windows?

Example 2

Mary works as a flower arranger. She is paid $143.75 for making 25 identical flower arrangements for a wedding. How much was she paid per arrangement?

SOLUTION

Find the unit rate. The easiest way to calculate this is to divide $143.75 by 25.

$143.75 ÷ 25 = $5.75

She is paid $5.75 per arrangement.

BUILD YOUR SKILLS

4. Jorge is an auto detailer. If each job costs the same amount and his office grossed $3048.00 on 12 jobs, what was the cost per job?

5. Karissa picked 18 quarts of strawberries and earned $67.50. How much did she earn per quart?

6. Joey is a freelance writer. He often writes articles for a local newspaper that pays $0.35 per word. How long was his article (expressed as the number of words) if he was paid $192.50?

Example 3

Ming works in a store that sells classic Chinese furniture such as roundback armchairs and corner-leg stone stools. Ming works on commission at a rate of 6.5% of his gross sales. If he sold $9865.00 worth of furniture last week, how much commission did he earn?

SOLUTION

Multiply his sales by his commission rate (expressed as a decimal).

$9865.00 × 0.065 = $641.23

His commission was $641.23.

BUILD YOUR SKILLS

7. Peter works in a sporting goods store and earns 12% commission on his sales. How much does he make on a bicycle that sells for $785.95?

8. When selling a home, a real estate agent makes 5% commission on the first $250 000.00 of the home's selling price and 2% on any amount over that. How much will Sue make if she sells a house worth $375 900.00?

9. David earns a salary of $375.00 per week plus 5% commission on his sales. If he sold $6521.00 of goods, how much did he make?

Example 4

Olaf earned $416.03 commission on his sales of $9245.00. What was his rate of commission?

SOLUTION

You need to find what percent $416.03 is of $9245.00. Use proportional reasoning.

$$\frac{\$416.03}{\$9245.00} = \frac{x}{100}$$

$$100 \times \frac{\$416.03}{\$9245.00} = \frac{x}{100} \times 100$$

$$100 \times \frac{\$416.03}{\$9245.00} = x$$

$$4.5 \approx x$$

His rate of commission was about 4.5%.

ALTERNATIVE SOLUTION

Divide Olaf's commission by his sales to find the rate of his commission as a decimal. Then multiply this by 100 to convert to a percentage.

$416.03 ÷ $9245.00 ≈ 0.045

$$0.045 \times 100 = 4.5$$

His rate of commission was 4.5%.

BUILD YOUR SKILLS

10. If Freddi earns $6.86 on a $95.95 sale, what was his rate of commission?

11. What is the rate of commission if you make $592.00 on sales of $12 589.00?

12. Don operates a small craft store in which he sells other people's crafts. He takes a 45% commission from the sales of all crafts. If he earned $958.00 commission last week, how much did he sell?

Example 5

Gurpreet is figuring out what he should charge for repairing the steps on a client's house. The cost of materials will be $785.96, and he will have to hire 2 workers for 8 hours each at a rate of $12.85/h. He wants to earn at least $450.00 for himself. What should he charge the client in the contract?

SOLUTION

Calculate all of Gurpreet's costs.

Cost of materials: $785.96

Cost of labour:

2 people × 8 hours × $\frac{\$12.85}{1 \text{ hour}}$ = $205.60

Gurpreet's income: $450.00

Add all of these costs to find the total cost of completing the repairs.

$785.95 + $205.60 + $450.00 = $1441.56

Gurpreet should charge $1441.56.

> Gurpreet would probably round this number. He might charge $1450.00.

BUILD YOUR SKILLS

13. Marcel is bidding on a contract to lay concrete on a patio. He decides to calculate his actual costs and then add 20% profit for himself. He needs 3 cubic yards of concrete at $100.00 per cubic yard delivered. He needs to pay 2 employees $12.45/h each for 4 hours to do the job. What should he charge the client?

14. Tien has three employees working for her. Each employee is paid the minimum wage in BC, $8.00/h, for an 8-hour day. They are also paid a commission of 12% on all sales they make. If the three employees made sales of $785.96, $452.87, and $616.42, how much must Tien pay in total for the day?

15. Kate works at the front desk for a sheet metal company that recently completed 5 contracts. The contracts were worth $5600.00, $2800.00, $7450.00, $1900.00, and $8900.00. Materials, salaries, and other expenses amounted to $23 750.00. What was the percentage of the profits?

Chapter 2 Earning an Income 95

PRACTISE YOUR NEW SKILLS

1. A farmer pays his son $8.25 for each bucket of wild blueberries he picks. He then sells them at a roadside stand for $15.00 per bucket.

   a) How much does his son earn if he picks 28 buckets of blueberries?

   $8.25 × 28 = $231

   b) How much does the farmer earn?

   $15.00/bucket − $8.25 = $6.75

   $6.75/bucket

2. A car company pays its salespeople 2% commission on the amount of their sales after cost. Joey sells a car for $23 000.00 that cost the company $15 000.00. How much did Joey make in commission?

   $\frac{2\%}{100\%} × \$23\,000 = \$460$

   Joey would earn $460

3. Larissa earns a base salary of $500.00 per week plus 4% commission on any sales. How much will she have to sell to earn $750.00 in a week?

   $750 − $500 = $250

   $\frac{250}{x} = \frac{4\%}{100\%}$ $\frac{250 \cdot 100}{4} = 6250$

4. Paulette has been hired to make bridesmaids' dresses for a wedding. She knows that it will take her approximately 9.5 hours to sew each dress and that the material for each dress costs $120.00. Paulette decides to charge $240.00 per dress. At this price, what is her hourly rate?

$240
−$120
―――――
$120 ÷ 9.5 = $12.63

Paulette earns $12.63/h

5. Jeff's bid on a contract was $15 980.00. His costs would be $12 250.00, plus he would have to pay a labourer for 36 hours at $12.45/h.

a) Jeff's potential client indicated that another contractor offered a bid that was 10% lower. Would Jeff be justified in lowering his contract price to the same amount? Why or why not?

b) Jeff calculated that he will put 50 hours into the job. If he lowers the bid, what will his hourly income be?

Additional Earnings 2.3

NEW SKILLS: WORKING WITH INCOME SUPPLEMENTS

A bonus is an extra amount earned for a job well done or for exceeding expectations, and is paid in addition to regular pay and/or overtime pay. It may be a lump sum or a percentage of earnings. Danger pay, isolation pay, a shift premium, and tips are also paid in addition to regular pay.

For more information, see page 72 of *MathWorks 10*.

Example 1

Marika works during the summer as a supervisor of a children's program at the local community centre. She has a good reputation with the children and her employer wants her to come back next year. Marika earned $3600.00 during the summer and her employer offers her a 15% signing bonus if she will sign up for next year. If Marika signs up, how much will she get as a signing bonus?

SOLUTION

Find 15% of Marika's wages.

0.15 × $3600.00 = $540.00

She will make $540.00 as a signing bonus.

BUILD YOUR SKILLS

1. Chester wants to clear out his used car sales lot in Surrey, BC. To do so, he offers his employees an incentive for each car they sell. They will receive bonuses in the following amounts:

   - $50.00 for each car they sell for more than $20 000.00
   - $40.00 for each car they sell between $15 000.00 and $19 999.00
   - $30.00 for each car they sell between $10 000.00 and $14 999.00
   - $25.00 for each car they sell below $10 000.00

   Gerry sells cars worth $14 895.00, $19 998.00, $15 675.00, $7250.00, and $15 229.00. What is his bonus pay?

2. Raymond receives isolation pay for working in Wabasca, AB. If his regular pay is $2245.00/month, and he is offered a bonus of 12% or $275.00/month, which should he take?

3. Darren works as a logging machine operator. His salary is $24.80/h. Due to the dangerous nature of his job, he makes 38% more per hour than Sean, who is a forklift operator. How much do Darren and Sean each make in an 8-hour day?

Example 2

Conchita works as a bus driver for a transit company. Since busy times of the day require more drivers than midday, the company requires that some employees work split shifts. The bus company offers a 12% shift premium for the second shift to anyone that has a 4-hour break between the end of one shift and the beginning of the next.

If Conchita earns $17.82/h, how much will she earn during the week?

Time Card: Conchita		
Day	Shift 1	Shift 2
Monday	6:15–11:00	3:30–6:45
Tuesday	6:15–10:15	3:30–7:15
Wednesday	12:00–4:00	6:00–9:00
Thursday	3:30–7:30	
Friday	8:00–11:00	2:00–4:45

SOLUTION

Determine the days on which Conchita will receive a shift premium.

Monday: $4\frac{1}{2}$ hours – Premium

Tuesday: $5\frac{1}{4}$ hours – Premium

Wednesday: 2 hours – No premium

Thursday: no break – No premium

Friday: 3 hours – No premium

Calculate the shift premium rate by find 112% of her regular wage (as a decimal, 1.12).

$1.12 \times \$17.82 = \$19.96$

Calculate the hours worked in each shift and the income per shift.

Time Card: Conchita		
Day	Shift 1	Shift 2
Monday	4.75 × $17.82 = $84.65	3.25 × $19.96 = $64.87
Tuesday	4 × $17.82 = $71.28	3.75 × $19.96 = $74.85
Wednesday	4 × $17.82 = $71.28	3 × $17.82 = $53.46
Thursday	4 × $17.82 = $71.28	
Friday	3 × $17.82 = $53.46	2.75 × $17.82 = $49.01

Calculate total income by adding.

$\$84.65 + 3(\$71.28) + 2(\$53.46) + \$64.87 + \$74.85 + \$49.01 = \$594.14$

Conchita will earn $594.14 during the week.

ALTERNATIVE SOLUTION

Determine the number of hours for which she earned regular pay.

Monday: 4.75 hours

Tuesday: 4 hours

Wednesday: 7 hours

Thursday: 4 hours

Friday: 5.75 hours

Total: 25.5 hours

Add up the number of hours for which she received a shift premium.

Monday: 3.25 hours

Tuesday: 3.75 hours

Total: 7 hours

Calculate her shift premium rate by finding 112% of her regular wage.

$112 \div 100 = 1.12$

$1.12 \times \$17.82 = \$19.96$

Calculate her regular income and her premium income, and then add the two.

Regular income:

$25.5 \text{ hours} \times \dfrac{\$17.82}{\text{hour}} = \$454.41$

Premium income:

$7 \text{ hours} \times \dfrac{\$19.96}{\text{hour}} = \$139.72$

$\$454.41 + \$139.72 = \$594.13$

Conchita will earn $594.13 during the week.

This answer differs from the first solution by $0.01, due to rounding in the first solution.

BUILD YOUR SKILLS

4. Regular hours at the computer repair shop where Denise works are 9:00 am to 5:00 pm, Monday to Friday. Her boss has offered a shift premium of $1.75/hour to anyone who will work after 5:00 pm or on Saturday. Last week, Denise worked the following hours:

   - Monday: 9:00 am–5:00 pm
   - Tuesday: 2:00 pm–8:00 pm
   - Wednesday: 2:00 pm–7:00 pm
   - Thursday: 12:00 pm–8:00 pm
   - Saturday: 9:00 am–3:00 pm

   If her regular pay was $15.25/h, how much did she earn last week?

5. Drivers for the Fast Delivery Parcel Company are offered a shift premium if they drive the night shift (after 8:00 pm) to deliver parcels by 9:00 the next morning. Baljeet's schedule last week was as follows:

   - Monday: 12:00 pm–7:00 pm
   - Tuesday: 9:00 am–5:00 pm
   - Wednesday: 6:00 pm–12:00 am
   - Thursday: 12:00 pm–8:00 pm
   - Friday: 3:00 pm–9:00 pm

   His regular pay is $12.75/h, and the shift premium is $7.00/h. How much did he make last week?

6. Chen is offered isolation pay of $1250.00 for a job in northern Manitoba. Alternatively, he can have a bonus payment of 28% of his salary. If his salary is $532.00/wk, which is the better option if it takes 10 weeks to complete the job?

Example 3

Suzette works as a waitress in a local café in Selkirk, MB. Yesterday she made $165.32 in tips. If this was 15% of the bills she collected, how much were the bills?

SOLUTION

Let x be the total of the bills. Use proportional reasoning.

$$\frac{15}{100} = \frac{165.32}{x}$$

$$100x\left(\frac{15}{100}\right) = \left(\frac{165.32}{x}\right)100x \quad \text{Multiply both sides by the product of the denominators.}$$

$$15x = 165.32 \times 100 \quad \text{Simplify.}$$

$$15x = 16\,532$$

$$\frac{15x}{15} = \frac{16\,532}{15} \quad \text{Divide both sides by 15 to isolate } x.$$

$$x = \$1102.13$$

Her orders totalled $1102.13.

ALTERNATIVE SOLUTION

You know that $165.32 equals 15% of the total orders. Use this to calculate 1% of the orders.

$165.32 ÷ 15 ≈ $11.0213

Multiply this number by 100 to get 100% of the total orders.

11.0213 × 100 = $1102.13

Suzette's orders totalled $1102.13.

BUILD YOUR SKILLS

7. Kirsten earns a base salary of $8.20/h plus tips. On a typical day, she bills her customers $950.00, and her tips average 15%. What is Kirsten's average daily income with tips for an 8-hour day?

8. Mandeep is at a restaurant in Prince Rupert, BC. He has decided that 15% is too much to leave for a waiter who did not provide good service. He left $3.00 on a meal that cost $24.75. What percentage tip did he leave?

9. Rosita earned $408.65 working 35 hours at $8.21/h plus tips. How much did she make in tips?

In most restaurants, 15% is the average expected tip amount. A quick way to estimate a 15% tip is to round off your bill, find 10% by moving the decimal one place to the left, and then add half of that number to itself.

For example, if the bill is $68.89, round up to $70.00.

10% is $7.00.

Half of $7.00 is $3.50.

$7.00 + $3.50 = $10.50

The total tip would be $10.50. This is slightly more than 15% because you rounded up, so you may want to pay about $79.00.

PRACTISE YOUR NEW SKILLS

1. Parminder is working at an isolated weather station in the Yukon. She earns an annual salary of $45 650.00 plus $780.00/month for isolation pay. If she works at the station for 8 months of the year, what will her annual income be?

   $780 / 8 months = $6240

   $45 650 + $6240
   = $51 890

2. Hilda works as a live-in nanny. She earns $11.25/h plus room and board. If Hilda works over 40 h in one week, her boss gives her a bonus of $8.50/h for each extra hour. If Hilda works 57.5 h in one week, how much does she earn?

   $11.25 · 40h = $450
   $8.50 · 17h = $144.50

   $450 + $144.50
   = $594.50

3. Restaurant sales totalled $40 568.00 one month, and the average tip was 15%.

   a) How much would each of the three waiters make in tips if they shared equally?

   $$\frac{15\%}{100\%} = \frac{x}{\$40\,568} = \frac{15 \cdot 40\,568}{100\%} = \$6085.20$$

   $$\$6085.20 \div 3 = \$2028.40$$

   b) If they give 25% of their tips to the kitchen staff, how much will each waiter make?

   $$\frac{25\%}{100\%} = \frac{x}{\$2028.40} = \frac{25 \cdot 2028.40}{100} = \$506.35$$

4. Franco earns $17.23/h, time and a half overtime, and a shift bonus of $2.65 for split shifts. If he worked a total of 43.5 hours, 18 of which were split shifts, how much did he earn if a regular work week was 38.5 hours?

   $17.23 \cdot 38.5 = \$663.35$
   $2.65 \cdot 18 = \$47.70$
   $5.5\text{hr} \cdot \$1.5 = \$8.25$

   $\$663.35 + \$47.70 + \$8.25 = \$719.30$

5. Horace works as a door-to-door salesman in rural Alberta and must use his own car. He is paid $0.45/km for each kilometre he drives, plus 8% of sales. If he drove 2354 km and sold $47 854.00 of merchandise, how much would his paycheque be?

   $2354 \text{ km} \cdot \$0.45 = \$1059.30$ ... $\$5231.11$

   $$\frac{8\%}{100\%} = \frac{x}{\$47\,854} = \frac{8 \cdot \$47\,854}{100} = \$3828.32$$

   $\$5231.11 + \$3828.32 = \$9059.43$

   his paycheque would be $9059.43

2.4 Deductions and Net Pay

NEW SKILLS: WORKING WITH NET INCOME

taxable income: income after before-tax deductions have been applied, on which federal and provincial taxes are paid

net income: income after all taxes and other deductions have been applied; also called take-home pay

Deductions are amounts of money taken off your gross pay for income tax (federal and provincial or territorial), union dues, disability insurance, employment insurance (EI), pension plans (including the Canada Pension Plan or CPP), and health or other benefits. Income tax is paid on your **taxable income**.

Each paycheque should list your gross pay, all deductions, and your **net income**. At the end of the year, your employer will supply you with a T4 slip that you will use to prepare your income tax return.

For more details, see page 79 of *MathWorks 10*.

Example 1

John's group life insurance is 1.5% of his salary of $450.00 every two weeks. How much does he pay for group life insurance?

SOLUTION

Change 1.5% to a decimal and multiply by his salary.

$$1.5 \div 100 = 0.015$$
$$0.015 \times \$450.00 = \$6.75$$

He pays $6.75 for group life insurance per paycheque.

Some deductions are taxable, and some are not. For example, union dues and company pension plans are before-tax deductions, and so they are not subject to federal and provincial taxes.

BUILD YOUR SKILLS

1. If the federal tax rate is 15%, how much is deducted from your $750.00 paycheque?

   Income tax rates vary with province or territory, salary, and family circumstances.

2. If your short-term disability insurance rate is 0.5%, what do you pay if your paycheque is $300.00?

3. If your Canada Pension Plan (CPP) contribution rate is 4.95% and your salary is $1578.00 every two weeks, what will be the CPP deduction?

Example 2

Jaar had a gross income of $785.00. His net income was $625.42. What percentage of his gross pay were his deductions?

SOLUTION

Calculate the amount of the deductions by subtracting his net income from his gross income.

$785.00 − $625.42 = $159.58

Calculate what percentage $159.58 is of $785.00.

159.58 ÷ 785.00 ≈ 0.2033

0.2033 × 100 = 20.33%

His deductions are about 20.3% of his gross pay.

BUILD YOUR SKILLS

4. Samara's monthly taxable income was $3276.54. If she paid $757.24 in taxes, what percentage of her taxable income did she pay?

5. Patricia's before-tax deductions amounted to $75.47 on a gross salary of $700.00.

   a) If she paid $93.68 in federal tax, what is her tax rate?

   b) If she paid $36.85 in territorial tax, what is her tax rate?

6. Hans paid $37.51 Employment Insurance (EI) on his taxable monthly income of $2168.21. What is the EI rate?

Example 3

Alphonso has a gross income of $852.00 per week. His before-tax deductions include union dues of 2.5% of his gross income and a company pension plan contribution of 3%. His federal tax rate is 16.2% and his provincial tax rate is 5.4%. He pays 4.95% to the CPP and 1.8% for EI. Calculate his net income.

SOLUTION

Calculate Alphonso's taxable income by subtracting his union dues and his company pension from his gross income.

First, calculate the amount of his union dues and company pension.

Union dues:

$$2.5 \div 100 = 0.025$$
$$0.025 \times \$852.00 = \$21.30$$

Company pension:

$$3 \div 100 = 0.03$$
$$0.03 \times \$852.00 = \$25.56$$

Next, subtract these amounts from his gross income to find his taxable income.

$$\$852.00 - (\$21.30 + \$25.56) = \$805.14$$

Calculate the amount of taxes, CPP, and EI using his taxable income.

Federal tax:

$$16.2 \div 100 = 0.162$$
$$0.162 \times \$805.14 = \$130.43$$

Provincial tax:

$$5.4 \div 100 = 0.054$$
$$0.054 \times \$805.14 = \$43.48$$

CPP:

$$4.95 \div 100 = 0.0495$$
$$0.0495 \times \$805.14 = \$39.85$$

EI:

$1.8 \div 100 = 0.018$

$0.018 \times \$805.14 = \$14.99$

Alphonso's net income will be his taxable income minus these deductions.

$\$805.14 - \$130.42 - \$43.48 - \$14.49 = \$576.89$

Alphonso's net income will be $576.89.

BUILD YOUR SKILLS

7. Randy works at two jobs. In one job, he earns $325.00/week, and has deductions of $56.67 federal tax, $13.12 provincial tax, $16.09 CPP, and $4.14 EI. At his other job, he earns $567.00/week and pays $79.42 federal tax, $16.82 provincial tax, and $18.12 CPP. What is his net income?

8. As a part-time college instructor, Kathy teaches an introductory course on Mexican history. She has a biweekly gross income of $3654.75. Her before-tax deductions include a short-term disability premium of 0.5%, union dues of 3.1%, and a pension amount of 4%. If she pays federal tax at a rate of 18.5%, provincial tax at a rate of 6.2%, CPP at 4.95%, and EI at 2.2%, what is her net income?

9. Consider the following pay statement.

Employee Name: Hank		
Company:	Pay Begin Date: 06/01/2010	Net Pay: ???
	Pay End Date: 06/15/2010	Cheque Date: 06/15/2010

General

Employee ID:	Job Title:
Address:	Pay Rate: $575.00
	Annual: $29 900.00

Taxes Data

Description	Federal
Claim Code	1

Hours and Earnings

	Current	
Description	Rate	Gross Earnings
Regular	$575.00/wk	$575.00

Taxes

Description	Current
Federal	$48.01
Provincial	$21.64
CPP	$25.13
EI	$9.95
Total	$104.73

a) What is Hank's gross weekly income?

b) What is his net income?

c) What percent of his taxable income did he pay in federal taxes?

PRACTISE YOUR NEW SKILLS

1. Juliana has an annual salary of $45 785.00.

   a) How much does she pay in union dues if the rate is 2.4%?

   b) How much does she pay in CPP if the rate is 4.95% and her taxable income is $44 686.16?

2. Mario had $685.74 deducted in federal tax. If his taxable income was $2981.52, what was his tax rate?

3. What will be your net pay if you have deductions of $105.30 federal tax, $23.76 provincial tax, $48.61 CPP, and $14.12 EI from your paycheque of $982.00?

   $982 − $105.30 − $23.76 − $48.61 − $14.12 = $790.21

   Your Net Pay would be $790.21

CHAPTER TEST

1. If Brenda earns $12.15/h and gets a 3.2% raise, how much will she earn per hour?

2. How much will you earn in a year as an apprentice metalworker if you are paid $750.00 every two weeks?

3. What is your annual salary if your monthly salary is $3568.00?

4. As a medical technician, Stephanie has been offered a job that pays $53 000.00 per year and another job that pays $25.50 per hour. Assuming a 40-hour work week and all other conditions being the same, at which job will she earn more?

5. Tommy made $20.55 commission on a $685.00 sale. What was his rate of commission?

6. Von works as a car salesman. He earns 8% commission on the after-cost profit when he sells a car. If he sells a car for $12 795.00 that cost the dealer $9280.00, how much does he make?

7. Jenny earns $12.42/h, but earns double time and a half when she works on a statutory holiday. If she works a 6-hour shift on a holiday, how much will she earn that day?

8. Harold works 40 hours regular time at $18.25 and 5.25 hours overtime at time and a half. How much does he earn?

9. Nanette crochets scarves and sells them for $15.95 each. If material cost her $7.52/scarf, how much does she make if she sells 9 scarves?

10. Cho bids $5750.00 for a contract. If he hires 4 men for 2 days (8 h/day) at a rate of $12.50/h and his materials cost him $1675.84, how much does he earn?

11. How much CPP will be taken off your $782.45 taxable income at 4.95%?

12. Padma has been offered isolation pay of $125.00/week to work as a park ranger in northern Alberta.

   a) How much will she make in a 40-hour work week if she is normally paid $21.52/h?

   b) Adding in the isolation pay, what is her hourly rate?

Chapter 3

Length, Area, and Volume

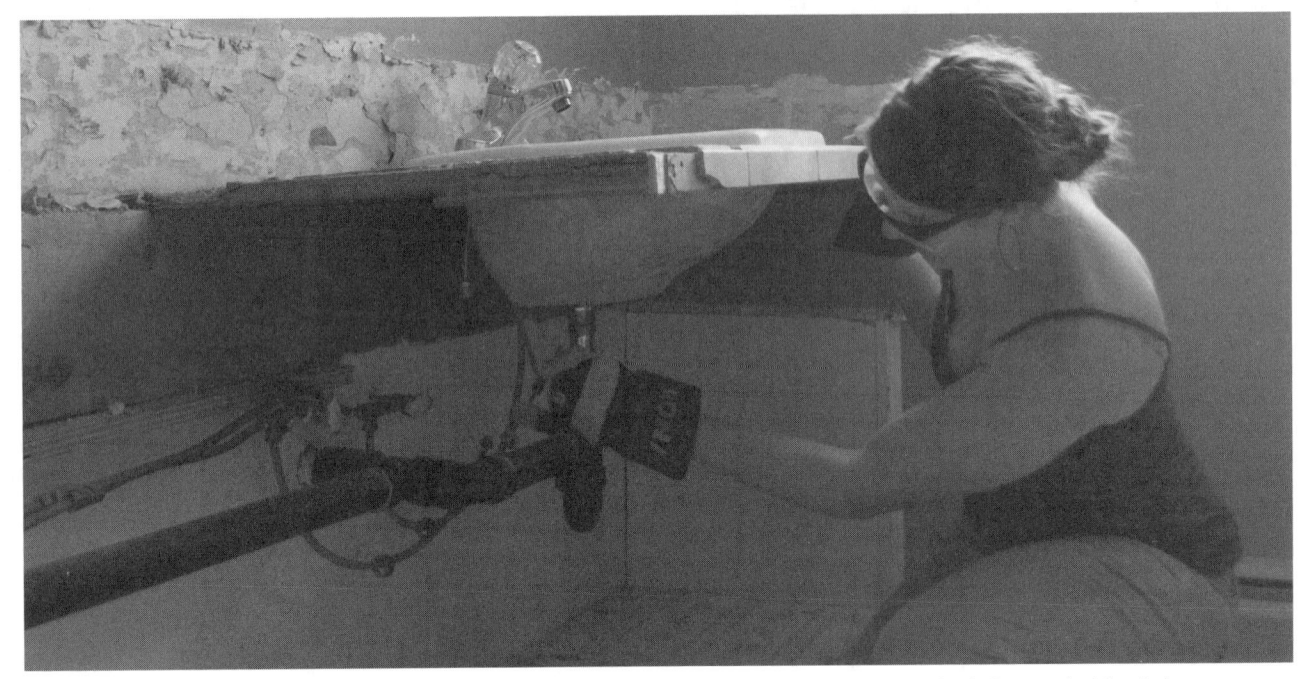

Kristi Hansen is a Red Seal plumber. Calculating the capacity of water lines, determining the length of pipe needed for drainage systems, and accurately predicting the volume of hot water a building's system will use are some of her tasks.

3.1 Systems of Measurement

REVIEW: WORKING WITH PERIMETER

perimeter: the sum of the lengths of all the sides of a polygon

In this section, you will calculate the **perimeter** of different shapes.

A square is a quadrilateral with 4 equal sides, so the perimeter can be found by the following formula:

$P = 4 \times (side\ length)$

The perimeter of a rectangle with length ℓ and width w can be found by the following formula:

$P = 2\ell + 2w$

$P = 2(\ell + w)$

Example 1

What is the perimeter of this figure?

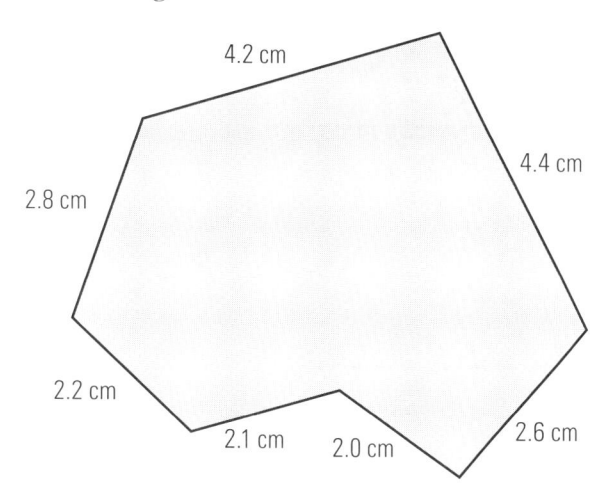

When the units of measurement are all the same, you can ignore them during calculations. Remember to add the units in at the end.

SOLUTION

This figure is a heptagon, which means it has 7 sides. Its perimeter, P, is the sum of the lengths of all 7 sides.

$P = 2.8 + 4.2 + 4.4 + 2.6 + 2.0 + 2.1 + 2.2$

$P = 20.3$ cm

The perimeter is 20.3 cm.

To make sure that you don't miss any sides when calculating the perimeter of a figure, start at one vertex and work your way around the figure.

BUILD YOUR SKILLS

1. Calculate the perimeters of the following diagrams.

A small square symbol in the corner of a diagram means that it is a right angle.

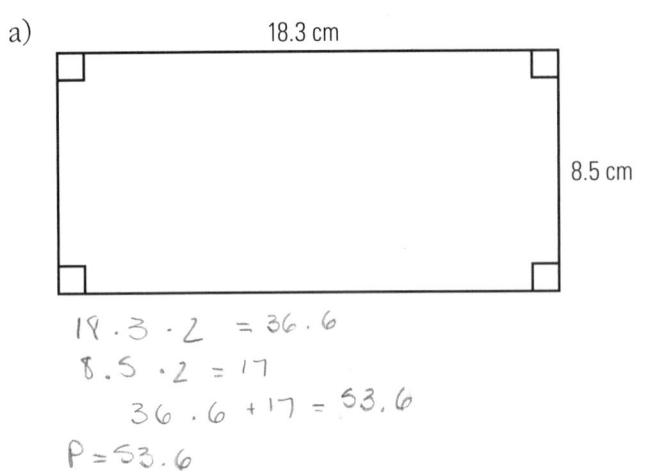

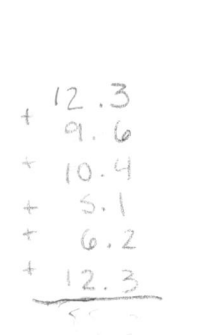

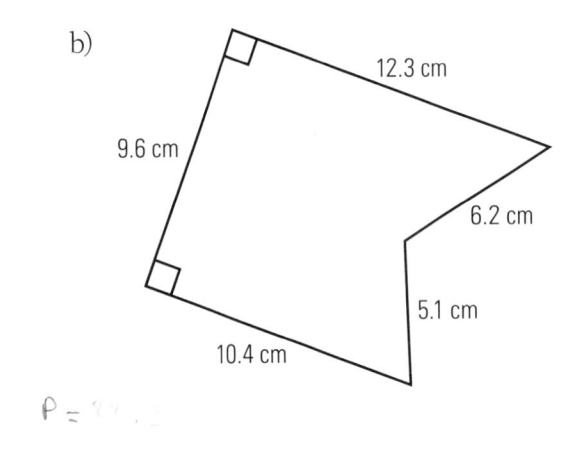

a) 18.3 cm, 8.5 cm

18.3 · 2 = 36.6
8.5 · 2 = 17
36.6 + 17 = 53.6
P = 53.6

b) 12.3 cm, 9.6 cm, 6.2 cm, 5.1 cm, 10.4 cm

12.3
+ 9.6
+ 10.4
+ 5.1
+ 6.2
+ 12.3

P =

c) 0.9 m, 0.9 m, 1.2 m, 2.3 m

0.9
+ 0.9
+ 2.3
+ 2.3
+ 1.2
7.6

P = 7.6

2. Darma is edging a tablecloth with lace. The tablecloth is 210 cm by 180 cm. How much lace does she need?

   210 · 2 = 420
   180 · 2 = 360
   420 + 360 = 780 cm

   Darma needs 780 cm of lace.

3. Garry installs a wire fence around a rectangular pasture. The pasture measures 15 m by 25 m, and he uses three rows of barbed wire. How much wire did he use?

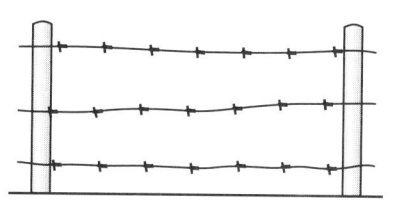

   15 · 2 = 30
   25 · 2 = 50
   80 m · 3 = 240

4. Chantal is building a fence around her swimming pool. The pool is 25 ft long and 12 ft wide, and she wants a 6-ft wide rectangular walkway around the entire pool. How much fencing will she need?

   25 · 2 = 50
   12 · 2 = 24
   74 ft · 6 = 444

Example 2

The sides of the flower garden shown below are 4 m long. Each end is a semi-circle with a diameter of 2 m. What is the perimeter of the flower garden?

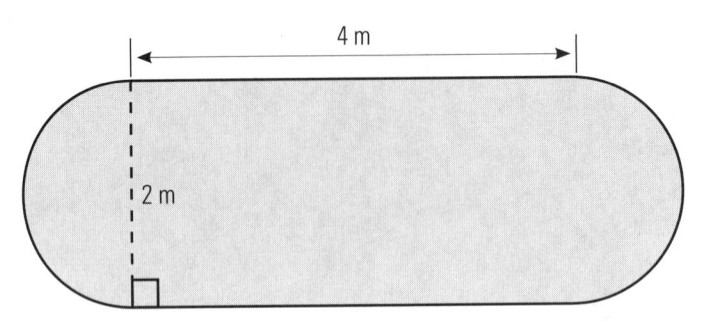

SOLUTION

Break this problem down into two parts, a circle and a rectangle.

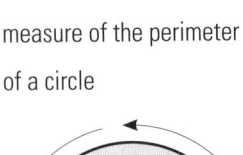

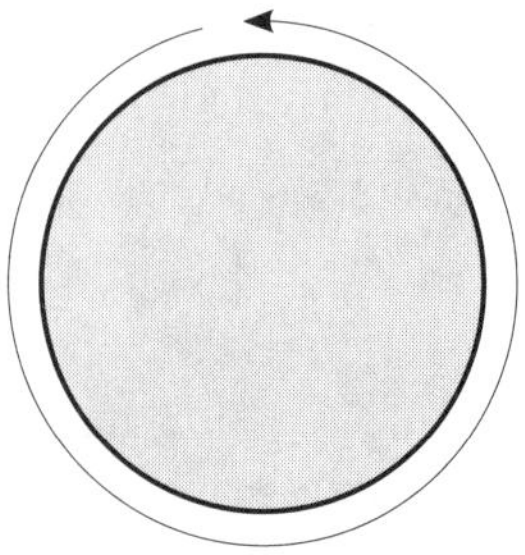

If you add the two end sections together, they form a circle. You can use the formula for the **circumference** to find the perimeter:

$C = \pi d$ or $2\pi r$

circumference: the measure of the perimeter of a circle

C is the circumference, r is the radius, d is the diameter, and π is a constant. In this example, the diameter is 2 m.

Find the circumference of the ends of the flower garden by using this formula.

$C = \pi d$

$C = \pi(2)$

$C \approx 6.28$

Add the lengths of the two straight parts to the circumference of the circle to calculate the perimeter.

$P \approx 6.28 + 4 + 4$

$P \approx 14.28$

The perimeter of the flower garden is about 14.28 m.

Chapter 3 Length, Area, and Volume   123

BUILD YOUR SKILLS

5. What is the circumference of a circular fountain if its radius is 5.3 m?

6. Johnny wants to put Christmas lights along the edge and peak of his roof. How many metres of lights will he need?

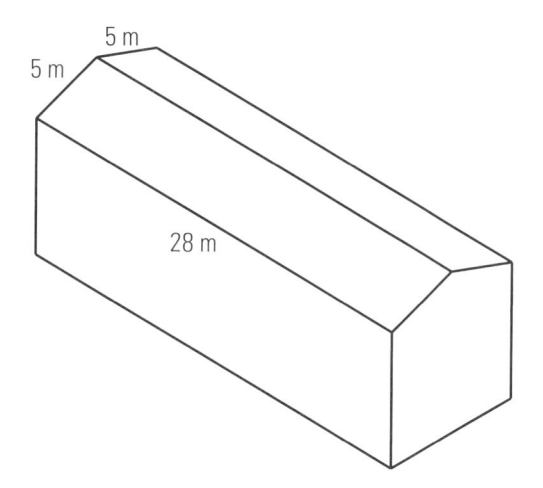

   (Diagram: prism-shaped roof with 5 m, 5 m edges and 28 m length)

7. Hershy uses coloured wire to make a model of the Olympic symbol (5 interlocking circles). If each circle has a radius of 35 cm, how much wire does he need for the rings?

   $C = 2 \cdot \pi \cdot 35 = 219.91 \text{ cm}$

   $219.91 \cdot 5 = 1099.55$

NEW SKILLS: WORKING WITH SYSTEMS OF MEASUREMENT

Système International (SI): the modern version of the metric system; uses the metre as the basic unit of length

imperial system: the system most commonly used in the United States; the standard unit of measurement for length is the foot

Although there are other systems of measurement, the two most common are the **Système International** (SI) and the **imperial system**. In Canada, the official system of measurement is the SI. Because of Canada's close proximity to the United States, you should be familiar with both systems. Both are used in certain contexts.

Below are listed some common imperial units of length and their relationships.

$$12 \text{ inches (in or ")} = 1 \text{ foot (ft or ')}$$

$$36 \text{ inches} = 1 \text{ yard (yd)}$$

$$3 \text{ feet} = 1 \text{ yard}$$

$$5280 \text{ feet} = 1 \text{ mile (mi)}$$

$$1760 \text{ yards} = 1 \text{ mile}$$

For more details, see page 94 of *MathWorks 10*.

If you look at a ruler marked in imperial units, you will notice that it is usually divided into halves, quarters, eighths, and sixteenths, whereas the SI system uses tenths.

Example 3

Wilhelmina, a seamstress, is sewing bridesmaids' dresses. She orders the fabric from the United States, where fabric is measured in yards. Each dress requires $3\frac{3}{4}$ yards of silk, $1\frac{1}{2}$ yards of lace fabric, and $7\frac{1}{4}$ yards of trim. How much of each type of material does Wilhelmina need to make 5 dresses?

SOLUTION

Multiply each amount by 5.

$\text{silk} = 3\frac{3}{4} \times 5$

$\text{silk} = \frac{15}{4} \times 5$ Convert to an improper fraction and multiply.

$\text{silk} = \frac{75}{4}$

$\text{silk} = 18\frac{3}{4}$ yd   Convert to a mixed fraction.

$\text{lace fabric} = 1\frac{1}{2} \times 5$

$\text{lace fabric} = \frac{3}{2} \times 5$ Convert to an improper fraction and multiply.

lace fabric = $\frac{15}{2}$

lace fabric = $7\frac{1}{2}$ yd   Convert to a mixed fraction.

trim = $7\frac{1}{4} \times 5$

trim = $\frac{29}{4} \times 5$ Convert to an improper fraction and multiply.

trim = $\frac{145}{4}$

trim = $36\frac{1}{4}$ yd   Convert to a mixed fraction.

Since fabric can be bought in partial yards, Wilhelmina will need to purchase $18\frac{3}{4}$ yd of silk, $7\frac{1}{2}$ yd of lace fabric, and $36\frac{1}{4}$ yd of trim.

ALTERNATIVE SOLUTION

Convert each mixed fraction to a decimal, and then multiply by 5.

silk = $3\frac{3}{4}$

silk = 3.75

silk = 3.75 × 5

silk = 18.75

lace fabric = $1\frac{1}{2}$

lace fabric = 1.5

lace fabric = 1.5 × 5

lace fabric = 7.5

trim = $7\frac{1}{4}$

trim = 7.25

trim = 7.25 × 5

trim = 36.25

Since fabric can be bought in partial yards, Wilhelmina will need to purchase 18.75 yd of silk, 7.5 yd of lace fabric, and 36.25 yd of trim.

A 2 by 4 is not exactly 2" by 4". The name comes from the dimensions of the lumber before it is dried; when the lumber dries, it shrinks and then is replaned to make it a standard size. A 2 by 4 is actually $1\frac{1}{2}$" by $3\frac{1}{2}$". Lumber and other building supplies are usually sold using imperial units.

BUILD YOUR SKILLS

8. Bernard is buying some lumber to finish a project. He needs 3 pieces of 2 by 4 that are each $4\frac{1}{2}$ feet long, and 10 pieces of 2 by 2 that are each $5\frac{1}{4}$ feet long. How much of each does he need in total?

9. Benjie is replacing some plumbing pipes. He needs 3 pieces of copper pipe: one piece is 2 feet long, one is 5 feet 7 inches long, and one is 4 feet long. How much copper pipe does he need if he loses 1 inch when he cuts the pipe and he can only buy it in even numbers of feet?

10. If each board in a fence is 6 inches wide, how many of them will José need to fence a playground that is 60 feet wide by 125 feet long?

board is 6" wide

Example 4

Fatima is trying to calculate how much baseboard she will need for the room shown below.

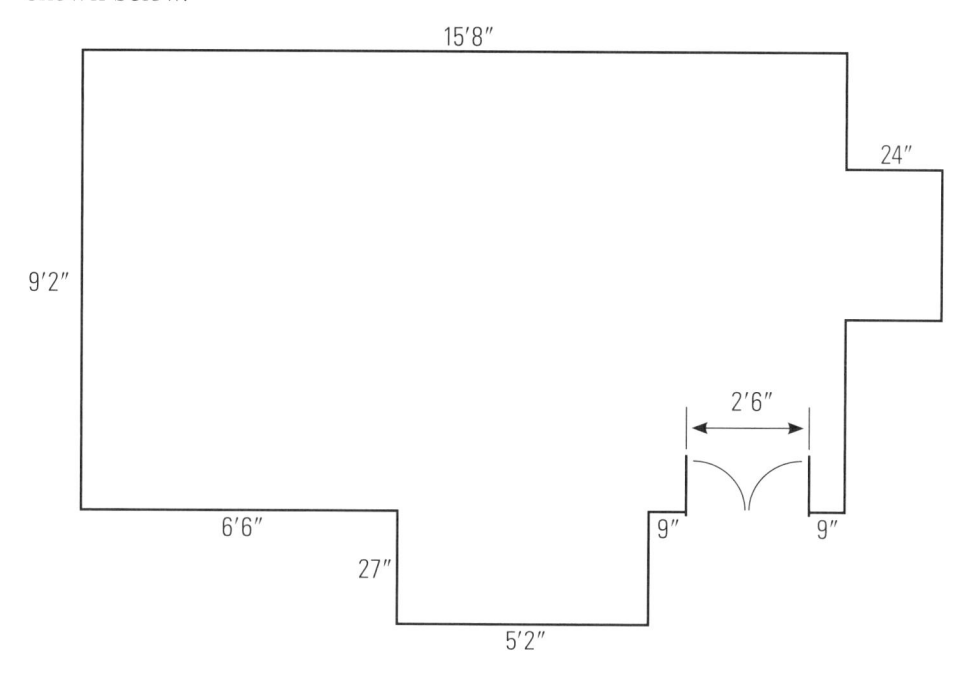

What is the minimum amount of baseboard she will need?

SOLUTION

Find the perimeter of the room. Since there is a door, no baseboard will be needed there. Measurements are given in feet and/or inches.

To find the perimeter of the room, start at any one point, such as the edge of the door, and work your way around the room.

P = 9″ + 27″ + 5′2″+ 27″+ 6′6″+ 9′2″+ 15′8″+ 9′2″+ 24″+ 24″+ 9″

Add feet to feet and inches to inches to get 44′140″.

Convert 140 inches to feet by dividing by 12 (because 12 inches equals 1 foot).

$\frac{140}{12}$ = 11 remainder 8, or 11′8″

Add this to the measure in feet.

44′ + 11′8″ = 55′8″

Therefore, she needs 55′8″ of baseboard.

> Where did the second 9′2″ come from?

ALTERNATIVE SOLUTION

Combine the lengths of the smaller wall segments to simplify the calculation, and subtract the width of the door.

P = 2(15′8″) + 2(9′2″) + 2(27″) + 2(24″) − 2′6″

P = 30′16″ + 18′4″ + 54″ + 48″ − 2′6″

P = 46′116″

Convert 116 inches to feet.

$\frac{116}{12}$ = 9, remainder 8, or 9′8″

Add this to the measure in feet.

46′ + 9′8″ = 55′8″

Therefore, she needs 55′ 8″ of baseboard.

BUILD YOUR SKILLS

11. A pet shop stores 5 pet cages that are 2′8″ wide, 3 cages that are 4′6″ wide, and 2 cages that are 1′8″ wide. Can these cages fit side by side along a wall that is 30′ long?

12. A circular garden is 6′4″ in diameter. To plant a geranium approximately every foot along the circumference, how many geraniums are needed?

13. The height of a basement ceiling is 7′2″. A 6″-deep heating pipe runs across the middle. To enclose it, there must be a 1-inch space between the pipe and the drywall. Will Craig, who is 6′6″ tall, be able to walk under the finished pipe?

PRACTISE YOUR NEW SKILLS

1. Convert the following measurements.

   a) 42 inches to feet

   b) 16 inches to feet and inches

   c) 96 inches to yards

   d) 5 miles to yards

2. You are building a fence around your vegetable garden in your backyard. If the garden is 12′8″ long and 4′6″ wide, what is the total length of fencing you will need?

3. Marjorie is building a dog run that is 25′8″ long and 8′8″ wide. How much fencing will she need if the opening is 3′6″ wide and will not need fencing?

4. A package of paper is 2″ high and 8.5″ wide. If a warehouse shelf is 1′5″ high and 2 yards long, how many packages of paper can be put on the shelf?

5. Jennine estimates that each step she takes is 18″ long and that she takes 1550 steps per block. How many blocks must she walk if she wants to walk 5 miles?

Converting Measurements 3.2

REVIEW: WORKING WITH VARIABLES WITHIN FORMULAS

In this section, you will practise substituting known values into formulas.

In this chapter, you will need to use the following formulas.

$A = \ell w$ Area of a rectangle, where ℓ is the length and w is the width.

$A = \pi r^2$ Area of a circle, where r is the radius and π is the constant, pi.

$A = \frac{1}{2} bh$ Area of a triangle, where b is the length of the base and h is the height.

$A = \pi rs$ Area of the surface of a cone, where r is the radius and s is the slant height.

$C = 2\pi r$ Circumference of a circle, where r is the radius.

Example 1

Sumo is a traditional Japanese martial art. The area of a circular sumo ring, or *dohyoi*, is 16.26 m². What is the radius of the ring?

SOLUTION

Use the formula for finding the area of a circle. You are given the area of the circle, so substitute it into the formula and solve for the unknown value, r.

$$A = \pi r^2$$

$$16.26 = \pi r^2$$

$$\frac{16.26}{\pi} = \frac{\pi r^2}{\pi} \quad \text{Divide both sides by } \pi \text{ to isolate } r^2.$$

$$\sqrt{\frac{16.26}{\pi}} = r$$

$$2.28 \approx r$$

The radius of a sumo ring is 2.28 m.

BUILD YOUR SKILLS

1. Ina is laying turf in a yard measuring 38 ft by 20 ft. What is the yard's area in square feet?

2. A store advertises a circular rug as being 4.9 m². Travis wants a rug to fit a rectangular space that is 2.6 m by 2.6 m. Will this rug fit?

   $A = l \cdot w$
   $4.9 = 2.6 \cdot 2.6$
   $ = 6.76$
   Yes, the rug will fit

3. You are designing a rectangular label for canned food. The can is 5 cm high, with a diameter of 9 cm. To plan your design, calculate the label's length. (The length is equal to the circle's cirumference.)

   $C = \pi \cdot 9 = 28.27$ cm

NEW SKILLS: WORKING WITH DIFFERENT SYSTEMS OF MEASUREMENT

The official system of measurement in Canada is the SI, but the United States uses imperial units. If you are buying products from the United States or are doing business with a US company, you will need to convert between the two systems of measurement.

Below are some common relationships between SI and imperial units of length.

   1 inch ≈ 2.54 centimetres

   1 foot ≈ 0.3 metres

   1 yard ≈ 0.9 metres

   1 mile ≈ 1.6 kilometres

For more details, see page 106 of *MathWorks 10*.

Example 2

Mary is delivering a load of goods from Vancouver, BC, to Seattle, WA, then in Seattle, she is picking up another load to deliver to Albuquerque, NM. The distance from Vancouver to Seattle is 220 km and the distance from Seattle to Albuquerque is 1456 mi. The odometer in Mary's truck records distance in kilometres.

a) What is the total distance she will travel, in kilometres?

b) If her odometer read 154 987 km when she left Seattle, what did it read when she left Vancouver?

c) What will her odometer read when she reaches Albuquerque?

SOLUTION

a) Find the distance in kilometres from Seattle to Albuquerque.

$$1 \text{ mi} \approx 1.6 \text{ km}$$

$$1456 \text{ mi} \approx 1456 \times 1.6$$

$$1456 \text{ mi} \approx 2330 \text{ km}$$

The distance from Seattle to Albuquerque is 2330 km.

Add this to the distance from Vancouver to Seattle to find the total distance.

$$220 \text{ km} + 2330 \text{ km} = 2550 \text{ km}$$

Her trip will be about 2550 km.

b) Subtract the distance she travelled from the odometer reading.

$$154\ 987 - 220 = 154\ 767$$

Her odometer read 154 767 when she left Vancouver

c) Add the distance from Seattle to Albuquerque to the odometer reading.

$$154\ 987 + 2330 = 157\ 317$$

Her odometer should read about 157 317 when she reaches Albuquerque.

BUILD YOUR SKILLS

4. Suzanne purchased tiles for her patio that are 8″ by 4″. She measured her patio in metres and wants to convert the tile dimensions to SI units. What are the dimensions of the tiles in centimetres?

5. Benjamin owns an older American truck. The odometer shows distance travelled in miles. On a recent trip to deliver produce for his employer, he drove 1564 mi. His employer pays him $0.89/km for the use of his own truck. How much will he be reimbursed for the use of his truck for the trip?

6. Marnie owns a carpet store and sells hallway runners for $9.52/linear foot.

   a) How much is this per linear yard?

   b) How much is this per linear metre?

   c) Ralph needs 3.9 m of the runner for his hallway. How much will it cost?

Example 3

Rebecca is planning to install sod in her backyard, which is 18.2 m by 9.8 m. If sod costs $0.28/ft², how much will it cost to sod the backyard?

SOLUTION

Change the measurements of the backyard to feet, and then find the area.

$0.3 \text{ m} = 1 \text{ ft}$

$18.2 \text{ m} = \frac{18.2}{0.3} \text{ ft}$

$\frac{18.2}{0.3} \approx 60.7 \text{ ft}$

Her yard is approximately 61 ft long.

Similarly, change 9.8 m (980 cm) to feet.

$1 \text{ m} = \frac{1}{0.3} \text{ ft}$

$9.8 \text{ m} = \frac{9.8}{0.3} \text{ ft}$

$\frac{9.8 \text{ ft}}{0.3} \approx 32.7 \text{ ft}$

Her yard is approximately 33 ft wide.

Calculate the area of her backyard. The area of a rectangle is calculated by multiplying the length by the width.

$A = \ell w$

$A = 61 \times 33$

$A = 2013 \text{ ft}^2$

She will need approximately 2013 square feet of sod at $0.28/ft².

$2013 \times \$0.28 = \$563.64$

It will cost about $563.64 to sod her backyard.

BUILD YOUR SKILLS

7. You could have solved Example 3 by determining the cost of the sod per square metre. Answer the question using this method. Is your answer the same? Why or why not?

8. Kuldeep has been hired to lay terracotta tiles on a floor that measures 4.2 m by 3.8 m. The tiles are 9″ by 9″ and come in boxes of 12.

   a) How many boxes must he buy? (He cannot buy a partial box.)

   b) If the tiles cost $18.95 per box, how much will the tiles cost in total?

9. Toula calculates the cost of cementing the bottom and sides of a circular pond. When all costs are considered, the job will cost $175.85 per square metre of finished area. If the pond has a radius of 3 feet and a depth of 2 feet, how much will she charge for the job?

PRACTISE YOUR NEW SKILLS

1. Juan is a picture framer. He is framing a picture that is 24 inches by 32 inches with a frame that is 2.5 inches wide. What is the outer perimeter of the framed picture:

   a) in inches?

   b) in feet and inches?

   c) in yards, feet, and inches?

2. Charlie drove from Calgary to Saskatoon, which is a distance of 620 km. How far is this in miles?

3. A school custodian must mark off a field that is 150 ft by 85 ft. His tape measure is marked in metres. What are the dimensions of the field in metres (to the nearest tenth of a metre)?

4. Jeff knows that his semi-trailer truck is 3.2 m high. A tunnel is marked as "Max height: 10'6"." Will Jeff's truck fit through the tunnel?

5. Carla needs 3.5 m of cloth. If the cloth she wants to purchase costs $9.78/yd, how much will the cloth cost?

6. Ari, a gardener, estimates the cost of seeding a 150 m by 210 m area with grass seed. He needs 3 pounds of seed per 100 000 square feet. How many pounds of seed will Ari need?

7. A room measures 12'8" by 10'9". Carpeting costs $45.98/m². A customer will have to purchase 10% more carpeting than floor area due to waste and he cannot purchase partial square metres. What is the minimum cost of the carpeting?

3.3 Surface Area

NEW SKILLS: WORKING WITH SURFACE AREA

surface area: the total area of all the faces, or surfaces, of a three-dimensional object; measured in square units

net: a two-dimensional pattern used to construct three-dimensional shapes

Surface area is the area that would be covered by a three-dimensional (3-D) object if you could lay it out flat. A **net** is a diagram of a 3-D object seen as a flat surface.

If you know how to find the area of 2-D shapes, you can find the surface area of 3-D objects by breaking them down to their component surfaces and adding the areas together.

For more details, see page 115 of *MathWorks 10*.

Example 1

Akiko has been hired to paint the exterior of a storage bin. If the bin is a rectangular prism that measures 2.3 yards by 4.4 yards by 2.8 yards, what is the surface area of the bin?

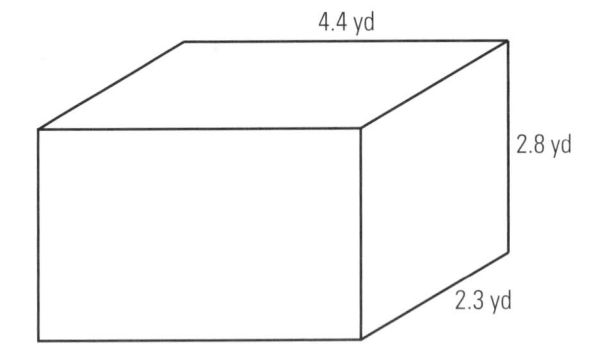

SOLUTION

Sketch a net of the bin.

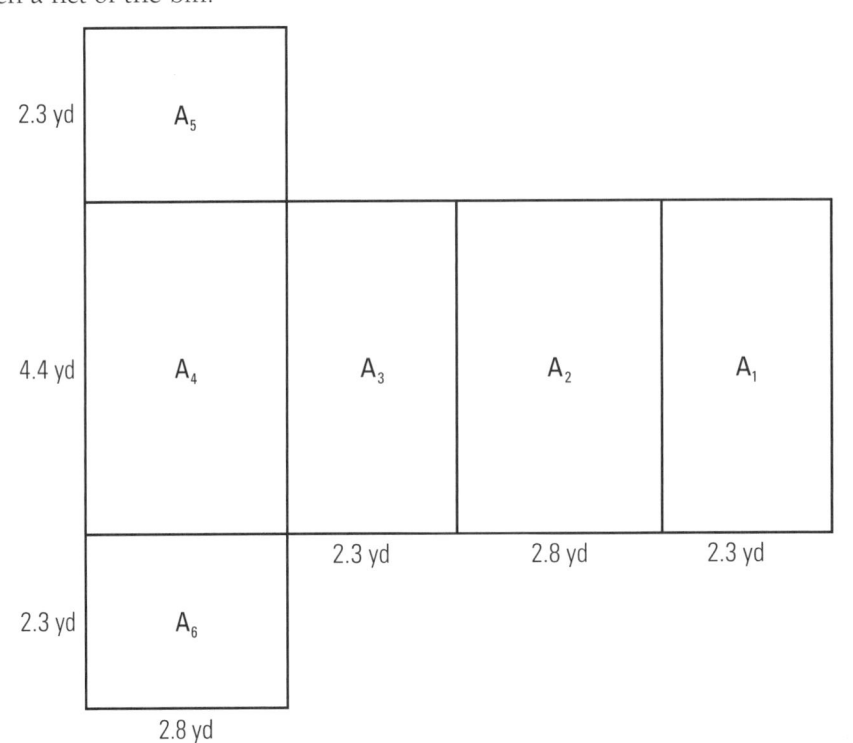

Calculate the area of each of the rectangles and add together to find the surface area (SA).

$A_1 = \ell w$

$A_1 = 4.4 \times 2.3$

$A_1 = 10.12 \text{ yd}^2$

The area of A_3 is the same as A_1.

$A_2 = \ell w$

$A_2 = 4.4 \times 2.8$

$A_2 = 12.32 \text{ yd}^2$

The area of A_4 is the same as A_2.

$A_5 = \ell w$

$A_5 = 2.3 \times 2.8$

$A_5 = 6.44 \text{ yd}^2$

The area of A_6 is the same as A_5.

Total surface area:

$SA = A_1 + A_2 + A_3 + A_4 + A_5 + A_6$

$SA = 10.12 + 12.32 + 10.12 + 12.32 + 6.44 + 6.44$

$SA = 57.76 \text{ yd}^2$

The bin has a surface area of 57.76 yd².

ALTERNATIVE SOLUTION

Many people prefer to measure the different surfaces of the object.

There are:

2 rectangles that are 4.4 yd by 2.8 yd (front and back)

2 rectangles that are 4.4 yd by 2.3 yd (top and bottom)

2 rectangles that are 2.3 yd by 2.8 yd (ends)

Find the area of each rectangle and then add.

$A_{1+3} = 2 \times 4.4 \text{ yd} \times 2.3 \text{ yd}$

$A_{1+3} = 20.24 \text{ yd}^2$

$A_{2+4} = 2 \times 4.4 \text{ yd} \times 2.8 \text{ yd}$

$A_{2+4} = 20.24 \text{ yd}^2$

$A_{5+6} = 2 \times 2.3 \text{ yd} \times 2.8 \text{ yd}$

$A_{5+6} = 12.88 \text{ yd}^2$

$SA = A_{1+3} + A_{2+4} + A_{5+6}$

$SA = 24.64 \text{ yd}^2 + 20.24 \text{ yd}^2 + 12.88 \text{ yd}^2$

$SA = 57.76 \text{ yd}^2$

The bin has a surface area of 57.76 yd².

BUILD YOUR SKILLS

1. Jim has been hired to make a jewellery box. If the box is 12 inches long, 6 inches deep, and 9 inches tall, how much veneer will it take to cover the exterior, assuming no waste?

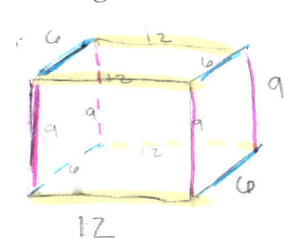

   $A_1 = l \cdot w = 6 \cdot 9 = 54 (2) = 108$"
   $A_2 = 12 \cdot 6 = 72 (2) = 144$
   $A_3 = 12 \cdot 9 = 108 (2) = 216$
   $A_4 = 9 \cdot 12 = 216$
   $A_5 = 6 \cdot 12 = 144$
   $A_6 = 9 \cdot 6 = 108$

   $= 936$

2. Anita is building a greenhouse onto the side of her garage. She wants it to be 6 feet long, 4 feet wide, and 3 feet high, with the 6-foot long side against the side of her garage. What area of glass will she need to complete the greenhouse? (Hint: No glass will be used along the side of the garage or for the floor.)

3. Vicki is tiling her 35″ by 35″ shower stall. The tiles reach the 8-foot ceiling on 3 sides. How many square inches of tiles should she purchase to tile the walls and floor?

Example 2

A canning factory wants to use as little metal as possible to make its cans. It considers two can sizes that each hold about the same amount. One is 4.5 inches tall with a radius of 4.2 inches and another is 9.6 inches tall with a radius of 2.8 inches.

Which can should they use? Why?

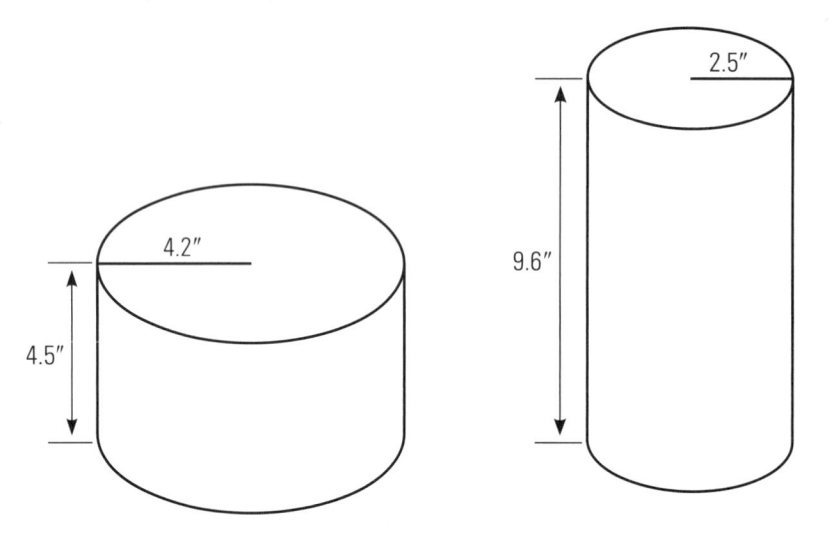

SOLUTION

To find out which can uses the least amount of metal, calculate the surface area of each can.

The top and bottom of the cans are circles. The area of a circle can be found by the following formula:

$A = \pi r^2$

If the side of the can is rolled out flat, it will form a rectangle, where the width is the height of the can and the length is the circumference of the circle.

Can #1

Top and bottom:

$A = 2\pi r^2$

$A = 2\pi(4.2)^2$

$A \approx 110.8 \text{ in}^2$

Side:

$A = 2\pi rh$

$A = 2\pi(4.2)(4.5)$

$A \approx 118.7 \text{ in}^2$

$SA = A_{top + bottom} + A_{side}$

$SA \approx 110.8 + 118.7$

$SA \approx 229.5 \text{ in}^2$

Can #2

Top and bottom:

$A = 2\pi r^2$

$A = 2\pi(2.8)^2$

$A \approx 49.2 \text{ in}^2$

Side:

$A = 2\pi rh$

$A = 2\pi(2.8)(9.6)$

$A \approx 168.8 \text{ in}^2$

$SA = A_{top + bottom} + A_{side}$

$SA \approx 49.2 + 168.8$

$SA \approx 218 \text{ in}^2$

Considering surface area, they should use the second can because it uses less material.

BUILD YOUR SKILLS

4. A cylindrical shipping tube is 48 inches tall and 6 inches in diameter.

   a) What is its surface area in square inches?

b) What is its surface area in square feet?

5. Sanjiv designs a cylindrical box to hold 4 tennis balls stacked one on top of the other. If a tennis ball is approximately $3\frac{1}{4}$ inches in diameter, what is the surface area of the box? (Ignore the thickness of the material.)

6. Jennifer must make a conical funnel out of sheet metal. If the funnel is 9 inches tall, has a slant height of 10.7 inches, and has a radius of 5.8 inches at the top, what is the surface area of the sheet metal in square feet?

Example 3

Harry has to paint the walls and ceiling of a room that is 12 ft long, 10 ft wide, and $8\frac{1}{2}$ ft high. There is a 6 ft by 4 ft window, a $2\frac{1}{2}$ ft by 7 ft doorway, and a mirrored closet door that is 6 ft by 7 ft. What surface area must he paint?

SOLUTION

Find the total area of the four walls and the ceiling and subtract the areas of the window and doors.

Area of ceiling:

$A_1 = 12 \text{ ft} \times 10 \text{ ft}$

$A_1 = 120 \text{ ft}^2$

Area of long walls:

$A_2 = 12 \text{ ft} \times 8\frac{1}{2} \text{ ft} \times 2$

$A_2 = 204 \text{ ft}^2$

Area of shorter walls:

$A_3 = 10 \text{ ft} \times 8\frac{1}{2} \text{ ft} \times 2$

$A_3 = 170 \text{ ft}^2$

Area of walls and ceiling, including openings:

$A_4 = A_1 + A_2 + A_3$

$A_4 = 120 \text{ ft}^2 + 204 \text{ ft}^2 + 170 \text{ ft}^2$

$A_4 = 494 \text{ ft}^2$

Calculate the areas of the window, door, and closet that will not be painted.

Area of window:

$A_5 = 6 \text{ ft} \times 4 \text{ ft}$

$A_5 = 24 \text{ ft}^2$

Area of door:

$A_6 = 2\frac{1}{2} \text{ ft} \times 7 \text{ ft}$

$A_6 = 17\frac{1}{2} \text{ ft}^2$

Area of closet door:

$A_7 = 6 \text{ ft} \times 7 \text{ ft}$

$A_7 = 42 \text{ ft}^2$

Total area that does not need painting:

$A_8 = A_5 + A_6 + A_7$

$A_8 = 24 \text{ ft}^2 + 17\frac{1}{2} \text{ ft}^2 + 42 \text{ ft}^2$

$A_8 = 83\frac{1}{2} \text{ ft}^2$

Total area to be painted:

$A_{total} = A_4 - A_8$

$A_{total} = 494 \text{ ft}^2 - 83\frac{1}{2} \text{ ft}^2$

$A_{total} = 410\frac{1}{2} \text{ ft}^2$

The total area to be painted is $410\frac{1}{2}$ ft².

BUILD YOUR SKILLS

7. Geneviève plans to apply two coats of paint to the walls of her garden shed. The shed is 8 feet long by 6 feet wide by 7 feet tall. If there are 3 windows that are 2 feet by 18 inches each, what will be the total area she paints?

8. A metal cylindrical canister is 1′3″ long and has a diameter of 4 inches. What is the total surface area of the cylinder?

9. Jerg is finishing the sides and bottom of a hot tub. The hot tub is 6′11″ long, 5′6″ wide, and 3′ deep. It has a bench going all the way around the inside that is 16″ high and 15″ wide that will not be finished. How much finishing material will Jerg need?

Example 4

The wood that Terrance wants to use to make a shelving unit costs $6.49/ft^2. How much will it cost him (assuming no wastage) to make a shelving unit that is 4 ft wide by 12 inches deep by 5 ft tall if there are 4 shelves (plus the top and bottom)?

SOLUTION

Sketch the unit.

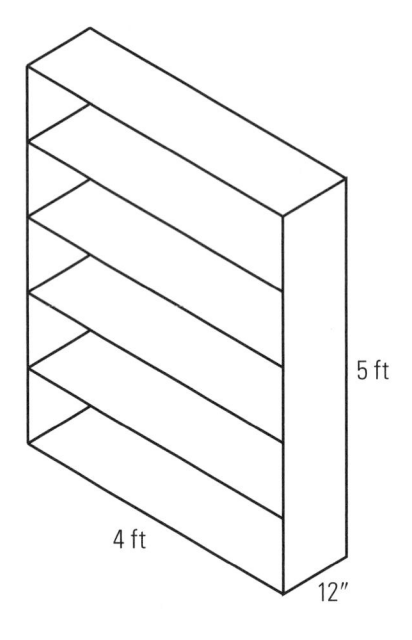

5 ft

4 ft

12"

There will be 6 pieces (shelves) that are 12" (or 1') by 4'.

There will be 2 pieces (ends) that are 1' by 5'.

There will be 1 piece (back) that is 4' by 5'.

Find the areas of each piece and add.

$A_1 = 6 \times 1 \text{ ft} \times 4 \text{ ft}$

$A_1 = 24 \text{ ft}^2$

$A_2 = 2 \times 1 \text{ ft} \times 5 \text{ ft}$

$A_2 = 10 \text{ ft}^2$

$A_3 = 1 \times 4 \text{ ft} \times 5 \text{ ft}$

$A_3 = 20 \text{ ft}^2$

Total area = 24 ft² + 10 ft² + 20 ft²

Total area = 54 ft²

Cost:

$6.49 × 54 = $350.46

The total cost of the wood will be $350.46.

BUILD YOUR SKILLS

10. Randi is installing flooring in her den. The room is 12 feet by 19 feet. A fireplace that is 6 feet wide juts out 2 feet into the room. Also, there are 2 built-in bookcases, each 1 foot deep and 3 feet wide. She needs to order 12% more flooring than required because of wastage and cutting. How much will it cost if the wood costs $5.25/ft^2?

11. Sheet metal costs $54.25/yd^2. How much will it cost Hamish to cover a conical roof if it has a radius of 2.2 yards and a slant height of 3.5 yards?

12. Ted is wallpapering his bedroom. The room is 10 ft long by 8 ft wide by $9\frac{1}{2}$ ft tall. There is a door measuring 3 ft by 7 ft and a window measuring 3 ft by 4 ft. Each double roll covers approximately 56 ft² and costs $29.95. How much will the wallpaper cost?

PRACTISE YOUR NEW SKILLS

1. A storage bin is a rectangular prism that measuring 114 cm long by 56 cm high by 56 cm deep. What is the surface area of the exterior, in square feet?

2. How much glass is needed to construct a hexagonal (6-sided) fish tank? The tank is 4 feet tall and each pane is $1\frac{1}{2}$ feet wide. (The tank's bottom is not made of glass.)

3. Stan is deciding between patio tiles that are 39 cm by 39 cm and tiles that are 18 cm by 27 cm. His patio is 3 m by 2.5 m. Considering area only, how many of each type of tile would he need?

4. A chocolate bar is in the shape of a triangular prism. The box is $8\frac{1}{2}$ inches long and the ends are equilateral triangles with sides measuring $1\frac{3}{4}$ inches. What is the surface area of the box? (Hint: You need to find the height of the triangle. Use the following formula, $A = \frac{1}{2}bh$)

5. Jocelyne is designing a logo for the outside of a cylindrical water bottle. She knows that the bottle is $7\frac{1}{2}$ in tall and has a diameter of $3\frac{3}{4}$ in. How large can the label on the water bottle be?

6. A conical paper cup has a slant height of $3\frac{1}{8}$ inches and a diameter of 3 inches. How much paper is needed to make the cup?

7. The Great Pyramid of Giza has a square base that, when built, was approximately 756 ft on each side. If the slant height of each triangular side was approximately 610 ft, what was the original surface area of the pyramid?

3.4 Volume

NEW SKILLS: WORKING WITH VOLUME

volume: the amount of space an object occupies

The **volume** of a solid is a measure of how much space it occupies. Volume is measured in cubic units.

The volume of a prism is calculated using the following formula.

$V = A_{base} \times h$

Volume is the product of the area of the base times the height of the object.

For more details, see page 124 of *MathWorks 10*.

Example 1

Alfred has a bulk container that holds 2000 cubic inches of dog biscuits. He plans to sell the biscuits in small boxes that measure 5″ by 8″ by 6″. How many boxes will he need to sell all the dog biscuits?

SOLUTION

Find the volume of the small box.

$V = \ell w h$

$V = 5″ \times 8″ \times 6″$

$V = 240$ cu in

Divide 2000 by 240.

$2000 \div 240 = 8.3$

Round up, so that all of the biscuits fit in boxes. Alfred would need 9 small boxes.

BUILD YOUR SKILLS

1. A fish tank is a rectangular prism that is 30 inches long, 24 inches deep, and 18 inches high. How much water will it hold:

   a) in cubic inches?

   $V = l \cdot w \cdot h$
   $= 30 \cdot 24 \cdot 18$
   $= \boxed{12960 \text{ in}^3}$

   b) in cubic feet?

   30 in = 2.5 ft $V = 2.5 \times 2 \times 1.5$
   24 in = 2 ft $= 7.5 \text{ ft}^3$
   18 in = 1.5 ft

2. Petra must stack boxes that are 3 ft by $2\frac{1}{2}$ ft by $1\frac{1}{2}$ ft onto a truck. What is the volume of each box?

3. Will the contents of a box that is 3 inches by 4 inches by 6 inches fit into a cube with sides of 4 inches?

Example 2

Paulino runs a landscaping business. He needs to cover an area that is 10.8 m by 9.5 m with 10 cm of topsoil. How much will it cost if the soil costs $18.75/yd³, and soil is available in multiples of $\frac{1}{2}$ yd³?

Remember:
10 cm = 0.1 m

SOLUTION

Find the volume of topsoil needed.

$V = \ell wh$

$V = 10.8$ m $\times 9.5$ m $\times 0.1$ m

$V = 10.26$ m³

Calculate how many yards are in 1 metre.

1 cm $= \frac{1}{2.54}$ in

100 cm $= \frac{100}{2.54}$ in

100 cm $= 39.37$ in

1 m $= 39.37$ in

1 in $= \frac{1}{36}$ yd

39.37 in $= \frac{39.37}{36}$ yd

1 m ≈ 1.09 yd

Calculate how many cubic yards are in a cubic metre by cubing both sides.

1 m³ $= 1.09$ yd³

1 m³ ≈ 1.3 yd³

Since he needs 10.26 cubic metres, change cubic metres to cubic yards.

10.26 m³ $= 10.26$ m³ $\times \frac{1.3 \text{ yd}^3}{1 \text{ m}^3}$

10.26 m³ ≈ 13.3 yd³

He needs 13.3 yd³, but Paulino will have to round up to the nearest $\frac{1}{2}$ yd³, to 13.5 yd³. Since each cubic yard costs $18.75, multiply the number of cubic yards by the cost per cubic yard.

13.5 × $18.75 = $253.13

The topsoil will cost $253.13.

ALTERNATIVE SOLUTION

Begin by changing the measurements to yards.

Using the calculations above, 1 m is approximately 1.09 yd.

    10.8 m = 10.8 × 1.09 yd

    10.8 m ≈ 11.8 yd

    9.5 m = 9.5 × 1.09 yd

    9.5 m ≈ 10.4 yd

    0.1 m = 0.1 × 1.09 yd

    0.1 m ≈ 0.1 yd

Find the volume in cubic yards.

    $V = \ell w h$

    $V = 11.8 \times 10.4 \times 0.1$

    $V = 12.3$ yd³

Paulino will need to round up to the nearest 0.5 cubic yard, so he will need 12.5 yd³.

Find the cost by multiplying the number of cubic yards by the cost per cubic yard.

12.5 × $18.75 = $234.38

It will cost approximately $234.38 for the topsoil. This answer is different from the first answer because you round at a different point in the calculation.

BUILD YOUR SKILLS

4. A garden bed is 4' by 3', and a 6" layer of soil will be spread over the garden. A bag of soil contains 2 ft³ of soil. How many bags are needed to cover the garden?

   Handwritten work:
   6 ÷ 12 = 0.5 ft
   V = 4 · 3 · 0.5
     = 6 ft³

   6 ft³ ÷ 2 = 3 ft³

5. Karl buys bales of hay that measure 15" × 24" × 36". He needs to buy 250 bales, and he needs to know if they will fit in his barn. What is the total volume of hay in cubic feet?

6. A computer measures 9 inches by 16 inches by $16\frac{1}{2}$ inches. It requires $1\frac{1}{2}$ inches of padding on each side to protect it during shipping. What is the volume of the packed box?

NEW SKILLS: WORKING WITH CAPACITY

The **capacity** of a container is the amount it can hold. Capacity is the volume of a container. Capacity is often used with liquid measures.

capacity: the maximum amount that a container can hold

In the SI, the basic unit of capacity is the litre. A litre is one one-thousandth of a cubic metre, or 1000 cubic centimetres.

In imperial units, capacity is measured in gallons.

$$4 \text{ quarts} = 1 \text{ gallon}$$

$$2 \text{ pints} = 1 \text{ quart}$$

$$2 \text{ cups} = 1 \text{ pint}$$

However, the gallon has two different sizes:

- The British gallon is approximately 4.5 litres and 1 pint is 20 fluid ounces.
- The American (US) gallon is approximately 3.8 litres and 1 pint is 16 fluid ounces.

In measuring liquids for recipes, the US system is often used.

$$1 \text{ teaspoon (tsp)} = 5 \text{ millilitres (mL)}$$

$$1 \text{ tablespoon (tbsp)} = 15 \text{ mL}$$

$$1 \text{ cup} = 250 \text{ mL}$$

1 cup is actually 237 mL, but in cooking it is rounded to 250 mL for easier measuring.

For more information, see page 124 of *MathWorks 10*.

Example 3

Paula is opening a French bakery and wants to make authentic French recipes. All the recipes are given in metric units, but she has imperial measuring devices. The crème brulée recipe requires 500 mL of cream and 1.25 mL of vanilla.

a) How much cream will she need, in cups?

b) How much vanilla will she need, in teaspoons?

c) How much cream will she need, in fluid ounces?

SOLUTION

a) Convert 500 mL to cups.

   1 cup = 250 mL

   $$500 \text{ mL} = 500 \text{ mL} \times \frac{1 \text{ cup}}{250 \text{ mL}}$$

   500 mL = 2 cups

   She will need 2 cups of cream.

b) Convert 1.25 mL to teaspoons.

   1 tsp = 5 mL

   $$1.25 \text{ mL} = 1.25 \text{ mL} \times \frac{1 \text{ tsp}}{5 \text{ mL}}$$

   1.25 mL = 0.25 tsp or $\frac{1}{4}$ tsp

   She will need $\frac{1}{4}$ tsp of vanilla.

c) Convert 500 mL to fluid ounces.

   500 mL = 2 cups

   2 cups = 1 pint

   1 pint = 16 fl oz

   She will need 16 fl oz of cream.

BUILD YOUR SKILLS

7. Serina is travelling through the US and her car's gas tank has a capacity of 55 litres.

   a) How much is this in American gallons?

   b) If gas costs $2.99/gal in Bellingham, WA, how much will it cost to fill her car (assuming that it is totally empty)?

   c) Assuming she has the same car in London, England, where gas costs $9.86/gal (converted from pounds), how much will it cost to fill her tank? (Remember that the British gallon is a different size.)

8. The box of Jakob's cube van has inside dimensions of 20 feet (length), 10 feet 8 inches (width), and 12 feet 6 inches (height). Calculate the volume of the interior.

9. Bev has two storage bins for grain. The first bin is 12 feet 8 inches by 8 feet 9 inches and is filled to a level height of 4 feet 6 inches. If she has to move the grain to a bin with a base measuring 9 feet by 9 feet, what will be the level height of the grain in the second bin?

PRACTISE YOUR NEW SKILLS

1. A storage container measures 6 feet by 3 feet by 4 feet.

    a) What is the volume in cubic feet?

    $V = 6 \cdot 3 \cdot 4$
    $= \boxed{72 \text{ ft}^3}$

    b) What is the volume in cubic yards?

    6 ft = 2 yd
    3 ft = 1 yd   ÷ by 3
    4 ft = 1.33 yd

    $2 \cdot 1 \cdot 1.33 = \boxed{2.66 \text{ yd}^3}$

2. A recipe calls for $2\frac{3}{4}$ cups of milk. How much is this in mL?

    $2.75 \cdot 250 = \boxed{687.5 \text{ mL}}$

3. What is the capacity of a 5-fl oz jar, in mL? (Hint: 1 fl oz = 30 mL.)

   5-fl oz · 30 mL
   = 150 mL

4. If your car's fuel consumption rate is 8.8 L/100 km, how many US gallons will you need for a trip of approximately 450 km?

   3.8 L

   $\dfrac{8.8 L}{100 km} = \dfrac{xL}{450 km}$

   $\dfrac{8.8 \cdot 450}{100} = 39.6 L$

   39.6 L ÷ 3.8 L = 10.42

5. In spring, a tree needs 10.5 fl oz of fertilizer. If fertilizer is sold in a 4.1-L bottles, how many bottles are needed to fertilize 15 trees?

6. The exterior of a concrete container will be 10 feet by 8 feet by 4 feet tall. The walls and the bottom are 6 inches thick. What will it cost to construct it if concrete is $98.95/cubic yard?

CHAPTER TEST

1. The tallest person in the world was Robert Pershing Wadlow. At the time of his death in 1940, he was 8′11.1″ tall. The record for the world's shortest adult was held by He Pingping; at the time of his death in 2010, he was 2′4.7″.

    a) What is the difference between their heights in feet and inches?

    b) Find the height of each man in metres.

    c) What is the difference between their heights in metres?

2. While driving in the United States, Franklin sees that the height of a tunnel is marked as 10′6″. He knows that his truck is 3.3 m tall. Can he drive through the tunnel?

3. Rachelle is buying panelling for wainscotting for her hall. The panels are 4′ by 8′. The wainscotting will be 4′ high and the room is 19′ by 13′. There are two doors measuring 30″ wide, and one 12′ window that will only need a 2′ panel of wainscotting under it. How many panels will she need, assuming no wastage?

4. Mario is laying tiles for the patio below and planting daffodils around the perimeter.

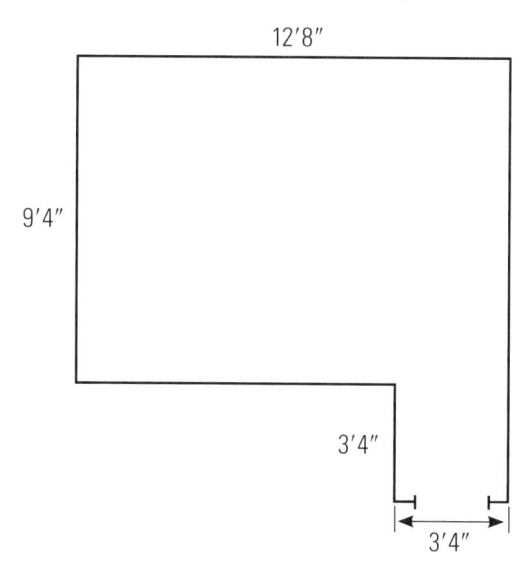

```
            12'8"
     ┌─────────────────┐
     │                 │
9'4" │                 │
     │                 │
     │          ┌──────┤
     └──────────┘ 3'4" │
                 ├──┤  │
                 3'4"
```

a) Assuming he needs to buy 10% more than the area due to wastage, how many 12" by 12" tiles will he need?

b) How many daffodils will he plant around the perimeter if there are no daffodils along the entrance and he plants them approximately 1 foot apart?

5. Louise needs to give the exterior of a cylindrical granary 2 coats of paint. If the granary is 10 feet tall and has a diameter of 14 feet, and paint covers approximately 375 square feet per gallon, how many gallons of paint will she need to buy? Assume that she can only buy full gallons, and will not be painting the roof.

6. Roberto is painting the exterior of a rectangular storage unit to protect it from rusting. If the unit is 7′6″ wide, 9′8″ long, and 8′2″ tall, what is the surface area in square feet? Roberto will be painting the sides and the roof.

7. A soccer field is 109 m long and 73 m wide. American soccer league rules state that a field should be no more than 120 yards long and 80 yards wide. Is the field within the specified dimensions?

8. What is the volume of water in a fish tank that is 90 cm by 55 cm if it is filled to a height of 32 cm?

9. A driveway is 36 ft long and 10 ft wide, and will be covered in gravel that is 2 in deep. How many cubic yards of gravel will be needed?

10. In the US, milk is commonly sold in jugs of 1 gal, $\frac{1}{2}$ gal, 1 quart, and $\frac{1}{2}$ pint. What are the equivalent sizes in millilitres?

11. A recipe for pumpkin cheesecake calls for a 5-US fl oz can of evaporated milk.

   a) What is this in cups?

   b) What is this in mL?

Chapter 4

Mass, Temperature, and Volume

To make good bread, the ingredients must be measured accurately and the dough stored and baked at the correct temperature. Cam McCaw, a Red Seal pastry chef, turns out hundreds of loaves of bread daily.

Temperature Conversions — 4.1

NEW SKILLS: WORKING WITH TEMPERATURE

If you travel to the United States, you will notice that a different temperature scale is used there. The US uses the Fahrenheit scale (°F) of the imperial system, while Canada uses the Celsius scale (°C) of the SI.

In the SI, water freezes at 0°C and boils at 100°C. In the imperial system, water freezes at 32°F and boils at 212°F. Since water freezes at 0°C and 32°F, the relationship between the two temperature systems can be calculated with the following formulas, where *C* represents degrees Celsius and *F* represents degrees Fahrenheit.

$$C = \frac{5}{9}(F - 32) \text{ or } F = \frac{9}{5}C + 32$$

For more details, see page 138 of *MathWorks 10*.

> The Celsius scale used to be called the centigrade scale, and it is sometimes referred to this way.

Example 1

When working with temperatures, convert them to the nearest tenth of a degree.

While visiting Florida, Kathy heard a local person say that it had been very cold overnight, as it was only 42°. At first, she thought this was not cold, but then Kathy realized the person meant degrees Fahrenheit. What was the temperature in degrees Celsius?

SOLUTION

Use the following formula, and substitute 42 for *F*.

$$C = \frac{5}{9}(F - 32)$$

$$C = \frac{5}{9}(42 - 32)$$

$$C = \frac{5}{9}(10)$$

$$C = \frac{50}{9}$$

$$C = \left(5\frac{5}{9}\right)°$$

Convert this mixed numeral to a decimal.

$$5\frac{5}{9} = 5 + \frac{5}{9}$$

$$\frac{5}{9} = 5 \div 9$$

$$\frac{5}{9} \approx 0.6$$

$$5\frac{5}{9} \approx 5.6$$

The temperature is about 5.6°C, which would be very cold in Florida.

BUILD YOUR SKILLS

1. A cake recipe says to bake at 350°F. Your oven only shows temperatures in degrees Celsius. At what temperature should you set your oven?

2. Sophie is making fudge in France, using an American cookbook. She needs to cook the chocolate until the temperature is 238°F, but her thermometer only shows temperatures in degrees Celsius. What temperature does her fudge mixture need to reach?

3. Firefighters can estimate the temperature of a burning fire by the colour of its flame. A clear orange flame has a temperature of about 2190°F. How hot is this in degrees Celsius?

Example 2

Sverre was paving a road with heated tar during a hot summer day. He noted that the external temperature of the tar was 48°C. What was this in degrees Fahrenheit?

SOLUTION

Use the formula for converting degrees Fahrenheit to degrees Celsius, and substitute 48 for C.

$F = \frac{9}{5}C + 32$

$F = \frac{9}{5}(48) + 32$

$F = \frac{432}{5} + 32$

$F \approx 86.4 + 32$

$F \approx 118.4$

The temperature was approximately 118.4°F.

BUILD YOUR SKILLS

4. The normal temperature for a dog is from 99°F to 102°F. Ashley's dog has a temperature of 40°C. Convert the temperature to Fahrenheit to calculate if it falls within the normal range.

   $F = \frac{9}{5}(40) + 32$

   $F = 72 + 32$

   $F = 104$

5. Roger is painting the exterior of a house. He should not apply the paint if the temperature is below 45°F. The temperature is 9°C. Is it safe to apply the paint?

6. Chinook winds are known to cause great changes in temperature over a short period of time. The most extreme temperature change in a 24-hour period occurred in Loma, Montana, on January 15, 1972. The temperature rose from −54°F to 49°F.

   a) What was the change in temperature in degrees Fahrenheit?

   b) What were the minimum and maximum temperatures in degrees Celsius?

   c) What was the change in temperature in degrees Celsius?

> A chinook wind is a warm, dry wind that blows east of the Rocky Mountains, often causing significant temperature increases in a short time in winter.

PRACTISE YOUR NEW SKILLS

1. Convert the following temperatures to degrees Fahrenheit.

   a) 35°C   b) −8°C

   c) 165°C   d) 21°C

   e) −40°C   f) 202°C

2. Convert the following temperatures to degrees Celsius.

   a) −20°F

   b) 80°F

   c) 375°F

   d) 2°F

   e) 0°F

   f) −2°F

3. Which is hotter: a blowtorch flame at 1300°C or a candle flame at 1830°F? By how much is one flame hotter than the other in each scale?

4. When Harry mixes different materials to pave a road, he knows that they must be kept at the following temperatures in degrees Fahrenheit. Calculate the temperatures in degrees Celsius.

   a) Bituminous material must be between 200°F and 260°F.

   b) Water solution must be between 65°F and 100°F.

   c) The mixing gel must be between 160°F and 210°F.

5. In 1992, the temperature in Pincher Creek, Alberta, rose from −19°C to 22°C in just one hour due to a chinook wind. What were these temperatures in degrees Fahrenheit?

6. When the human body reaches a temperature of 41°F, it is said to be in a state of "medical emergency." What is this temperature in degrees Celsius?

7. On May 26, 1991, Mount Logan, YT, recorded the coldest temperature outside of Antarctica at −106.6°F. What is this temperature in degrees Celsius?

8. Some of the tiles on the outside of a space shuttle are able to withstand temperatures of 2300°F. What is this in degrees Celsius?

Mass in the Imperial System 4.2

NEW SKILLS: WORKING WITH WEIGHT

The **mass** of an object refers to the quantity of matter in it, and it remains constant, no matter where the object is located. The **weight** of an object is a measure of the force of gravity on the object. On earth, the mass and the weight of an object are essentially the same; on other planets where the pull of gravity is different, weight and mass will not be the same.

mass: a measure of the quantity of matter in an object

weight: a measure of the force of gravity on an object

The basic units of weight in the imperial system are ton (tn), pound (lb), and ounce (oz).

  1 ton (tn) = 2000 pounds

  1 pound (lb) = 16 ounces (oz)

For more details, see page 146 of *MathWorks 10*.

Example 1

Manuela needs 1 pound 2 ounces of Gruyère cheese, 12 ounces of cheddar cheese, and 11 ounces of Swiss cheese for a fondue recipe. How many pounds of cheese does she need in all?

SOLUTION

Add pounds to pounds and ounces to ounces.

$$1 \text{ pound} + 2 \text{ ounces}$$
$$+ 12 \text{ ounces}$$
$$+ 11 \text{ ounces}$$
$$\overline{1 \text{ pound } 25 \text{ ounces}}$$

Change 25 ounces to pounds.

  16 ounces = 1 pound

  25 ounces = (16 + 9) ounces

  25 ounces = 1 pound 9 ounces

Total weight = 1 pound 25 ounces

Total weight = 1 pound + 1 pound 9 ounces

Total weight = 2 pounds 9 ounces

Manuela needs 2 lb 9 oz of cheese for her recipe.

ALTERNATIVE SOLUTION 1

Change 1 pound 2 ounces to ounces.

1 lb 2 oz = 16 oz + 2 oz

1 lb 2 oz = 18 oz

Add all the weights.

18 oz + 12 oz + 11 oz = 41 oz

Change to pounds by dividing by 16.

$41 \text{ oz} = 41 \text{ oz} \times \frac{1 \text{ lb}}{16 \text{ oz}}$

$41 \text{ oz} = \left(\frac{41}{16}\right) \text{ lb}$

$41 \text{ oz} = \left(2\frac{9}{16}\right) \text{ lb}$

41 oz = 2 lb 9 oz

ALTERNATIVE SOLUTION 2

You could also change the ounces to pounds and work with decimals or fractions.

1 lb 2 oz of Gruyère equals 1 plus $\frac{2}{16}$ lb, or 1.125 lb.

12 oz of cheddar equals $\frac{12}{16}$ lb, or 0.75 lb.

11 oz of Swiss equals $\frac{11}{16}$ lb, or 0.6875 lb.

Total weight = 1.125 + 0.75 + 0.6875

Total weight ≈ 2.56 lb

BUILD YOUR SKILLS

1. Rochelle gave birth to twin boys weighing 6 lb 5 oz and 5 lb 14 oz. What was their total weight?

2. The weight of water is approximately 2 pounds 3 ounces per litre. How much will 8 litres of water weigh?

3. If a basket of raspberries weighs 12 ounces and you need 4 pounds to make jam, how many baskets do you need to buy?

Example 2

The cab of Arthur's semi-trailer truck weighs 8.7 tons and the trailer weighs 6.4 tons. If the loaded gross weight of the truck is 21.3 tons, what is the weight of the load:

a) in tons?

b) in pounds?

SOLUTION

a) The total weight of the truck is found by adding the weight of the cab and the trailer.

8.7 tn + 6.4 tn = 15.1 tn

Subtract this amount from the gross weight to get the weight of the load.

21.3 tn − 15.1 tn = 6.2 tn

The weight of the load is 6.2 tons.

b) Since 1 ton equals 2000 pounds, find the weight in pounds by multiplying.

$$6.2 \text{ tn} = 6.2 \text{ tn} \times \frac{2000 \text{ lb}}{1 \text{ tn}}$$

6.2 tn = 12 400 lb

The weight of the load is 12 400 pounds.

BUILD YOUR SKILLS

4. An elevator has a maximum load restriction of 1.5 tons. Is it safe for two tile layers weighing 195 lb and 210 lb to load it with 65 boxes of tile weighing 42 lb each?

5. A small truck weighs approximately 1300 lb. It is loaded with cement slabs that weigh 150 lb each. If the maximum loaded weight of the truck is 2.75 tons, how many slabs can be loaded?

6. Kurt is planting wheat at the rate of 90 pounds per acre. If he plans to plant 320 acres of wheat, how many tons of wheat will he use?

Example 3

A 12-ounce can of vegetables costs $1.49. A 1 lb 2-oz can of the same vegetables costs $2.19. Which is the better buy?

SOLUTION

Use unit pricing to find the cost per ounce.

12 ounces cost $1.49.

$$12 \text{ oz} = \$1.49$$

$$\left(\frac{12}{12}\right) \text{ oz} = \frac{\$1.49}{12}$$

$$1 \text{ oz} = \frac{\$1.49}{12}$$

$$1 \text{ oz} = \$0.1242$$

1 lb 2 oz costs $2.19.

$$1 \text{ lb } 2 \text{ oz} = 16 \text{ oz} + 2 \text{ oz}$$

$$1 \text{ lb } 2 \text{ oz} = 18 \text{ oz}$$

$$18 \text{ oz} = \$2.19$$

$$\left(\frac{18}{18}\right) \text{ oz} = \frac{\$2.19}{18}$$

$$1 \text{ oz} = \frac{\$2.19}{18}$$

$$1 \text{ oz} \approx \$0.1217$$

The 1 lb 2-oz can is the better buy.

BUILD YOUR SKILLS

7. An 18-oz jar of peanut butter costs $3.29, a 28-oz jar costs $4.79, and a 2.5-lb jar costs $5.99. Which is the best buy?

8. If knitting yarn costs $6.24 per 3-oz skein, how much will it cost to knit a sweater that requires 1 pound of yarn? (You cannot buy partial skeins.)

9. About 200 cocoa beans are used to make 1 lb of chocolate. Beans are shipped in 200-lb sacks, which contain about 88 000 beans. How many 1.5-oz chocolate bars can be made from one sack of beans?

Example 4

Valérie bought 4 pounds 6 ounces of steak for dinner at $2.74/lb. After removing the excess fat, she had only 4 pounds of meat. What was her true cost per pound?

SOLUTION

Change 6 ounces to pounds.

1 lb = 16 ounces

6 oz = (6 ÷ 16) lb

6 oz = 0.375 lb

She bought 4.375 pounds of meat at $2.74/lb.

Total cost:

4.375 × $2.74 = $11.99

Since only 4 pounds were usable, calculate how much each pound cost her.

$11.99 ÷ 4 = $3.00

Valérie paid approximately $3.00/lb for the steaks.

BUILD YOUR SKILLS

10. Zara buys 8 pounds 12 ounces of strawberries at $1.98/lb. What is her true cost per pound if 10% of the berries rot before she uses them?

11. Mark bought 8 bags of sand, each weighing 25 lb, for $1.68/bag. One bag ripped and he lost all the sand. What was his true price per pound of sand?

12. Alyson paid $28.45 for 24 ounces of coffee beans, but when she checked, the actual weight was 22 ounces. What was her true cost per ounce?

PRACTISE YOUR NEW SKILLS

1. Calculate the conversions.

   a) 24 oz = __1.5__ lb

   b) 7890 lb = __3.945__ tn

   $\dfrac{1\,lb}{16} = \dfrac{x}{24}$

   7890
   2000

   c) 54 oz = _____ lb _____ oz

   d) 6 lb 2 oz = _____ oz

   e) 4.54 tn = _____ lb

   f) 654 oz = _____ lb _____ oz

2. What is the total weight, in pounds and ounces, of six books on a shelf if they weigh 12 oz, 1 lb 7 oz, 1 lb 2 oz, 15 oz, 9 oz, and 1 lb 3 oz?

3. A bakery uses a recipe for oatmeal cookies that calls for 1 lb 4 oz of flour to make 9 dozen cookies. How many ounces of flour are needed to make 3 dozen cookies?

4. Kris needs to transport 5 slabs of concrete to an apartment work site. If each slab weighs 46 pounds, Kris weighs 195 pounds, and the truck weighs 1.5 tons, what is the total weight of the loaded truck in pounds?

5. Harinder is concerned about the weight that paint might add to a delicate structure he built. He estimates that he needs 1.5 gal of paint and that the structure can withstand 15 lb of weight. The weight of a particular paint is 9 lb/gal. When it dries, the weight is only 5.4 lb/gal. Can Harinder paint his structure without having it collapse?

6. U-pick organic blueberries sell for $20.00 for a 12-pound box.

   a) How much would 1 pound cost?

   b) How much would 12 ounces cost?

7. What is the true cost per pound of a 10-pound box of oranges if the original price of the box was $12.99 and $\frac{1}{4}$ of them had to be thrown away because they were mouldy?

Mass in the Système International

4.3

NEW SKILLS: WORKING WITH SI UNITS OF MASS

In the Système International (SI), the **kilogram** is the basic unit of mass, but it is often used for weight as well. The correct unit of weight in the SI is the newton. Here, you will work with mass.

kilogram: the mass of one litre of water at 4°C

1000 grams (g) = 1 kilogram (kg)

1000 milligrams (mg) = 1 gram

1 tonne (t) = 1000 kilograms

For more details, see page 154 of *MathWorks 10*.

Note that a tonne (t) is not the same as a ton (tn). A tonne is sometimes referred to as a metric ton.

Example 1

A recipe for cornbread calls for 120 g of flour, 170 g of cornmeal, and 50 g of sugar. If you double the recipe, what is the total mass of the dry ingredients?

SOLUTION

You can either add the masses together and then double the sum, or double the masses and then add them together.

Flour: 2 × 120 g = 240 g

Cornmeal: 2 × 170 g = 340 g

Sugar: 2 × 50 g = 100 g

Add the masses of all the ingredients.

240 g + 340 g + 100 g = 680 g

There are 680 g of dry ingredients in the doubled recipe.

BUILD YOUR SKILLS

1. What is the total mass of a loaded truck if the truck has a mass of 2.6 tonnes and it is loaded with 15 skids of boxes that have masses of 210 kilograms each? Give your answer in tonnes.

2. Irène needs 1.6 kg of tomatoes to make her grandmother's recipe for ratatouille. She has baskets of tomatoes that have masses of 256 g, 452 g, 158 g, and 320 g. How many more grams of tomatoes does she need?

3. Genoa salami sells for $1.79/100 g at the deli.

    a) How much will 350 g cost?

    b) What is the price per kilogram?

NEW SKILLS: WORKING WITH MASS/WEIGHT CONVERSION BETWEEN IMPERIAL AND SI

In this section, you will need to work with the relationship between the SI and the imperial units of weight/mass. One kilogram weighs about 2.2 lb. You can also use this information to convert from grams to ounces and tonnes to tons.

For more details, see page 157 of *MathWorks 10*.

> To estimate a conversion from pounds to kilograms, you can think of a pound as being about $\frac{1}{2}$ kg.

Example 2

Lorinda is baking apple pies. According to her recipe, she needs 6 pounds of apples. The bag of apples she bought only shows the mass in kilograms. How many kilograms of apples does she need?

SOLUTION

$$2.2 \text{ lb} = 1 \text{ kg}$$

$$1 \text{ lb} = \frac{1 \text{ kg}}{2.2}$$

$$6 \text{ lb} = 6 \times \frac{1 \text{ kg}}{2.2}$$

$$6 \text{ lb} \approx 2.7 \text{ kg}$$

She will need approximately 2.7 kg of apples.

BUILD YOUR SKILLS

4. A recipe calls for 180 g of flour. How much is this in ounces?

5. A baby weighed 7 pounds 12 ounces at birth. What is its mass in grams?

6. Chen has a mass of 68 kg. How much does he weigh in pounds?

Example 3

The cost of bananas is $0.49/lb at one store, but you see an advertisement for bananas on sale at another store for $1.05/kg. Which is the better buy?

SOLUTION

Convert the price of bananas at the first store to kilograms.

1 lb costs $0.49.

1 kg = 2.2 lb

Therefore, 1 kg costs 2.2 times the cost of 1 lb.

2.2 × $0.49 = $1.08

One kilogram of bananas at the first store costs about $1.08. The sale at the second store is a better buy.

BUILD YOUR SKILLS

7. How much does 1 pound of beef cost if the butcher shop sells it for $9.74/kg?

8. Which is the better buy: 200 g of coffee beans at $3.85 or 1 pound at $9.60?

9. The dosage of a certain medicine is 0.05 mg/kg of the patient's mass. Tom weighs 185 lbs.

   a) How many milligrams of the medicine should he take?

   b) If the medicine costs $1.95/mg, what will his dosage cost?

PRACTISE YOUR NEW SKILLS

1. Convert the following weights/masses.

   a) 2.5 t = _____ kg

   b) 2.8 kg = _____ g

   c) 125 g = _____ kg

d) 2.4 g = _____ kg

e) 1 t = _____ lb

f) 3.6 tn = _____ kg

2. How many tons are in 1 tonne?

3. What is the total mass in grams of these 3 packages of nuts: 1.2 kg, 0.75 kg, and 1.5 kg?

4. Win has a mass of 78 kg and his dog has a mass of 18 kg. If his truck's mass is 1.9 t and there are 5 boxes of books each with a mass of 9.8 kg in the truck, what is the total mass of the truck, including Win, his dog, and the books?

5. Karen is making a batch of potato soup. She needs 8 potatoes, and each potato is about 375 g. How many pounds of potatoes does she need?

6. If a 10-lb bag of grass seed costs $75.45, how much does the seed cost per kilogram?

7. How many quarter-pound (before cooking) hamburgers can you make from 1.9 kg of ground beef?

Making Conversions 4.4

NEW SKILLS: WORKING WITH CONVERSIONS BETWEEN MEASURES OF VOLUME AND WEIGHT/MASS

You have converted measures from one unit to another, within the SI or imperial system, or between them.

Here, you will convert from a unit of volume to a unit of weight or mass. For example, grain is often measured in bushels, a volume measure, but its weight may be needed to judge whether it is a safe load for a truck. Each grain has a different weight, so conversions between bushels and weight depend on knowing the conversion factor.

1 bushel = 2220 in^3 or approximately 8 gallons.

For more details, see page 162 of *MathWorks 10*.

Example 1

How many bushels (bu) of flax seed are there in 2.4 tonnes, if the conversion factor is 39.368 bushels/tonne?

SOLUTION

A conversion factor of 39.368 means that there are 39.368 bushels of flax seed per tonne. To find the number of bushels, multiply.

$$2.4 \text{ t} \times \frac{39.368 \text{ bu}}{1 \text{ t}} = x \text{ bu}$$

$$2.4 \times 39.368 = 94.5$$

There are approximately 94.5 bushels of flax seed.

BUILD YOUR SKILLS

1. Laila bought 5 bushels of sunflower seeds. If the conversion factor is 73.487 bu/t, what is the weight or mass of the sunflower seeds:

   a) in kilograms?

   b) in pounds?

2. The conversion factor for white beans is 36.744, and for corn it is 39.368. Which weighs more per unit volume?

3. If Jore gets $195.76 per metric ton for wheat, how much does he earn per bushel (conversion factor 36.744 bu/t)?

4. If one bushel of triticale grain is about 2220 cubic inches, how many bushels are in a pile that measures approximately 8 feet by 6 feet by 5 feet?

5. How many tonnes of rye are there is 900 bushels if there are 39.368 bushels/tonne?

6. Wheat is 36.744 bushels/tonne and sunflower seeds are 73.487 bushels/tonne. What does this tell you about the relative masses of wheat and sunflower seeds?

NEW SKILLS: WORKING WITH CONVERSION BETWEEN SI AND IMPERIAL UNITS OF WEIGHT/MASS

You can use the following equivalencies to convert between SI and imperial units.

1 lb ≈ 0.45 kg

1 oz ≈ 28.3 g

1 tn ≈ 0.9 t

BUILD YOUR SKILLS

7. Alphonse is making chicken kebabs for 14 people. His recipe suggests about 7 oz of chicken per person. At the grocery store, the mass of chicken is labelled in kilograms. How much chicken does Alphonse need to buy?

8. A crane can lift a maximum of 5 t. Sandstone weighs about 150 lb per cubic foot, and a container contains 70 cubic feet of sandstone. Can the crane be used to load the container onto a train?

9. Josephine is sending a gift of a bottle of maple syrup that weighs 3 lb, and 3 packages of smoked salmon jerky that are each 100 g. If the package's total mass is less than 2 kg, she can ship it at a cheaper rate. Will she be able to do so?

PRACTISE YOUR NEW SKILLS

1. If 1 bushel is approximately 2220 cubic inches, approximately how many bushels of grain are there in a bin that is 8 feet by 8 feet by 4 feet?

2. A truck has a maximum load limit of 5000 kg. Can it safely carry 230 bushels of canola, if the conversion factor is 44.092 bushels/tonne?

3. How many kilograms are in 1 ton?

4. A sign posted in an elevator says "Maximum capacity 1400 lb." If the average mass of an adult is 80 kg, how many average-mass adults can the elevator carry?

5. Recall that 1000 cubic centimetres equal 1 litre. How many millilitres are in a box that is 10 cm by 5 cm by 3 cm?

6. A hectare (ha) is an area measure of 10 000 square metres. How many hectares are there in a field that is 620 m by 380 m?

CHAPTER TEST

1. Convert the following temperatures.

    a) 25°C = _____ °F

    b) 25°F = _____ °C

    c) −40°C = _____ °F

    d) −25°F = _____ °C

    e) 405°F = _____ °C

    f) 45°C = _____ °F

2. A welder's electrical arc has a temperature ranging from 500°C to 20 000°C. What is this in degrees Fahrenheit?

3. Convert the following weights/masses.

   a) 12 lb 4 oz = _____ oz

   b) 2.3 tn = _____ lb

   c) 5284 lb = _____ tn _____ lb

   d) $3\frac{3}{4}$ lb = _____ oz

   e) 165 oz = _____ lb

   f) 454 g = _____ lb

4. It is estimated that recycling 1 ton of paper saves about 17 trees. About how many trees are saved if 8254 tons of paper are recycled?

5. Eva bought 3 rainbow trout for dinner. They weighed 3 lb 5 oz, 2 lb 12 oz, and 3 lb 8 oz. She cut off the heads and the tails and was left with 8 lb 2 oz. What was the amount of waste?

6. The weight of a piece of raw silk that is 100 yards long by 1.25 yards wide (standard width) is about 38 pounds. The weight of an equal amount of habutai silk is about 12 pounds. If Katharine bought pieces of raw silk and habutai silk that were both 12.5 yards long, how much would they weigh together?

7. A robin's egg has a mass of about 70 g. How many eggs would it take to make 1 kilogram?

8. Huang bought 12 boxes of floor tiles that weigh 288 pounds each. How much is this in kilograms?

9. Soybeans have a conversion factor of 36.744 (bu/t). How much do 45 bushels weigh?

Chapter 5

Angles and Parallel Lines

Angles and parallel lines provide BC's Liard River Bridge with strength, stability, and visual appeal. The bridge was built in 1942.

5.1 Measuring, Drawing, and Estimating Angles

REVIEW: WORKING WITH ANGLES

In this section, you will review types of angles and how to classify them.

An angle is formed when two rays meet at a point called the vertex. Angles are usually measured in degrees using a protractor. Angle measures range from 0° to 360°.

Angles are:

- acute, if their measure is between 0° and 90°;
- right, if their measure is 90°; the two rays are perpendicular to each other;
- obtuse, if their measure is between 90° and 180°;
- straight, if their measure is 180°; and
- reflex, if their measure is between 180° and 360°.

Example 1

Identify the type of angle: acute, right, obtuse, straight, or reflex.

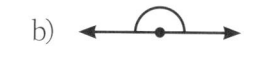

a) 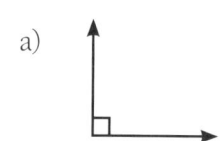   b)   c)

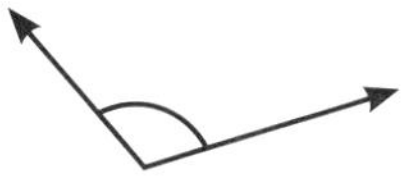

d) 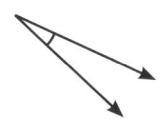   e)

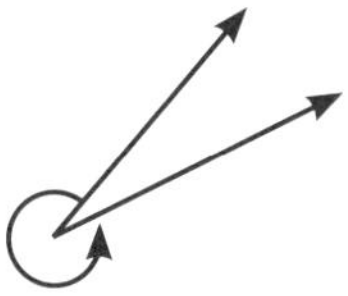

SOLUTION

a) This is a right angle.

b) This is a straight angle.

c) This is an obtuse angle.

d) This is an acute angle.

e) This is a reflex angle.

BUILD YOUR SKILLS

1. Identify the type of angle: acute, right, obtuse, straight, or reflex.

   a) 68°   b) 215°   c) 91°   d) 32°

   e) 180°   f) 99°   g) 195°   h) 265°

NEW SKILLS: WORKING WITH REFERENT ANGLES

In many jobs, people have to draw angles or estimate their measure. To estimate the size of an angle, you can use referent angles, which are angles that are easy to visualize. You can use these referents to determine the approximate size of a given angle.

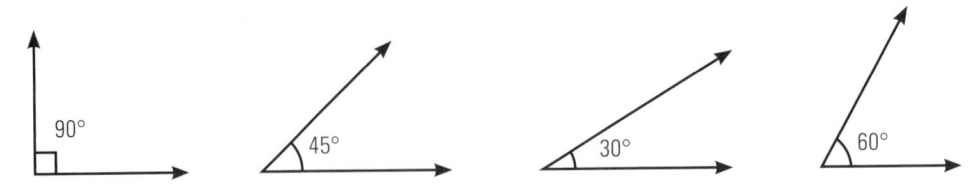

For more details, see page 174 of *MathWorks 10*.

Example 2

Use the referents above to estimate the size of each of the following angles. Use a protractor to check your answers.

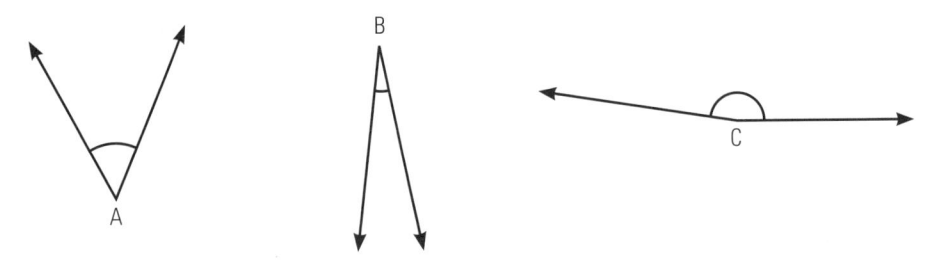

SOLUTION

$\angle$ is a symbol used to indicate an angle.

$\angle A$ is slightly bigger than the 45° referent. It is probably about 50°.

$\angle B$ is less than 30°, so it is probably between 15° and 20°.

$\angle C$ is close to a straight angle but it is probably about 10° less. Therefore, $\angle C$ is approximately 170°.

Using a protractor, measure the angles.

$\angle A$ is 52°.

$\angle B$ is 18°.

$\angle C$ is 172°.

BUILD YOUR SKILLS

2. Use the referents to determine the approximate size of the following angles.

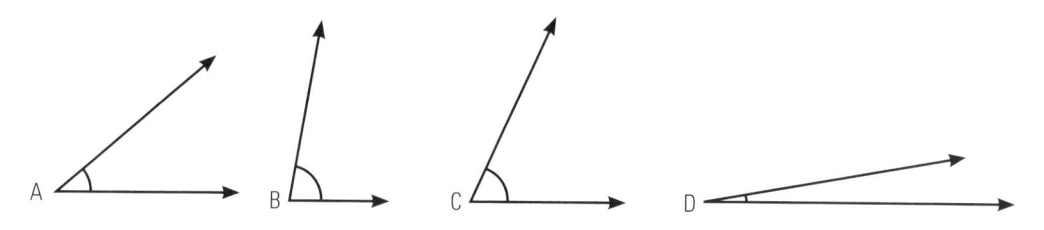

3. What is the approximate angle of the railing on the stairs?

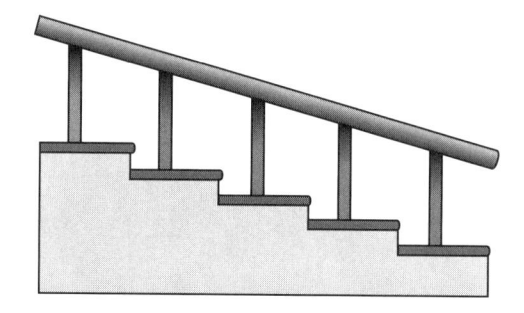

4. Use the referents in the New Skills section to determine the approximate size of the following angles.

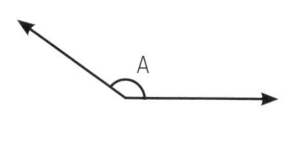

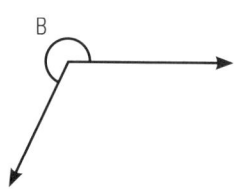

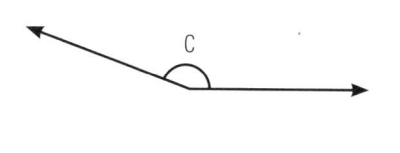

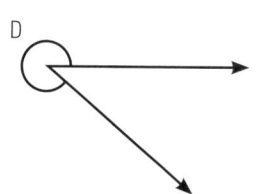

5. Jason is doing a survey of a city block. What is the approximate angle between his sightings of the two buildings?

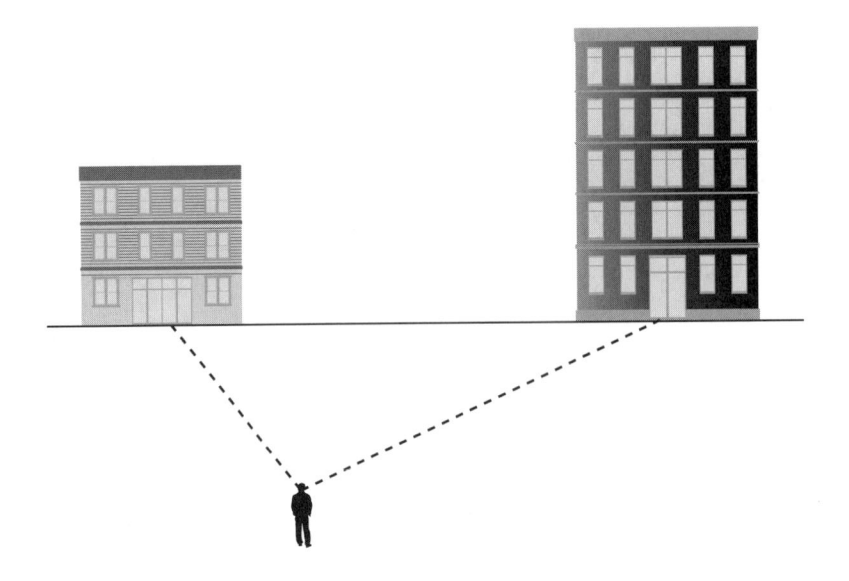

Example 3

complementary angles:
two angles that have measures that add up to 90°

supplementary angles:
two angles that have measures that add up to 180°

Given each of the following angles, determine the size of the **complement** and/or the size of the **supplement** (if they exist).

a) 75°

b) 43°

c) 103°

d) 87°

e) 300°

Two angles with the same measure are referred to as congruent.

SOLUTION

To find the complement, subtract the angle measure from 90°.

To find the supplement, subtract the angle measure from 180°.

a) Complement:

 90° − 75° = 15°

 Supplement:

 180° − 75° = 105°

b) Complement:

 90° − 43° = 47°

 Supplement:

 180° − 43° = 137°

c) Complement: The angle is already greater than 90° so there is no complement.

 Supplement:

 180° − 103° = 77°

d) Complement:

 90° − 87° = 3°

 Supplement:

 180° − 87° = 93°

e) The angle is greater than 180°, so it has no complement or supplement.

BUILD YOUR SKILLS

6. Fill in the chart with the complement and the supplement of each angle, if they exist. If they don't exist, state why.

ANGLE COMPLEMENTS AND SUPPLEMENTS		
Angle	Complement	Supplement
45°		
78°		
112°		
160°		
220°		

7. The complement of an angle is 58°.

   a) What is the size of the angle?

   b) What is the supplement of the angle?

8. The complement of an angle is 0°.

   a) What is the size of the angle?

   b) What is the size of the supplement of the angle?

NEW SKILLS: WORKING WITH TRUE BEARING

In navigation and map-making, people often measure angles from the vertical, or north. The angle, measured in a clockwise direction from a line pointing north, is referred to as the **true bearing**. Straight north has a bearing of 0°.

For more details, see page 182 of *MathWorks 10*.

true bearing: the angle measured clockwise between true north and an intended path or direction, expressed in degrees

Example 4

A boat is heading directly southwest. What is its true bearing?

SOLUTION

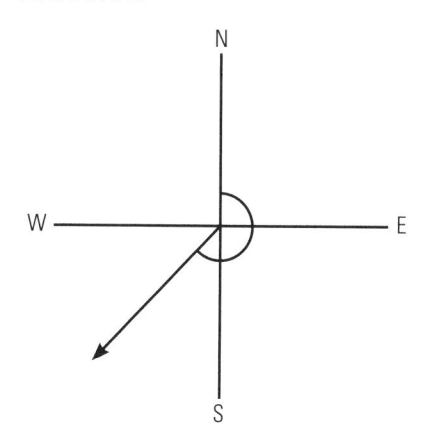

If the boat is heading southwest, measuring from the vertical will give you an obtuse angle of 225° (45° beyond a straight angle).

BUILD YOUR SKILLS

9. If a boat is travelling 25° south of straight east, what is its true bearing?

10. What is the true bearing of a boat travelling south?

11. What is the true bearing of a boat travelling north-northwest?

PRACTISE YOUR NEW SKILLS

1. Identify the type of angle: acute, right, obtuse, straight, or reflex.

    a) 56°

    b) 91°

    c) 270°

    d) 170°

    e) 43°

    f) 192°

2. Estimate, using referents, the size of the angles indicated in the diagrams.

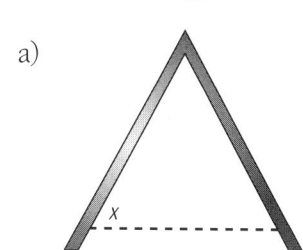

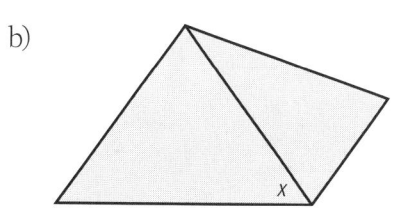

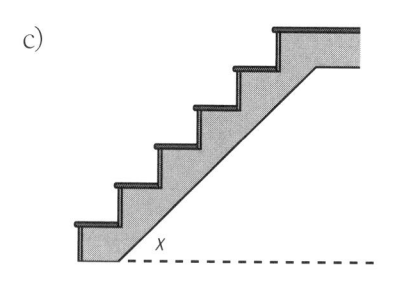

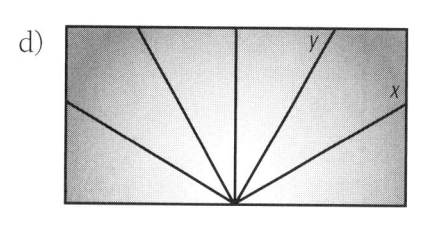

   a)

   b)

   c)

   d)

3. If Renata cuts a rectangular tile diagonally, one of the acute angles formed is 65°. What is the size of the other acute angle?

4. Pete is laying irregularly shaped paving stones. He needs to find one to fit in position A. Approximately what size of angle will it have?

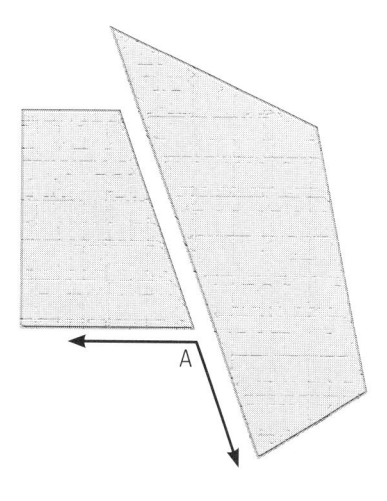

5. On the map below, what is the bearing from the following points?

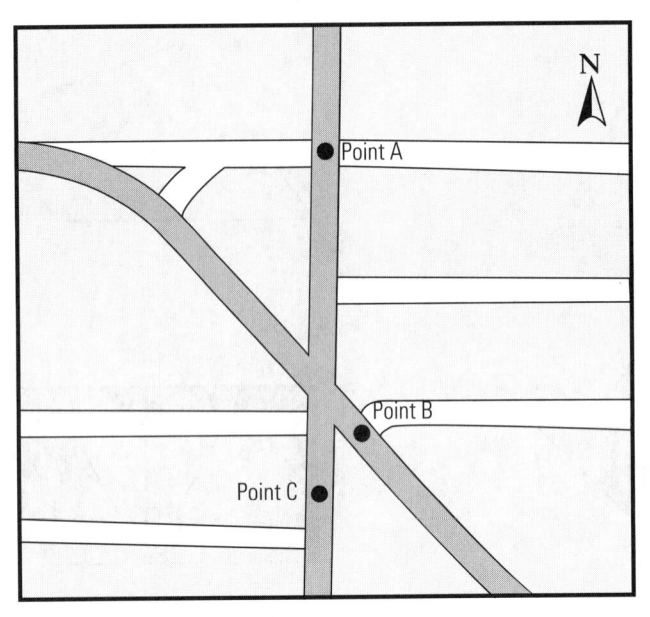

a) A to B

b) B to C

Angle Bisectors and Perpendicular Lines   5.2

NEW SKILLS: WORKING WITH ANGLE BISECTORS

To bisect something is to cut it into two equal parts. An angle is bisected by a ray that divides it into two angles of equal measure. The ray that divides the angle is called an **angle bisector**.

angle bisector: a segment, ray, or line that separates two halves of a bisected angle

Perpendicular lines are two lines that form a right angle. A right angle (90°) can be thought of as a bisected straight (180°) angle. The process used to draw perpendicular lines is the same as drawing angle bisectors because a perpendicular line bisects a straight angle.

For more details, see page 187 of *MathWorks 10*.

Point C bisects AB if AC is equal to CB.

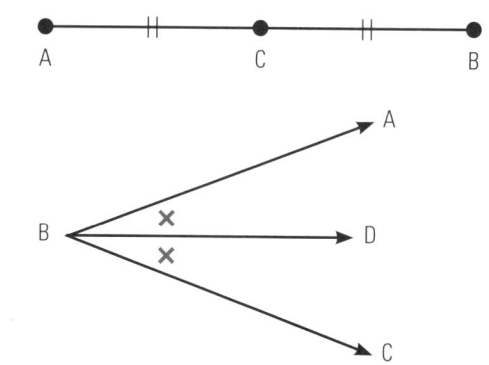

Ray BD bisects ∠ABC if ∠ABD is equal to ∠DBC.

Example 1

Bisect ∠ABC using a straight edge and compass.

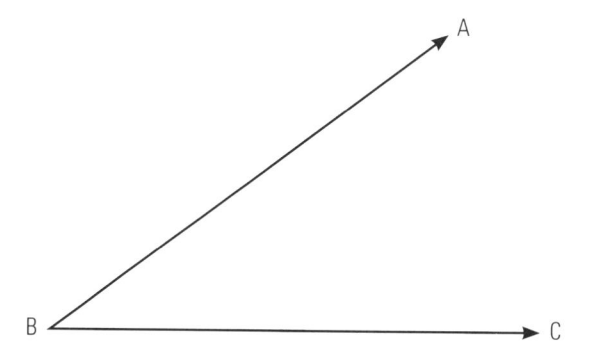

226 MathWorks 10 Workbook

SOLUTION

To draw a ray, BD, that bisects ∠ABC, follow these steps:

- With the compass point at B, draw an arc to intersect BA and BC at X and Y, respectively.

- With the compass point at X and the radius more than half of XY, draw a small arc in the interior of ∠ABC.

- With the same radius and compass point at Y, draw a small arc to intersect this arc at D.

- Join B and D.

BD is the bisector of ∠ABC.

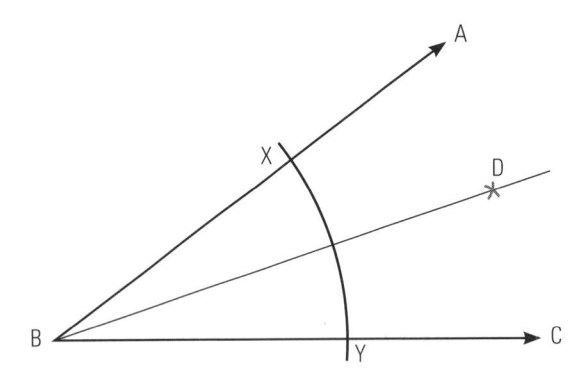

BUILD YOUR SKILLS

1. If a right angle is bisected, what is the size of each angle?

   45°

2. Bisect the given angles using a straight edge and compass.

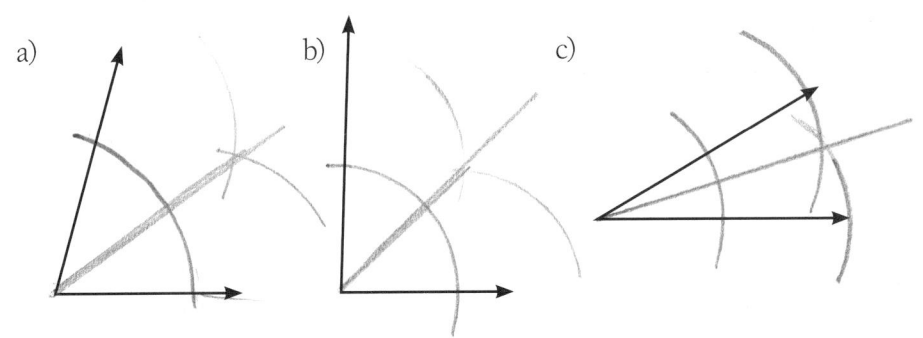

   a)   b)   c)

3. An angle is bisected. Each resulting angle is 78°. How big was the original angle?

4. The size of one resulting angle after the original angle is bisected is equal to the supplement of the original angle. What is the measure of the original angle?

Example 2

Using a protractor, determine which of the following lines are perpendicular.

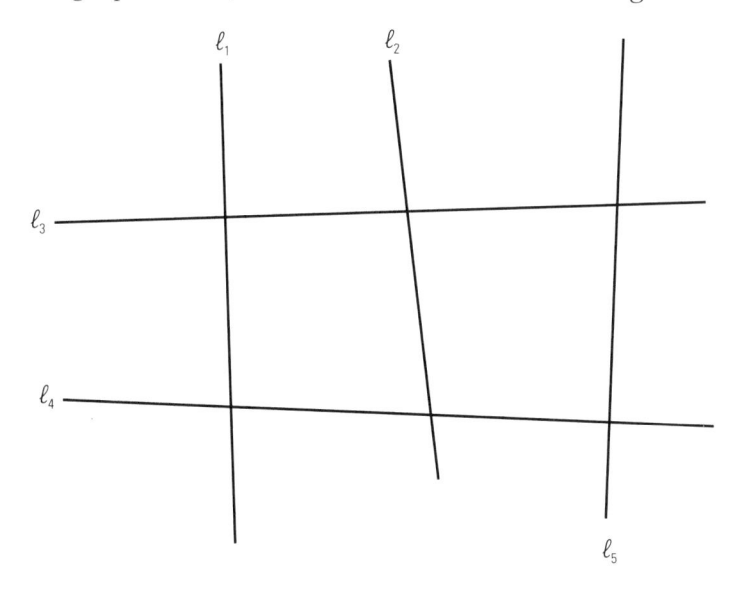

In the workplace, carpenters often use framing squares and levels to ensure that they have right angles. A framing square is a tool that is a right angle.

SOLUTION

The angles formed between ℓ_1 and ℓ_3 are each 90°, so ℓ_1 and ℓ_3 are perpendicular.

The angles formed between ℓ_1 and ℓ_4 are not 90°, so ℓ_1 and ℓ_4 are not perpendicular.

The angles formed between ℓ_2 and ℓ_3 are not 90°, so ℓ_2 and ℓ_3 are not perpendicular.

The angles formed between ℓ_2 and ℓ_4 are not 90°, so ℓ_2 and ℓ_4 are not perpendicular.

The angles formed between ℓ_5 and ℓ_3 are not 90°, so ℓ_5 and ℓ_3 are not perpendicular.

The angles formed between ℓ_5 and ℓ_4 are each 90°, so ℓ_5 and ℓ_4 are perpendicular.

BUILD YOUR SKILLS

5. A crooked table leg makes an angle of 86.7° with the tabletop. How much must the carpenter move the leg so that it is perpendicular to the tabletop?

6. At what approximate angle does the hill incline from the horizontal?

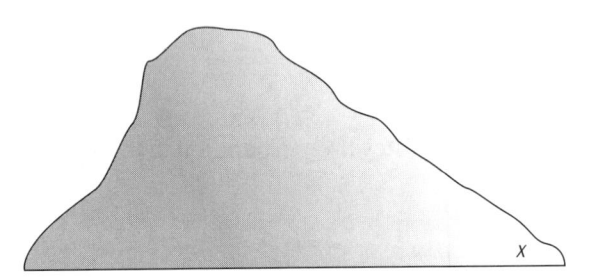

7. A carpenter is inlaying different types of wood on a tabletop. What must be the size of angles a, b, c, and d?

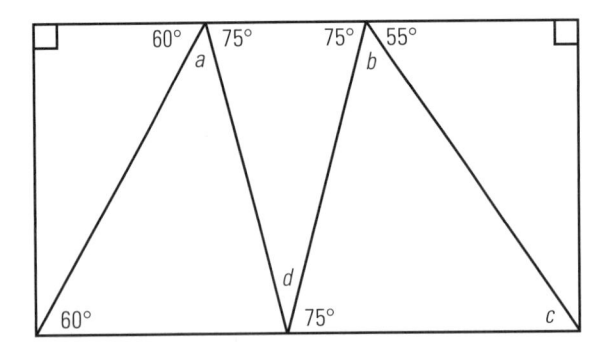

PRACTISE YOUR NEW SKILLS

1. Use a protractor to determine whether these lines are perpendicular.

   a)

   b)

   c)

   d)

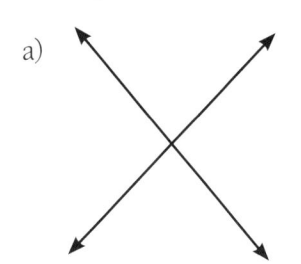

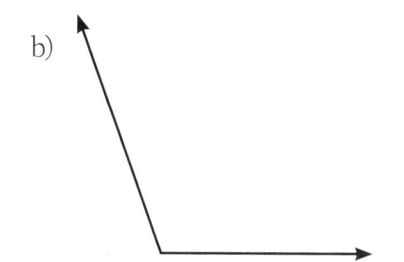

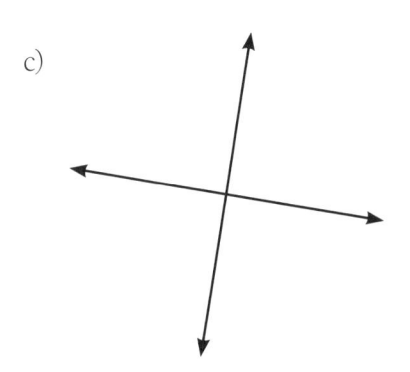

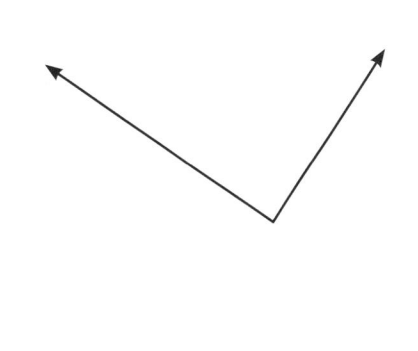

2. Complete the following table.

ANGLE CALCULATIONS			
Angle	Complement	Supplement	Resulting angle measure after the angle is bisected
73°			
	12°		
15°			
		132°	
90°			
			34°
	49°		
			68°
		100°	
			127°

3. Kaleb is edging a garden bed with square tiles. In the corner shown below, he wants two congruent tiles. At what angle must he cut the tiles so that they fit?

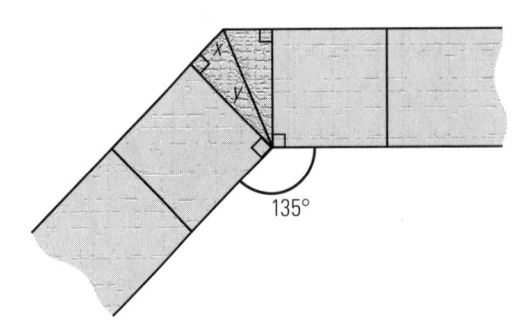

4. Calculate the size of the indicated angles. Name as many pairs of complementary and supplementary angles as possible.

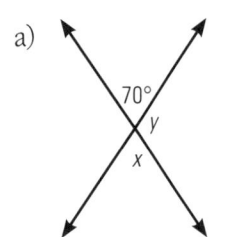

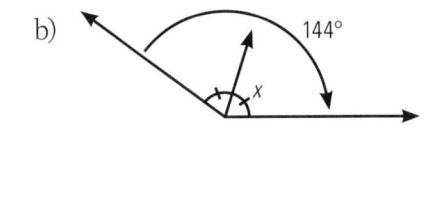

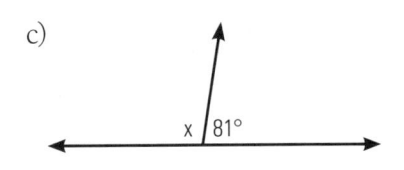

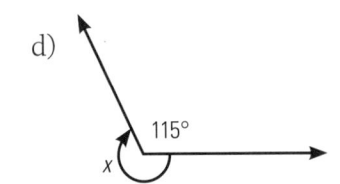

a) 70°, y, x

b) 144°, x, x

c) x, 81°

d) 115°, x

5. The angle at the peak of a roof is 135°. Calculate the measure of the angle formed by the rafter and the king post.

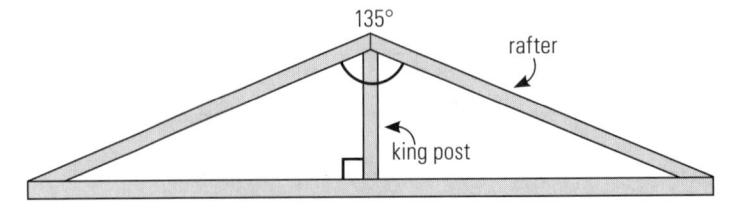

Non-Parallel Lines and Transversals   5.3

NEW SKILLS: WORKING WITH ANGLES FORMED BY INTERSECTING LINES

A line that intersects two other lines at two distinct points is a **transversal**. When two non-parallel lines are intersected by a transversal, they form angles of varying sizes.

Consider the diagram below: t is a transversal that intersects ℓ_1 and ℓ_2.

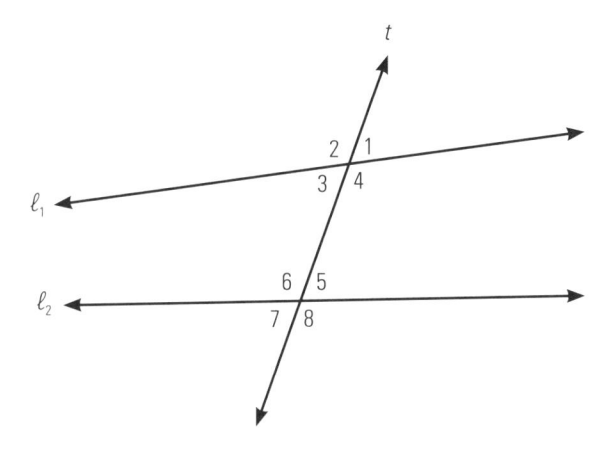

Eight angles are formed.

- ∠1 and ∠5, and ∠4 and ∠8, ∠2 and ∠6, and ∠3 and ∠7 are pairs of **corresponding** angles.

- ∠1 and ∠3, and ∠2 and ∠4, ∠5 and ∠7, and ∠6 and ∠8 are pairs of **vertically opposite angles**.

- ∠3 and ∠5, and ∠4 and ∠6 are pairs of **alternate interior angles**.

- ∠2 and ∠8, and ∠1 and ∠7 are pairs of **alternate exterior angles**.

- ∠3 and ∠6, and ∠4 and ∠5 are pairs of interior angles on the same side of the transversal.

- ∠1 and ∠8, and ∠2 and ∠7 are pairs of exterior angles on the same side of the transversal.

For more details, see page 198 of *MathWorks 10*.

---

transversal: a line that intersects two or more lines

corresponding angles: two angles that occupy the same relative position at two different intersections

vertically opposite angles: angles created by intersecting lines that share only a vertex

alternate interior angles: angles in opposite positions between two lines intersected by a transversal and also on alternate sides of the same transversal

alternate exterior angles: angles in opposite positions outside two lines intersected by a transversal

Example 1

In the following diagram, identify each of the following, and specify which lines and transversals you are using.

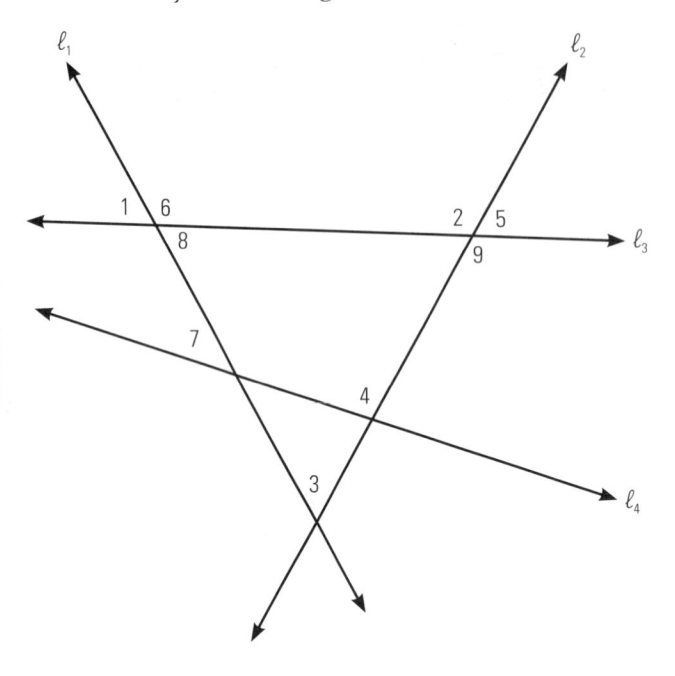

> A transversal is not necessarily one line segment in a specific drawing. In this figure, there are several lines that intersect other lines. These can be considered transversals.

a) an interior angle on the same side of the transversal as ∠6

b) an angle corresponding to ∠2

c) an angle corresponding to ∠4

d) an alternate interior angle to ∠4

SOLUTION

a) Using ℓ_1 and ℓ_2, with transversal ℓ_3, ∠2 and ∠6 are interior angles on the same side of the transversal.

b) Using ℓ_1 and ℓ_2, with transversal ℓ_3, ∠1 corresponds to ∠2.

c) Using ℓ_1 and ℓ_2, with transversal ℓ_4, ∠7 corresponds to ∠4.

d) Using ℓ_3 and ℓ_4, with transversal ℓ_2, ∠4 and ∠9 are alternate interior angles.

BUILD YOUR SKILLS

1. In the diagram below, identify the relationship between each pair of angles.

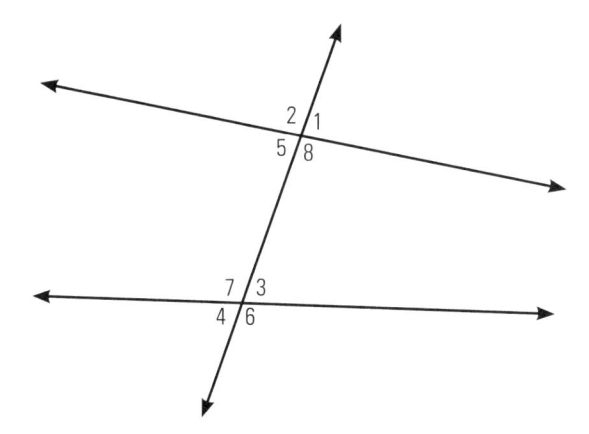

   a) ∠7 and ∠8

   b) ∠2 and ∠7

   c) ∠1 and ∠6

   d) ∠5 and ∠7

2. Given the diagram below, identify the following angles.

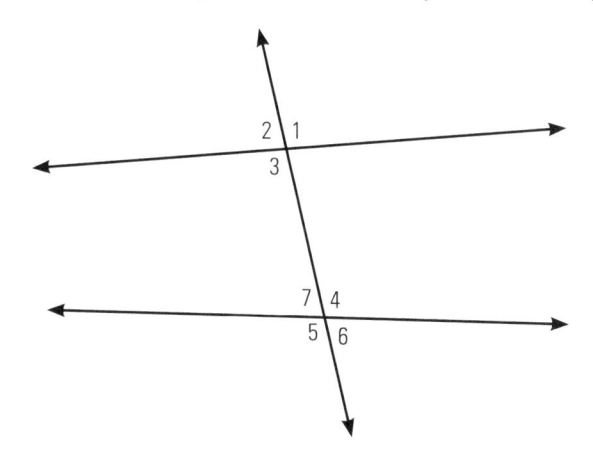

   a) an alternate exterior angle to ∠2

   b) an interior angle on the same side of the transversal as ∠7

   c) an alternate interior angle to ∠4

   d) an angle corresponding to ∠5

3. Identify each of the following angles. Name the two lines and the transversal you are using.

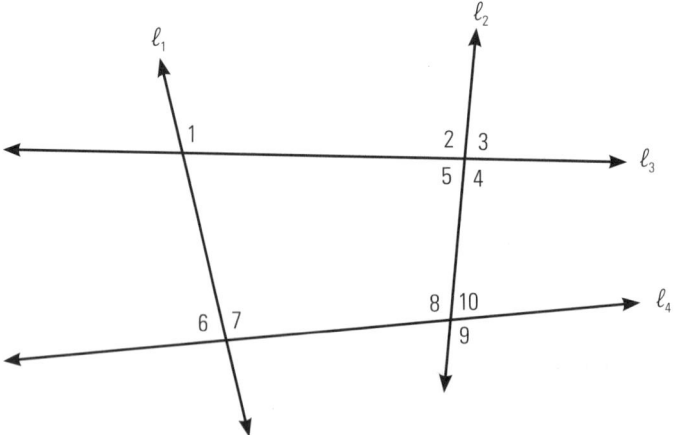

   a) two angles corresponding to ∠1

   b) an interior angle on the same side of the transversal as ∠10

   c) an alterate interior angle to ∠5

   d) two interior angles on the same side of the transversal as ∠8

Example 2

In the diagram below, measure and record the sizes of the angles. Identify pairs of equal angles and state why they are equal.

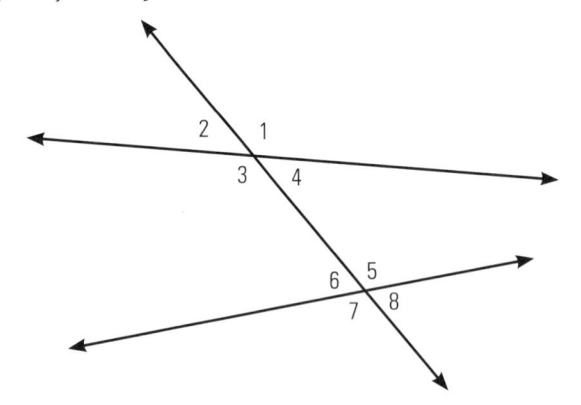

SOLUTION

Use a protractor to measure the angles.

∠1 and ∠3 measure 125°

∠2 and ∠4 measure 55°

∠5 and ∠7 measure 120°

∠6 and ∠8 measure 60°

These are each pairs of vertically opposite angles.

BUILD YOUR SKILLS

4. Look at the diagram below. Identify two transversals that intersect both AB and AD.

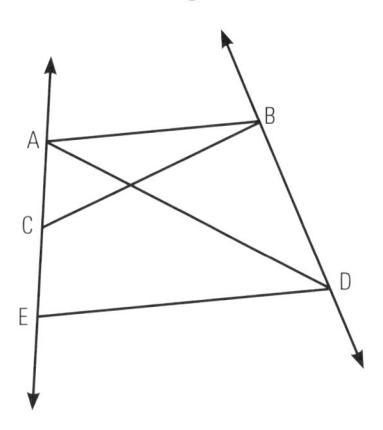

5. In the diagram below, can t be a transversal that intersects ℓ_1 and ℓ_2? State why or why not.

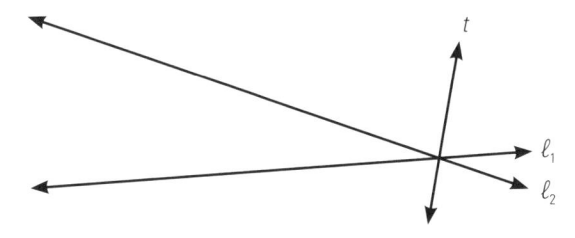

6. In the diagram below, t is a transversal that intersects ℓ_1 and ℓ_2. Name another pair of lines and their transversal.

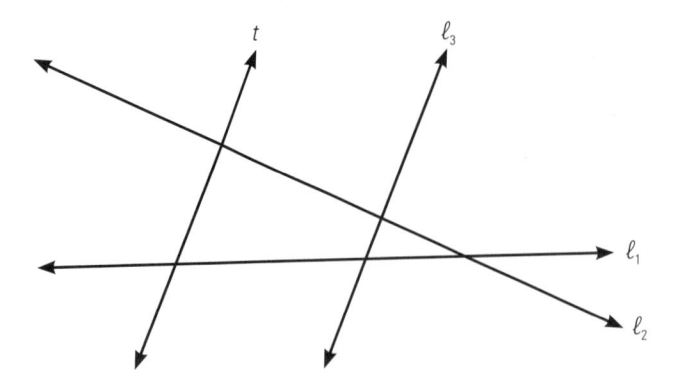

PRACTISE YOUR NEW SKILLS

1. In the diagram below, where t is the transversal, identify two pairs of each of the following angles.

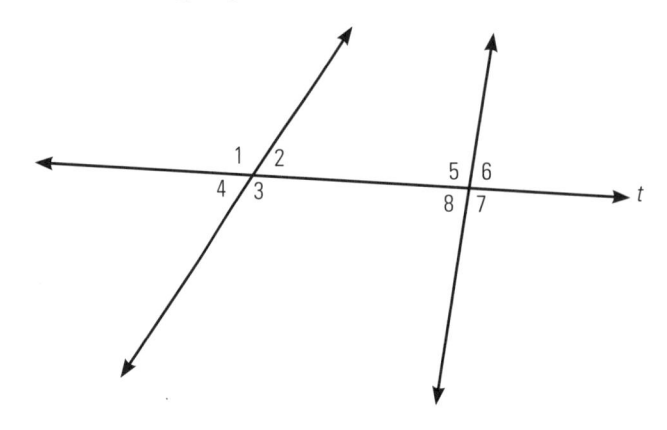

   a) alternate interior angles ∠5 ∠3

   b) corresponding angles ∠4 ∠8

   c) interior angles on the same side of the transversal ∠3 ∠8

Chapter 5 Angles and Parallel Lines 237

2. A flashlight shines down onto a floor as shown in the diagram below. If the outer rays are considered to be two lines and the floor is a transversal, name a pair of corresponding angles.

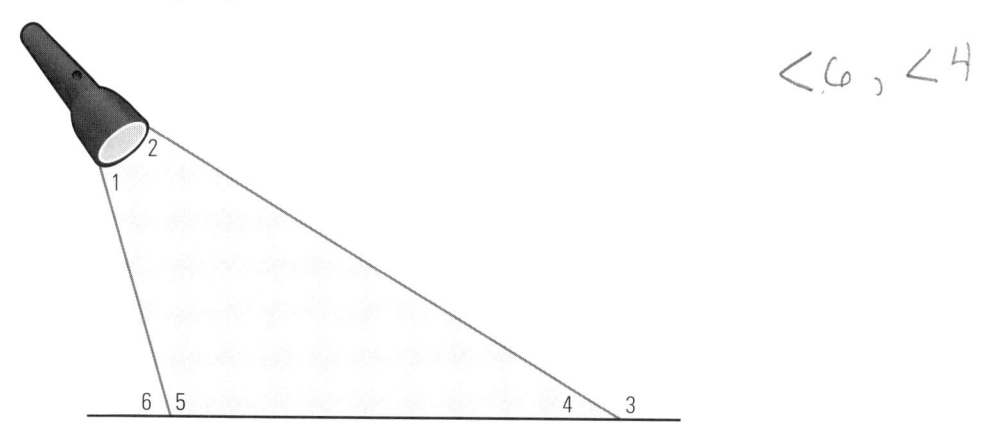

∠6, ∠4

3. In the diagram below, identify which line is a transversal that intersects ℓ_1 and ℓ_2 that makes the following relationships between the pairs of angles.

   a) ∠1 and ∠2 a pair of corresponding angles

   b) ∠3 and ∠4 a pair of alternate interior angles

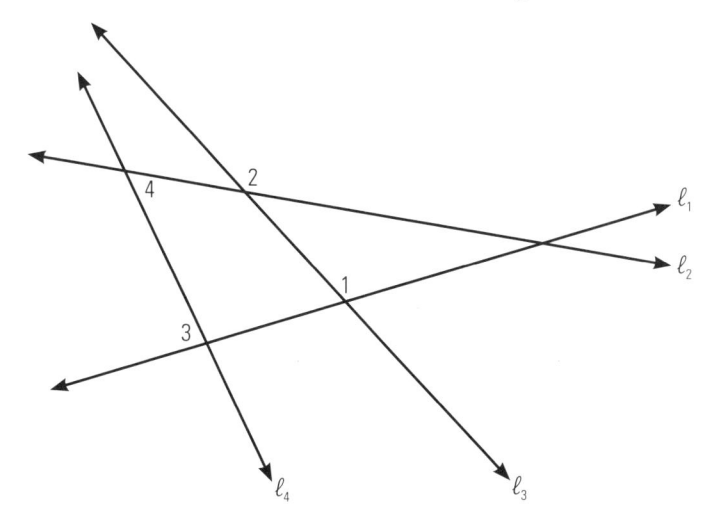

4. In the diagram below, calculate the sizes of each of the interior angles. What is their sum?

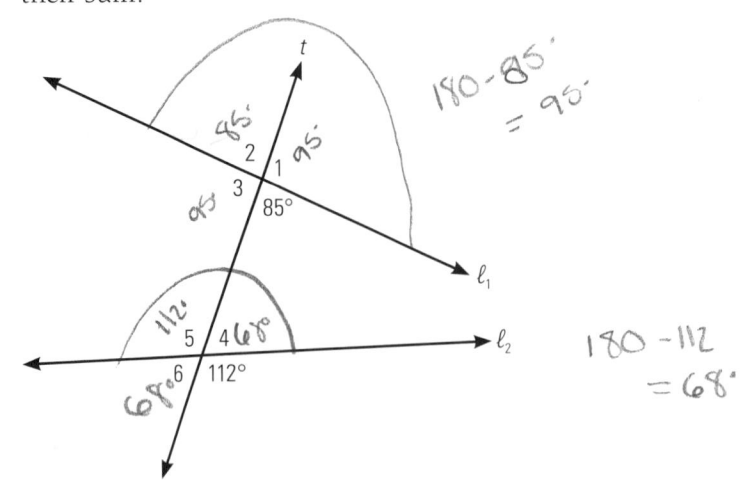

Annotations on diagram:
- angle 1 = 95°
- angle 2 = 85°
- angle 3 = 95°
- 85° (given)
- angle 4 = 68°
- angle 5 = 112°
- angle 6 = 68°
- 112° (given)

180 − 85° = 95°

180 − 112 = 68°

5. Calculate the sizes of the six angles indicated in the figure.

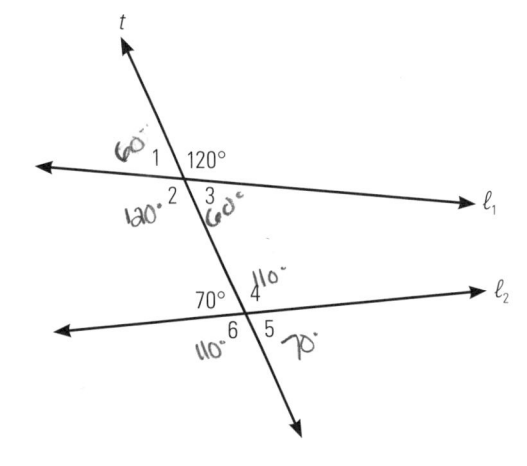

Annotations on diagram:
- angle 1 = 60°
- 120° (given)
- angle 2 = 120°
- angle 3 = 60°
- 70° (given)
- angle 4 = 110°
- angle 6 = 110°
- angle 5 = 70°

Parallel Lines and Transversals 5.4

NEW SKILLS: WORKING WITH ANGLES FORMED BY PARALLEL LINES INTERSECTED BY A TRANSVERSAL

If two parallel lines are intersected by a transversal:

- the alternate interior angles are equal;
- the corresponding angles are equal; and
- the interior angles on the same side of the transversal are supplementary.

If you know that, given two lines cut by a transversal:

- alternate interior angles are equal; or
- corresponding angles are equal; or
- interior angles on the same side of the transversal are supplementary;

then you can conclude that the lines are parallel.

For more details, see page 209 of *MathWorks 10*.

Example 1

Consider the diagram below, in which ℓ_1 is parallel to ℓ_2. What are the measures of the three indicated angles? Explain how you reached your answers.

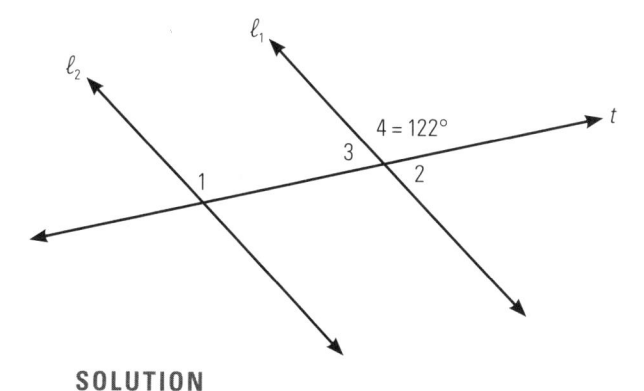

SOLUTION

∠1 measures 122° because it corresponds to ∠4.

∠2 measures 58° because it forms a straight angle with ∠4.

∠3 measures 58° because it is vertically opposite ∠2.

ALTERNATIVE SOLUTION

There may be more than one reason for stating why two angles are equal.

∠3 is 58° because it forms a straight angle with ∠4.

∠2 is 58° because it is vertically opposite ∠3.

∠1 is 122° because it is an interior angle on the same side of a transversal as ∠3.

> The order in which you find the angle measures is important in explaining your reasoning.

BUILD YOUR SKILLS

1. In the diagram below, ℓ_1 is parallel to ℓ_2. State the measures of the indicated angles and explain your reasoning.

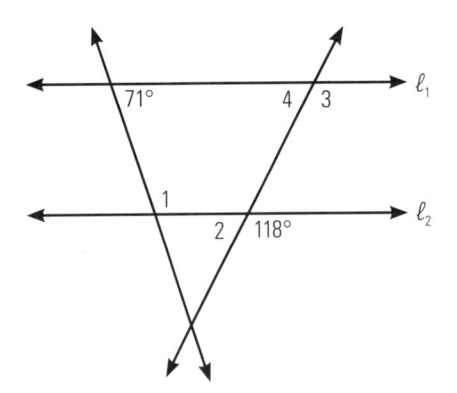

2. What are the measures of the interior angles in the trapezoid shown below? (Hint: Be careful of the order in which you calculate the angles.)

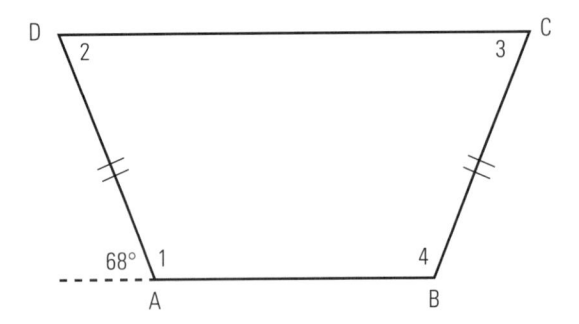

3. Quadrilateral ABCD is a parallelogram in which ∠B measures 74°. Determine the measures of the other angles and state your reasons.

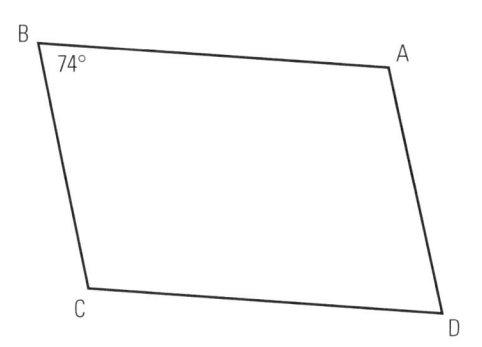

Example 2

Given the diagram below, identify all the pairs of parallel lines and explain your selection.

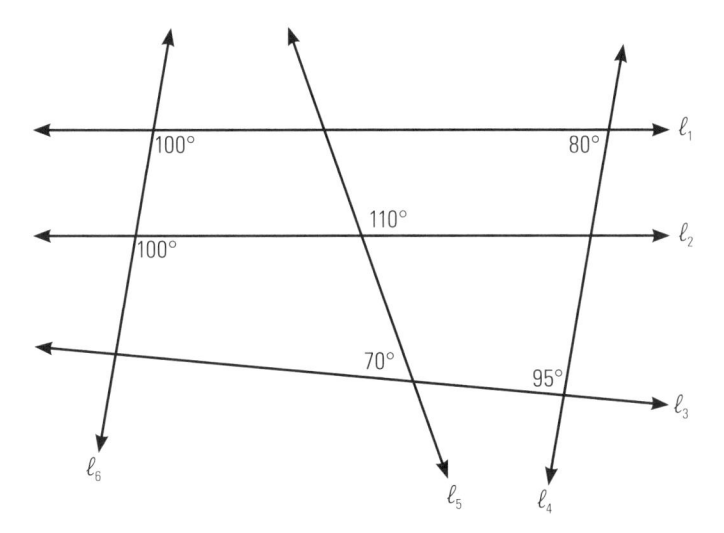

SOLUTION

ℓ_6 is parallel to ℓ_4. If you consider ℓ_1 to be a transversal, 100° and 80° are interior angles on the same side of the transversal.

ℓ_1 is parallel to ℓ_2. If ℓ_6 is a transversal, the two 100° angles are corresponding angles.

BUILD YOUR SKILLS

4. Find a pair of parallel lines in the following diagram. On the diagram, mark all the angles necessary to determine this.

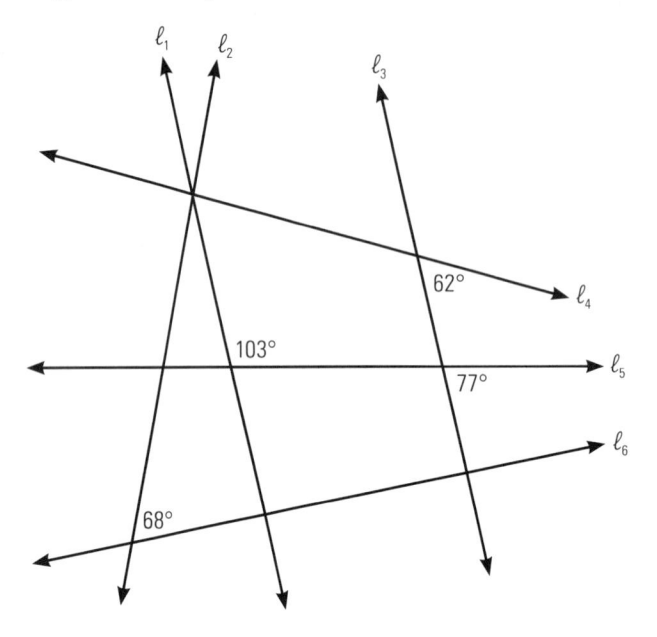

5. What size must ∠1 be if ℓ_1 is parallel to ℓ_2?

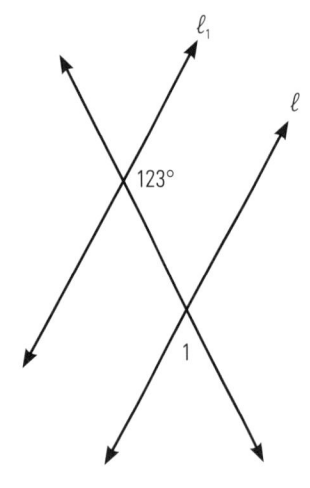

6. The two vertical pipes in the diagram need to be moved to be parallel to each other. By what angle must the plumber move the second pipe?

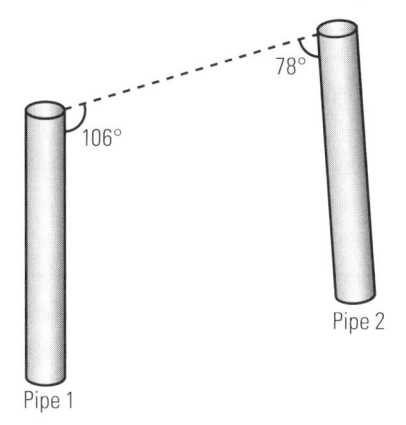

Example 3

Given parallelogram ABCD, determine the values of ∠B, ∠C, and ∠D in that order, stating your reason for each measure.

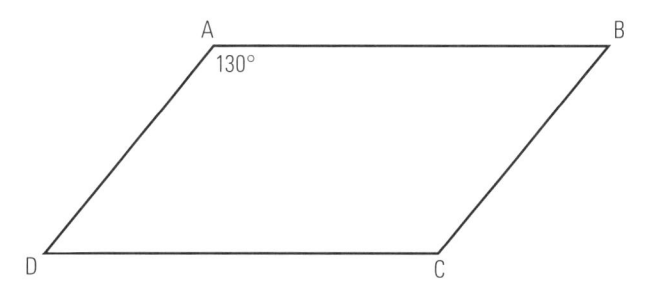

SOLUTION

In a parallelogram, opposite sides are parallel.

AD is parallel to BC, and they are intersected by transversal AB. ∠B is an interior angle on the same side of the transversal as ∠A. Therefore, it is complementary to ∠A.

$180° - 130° = 50°$

∠B is 50°.

> You can use the notation AD ∥ BC to indicate that AD and BC are parallel.

AB is parallel to DC, and they are intersected by transversal BC. You know that ∠B is 50°. ∠C is an interior angle on the same side of the transversal as ∠B, so they are complementary. ∠C measures 130°.

AB is parallel to DC, and they are intersected by transversal AD. You know that ∠A measures 130° and is complementary to ∠D. Therefore, ∠D measures 50°.

BUILD YOUR SKILLS

7. If ℓ_1 and ℓ_2 are parallel and are intersected by transversals t_1 and t_2, what are the measures of the indicated angles? Solve for the measures in the given order, stating your reasoning.

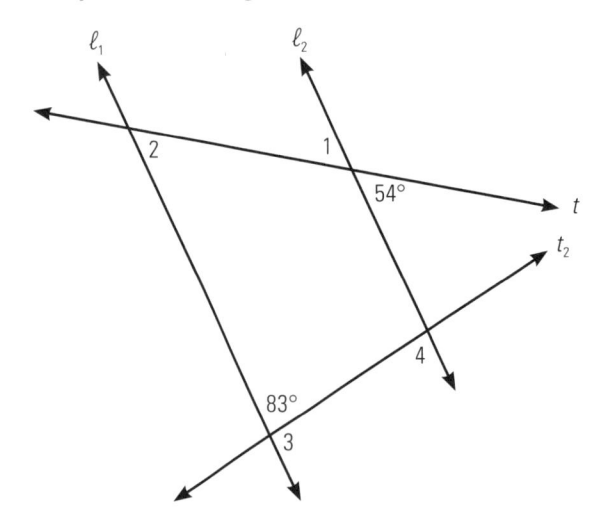

SOLVING ANGLE MEASURES	
Angle Measure	Reason
∠1 =	
∠2 =	
∠3 =	
∠4 =	

8. In the diagram below, if the side of the house and the side of the shed are parallel, what are the measures of ∠1 and ∠2?

9. A plumber must install pipe 2 parallel to pipe 1. He knows that ∠1 is 53°. What is the measure of ∠2?

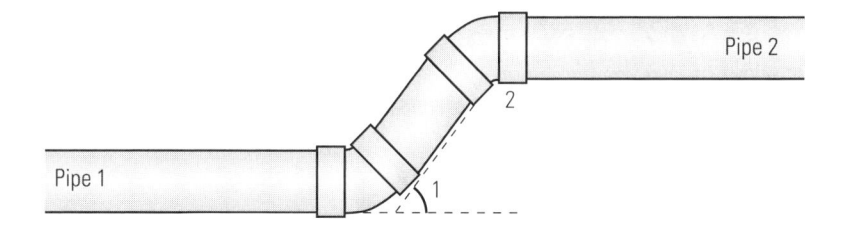

PRACTISE YOUR NEW SKILLS

1. Given the diagram below, where ℓ_1 is parallel to ℓ_2, find the measures of the indicated angles and state your reasons.

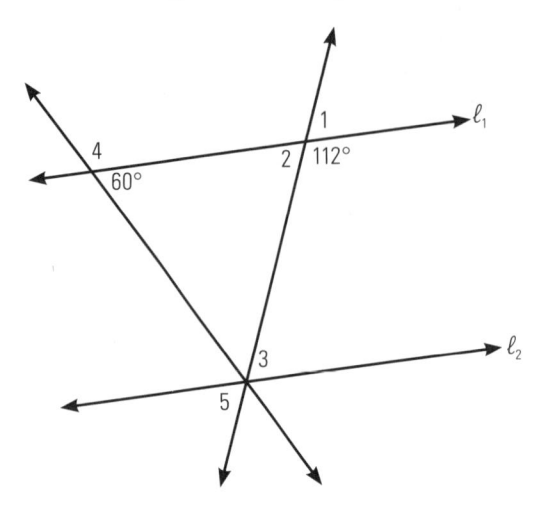

2. In the diagram below, the top of the bridge is parallel to the deck, and the brace in the middle is vertical, perpendicular to the deck, determine the size of ∠1 and ∠2.

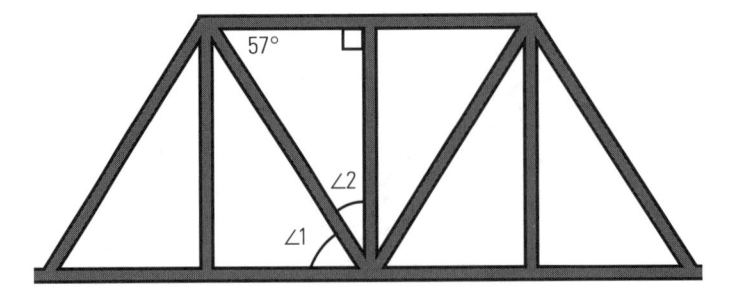

3. Identify the pairs of parallel lines in the following diagram. (Hint: The lines can be extended.)

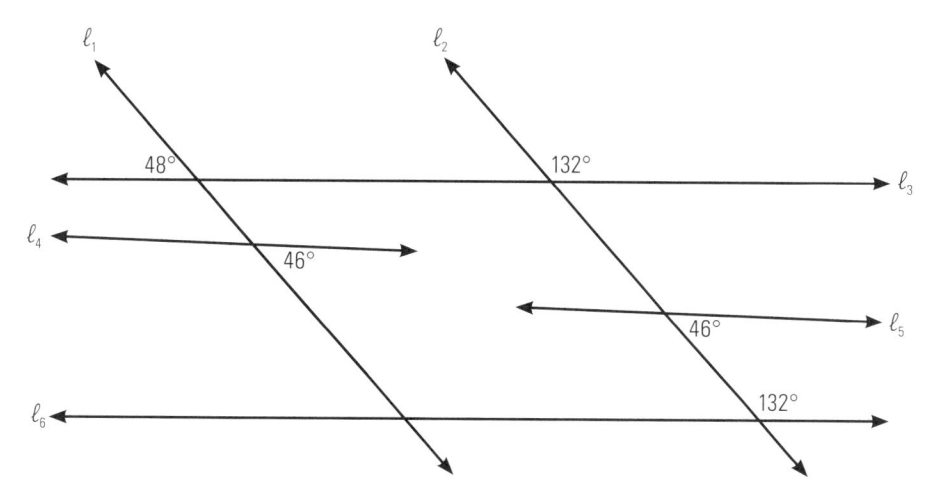

4. Examine the following diagram. By how many degrees do the studs need to be moved in order to be parallel to each other? What direction do they need to move in? (The studs are indicated by the capital letters.)

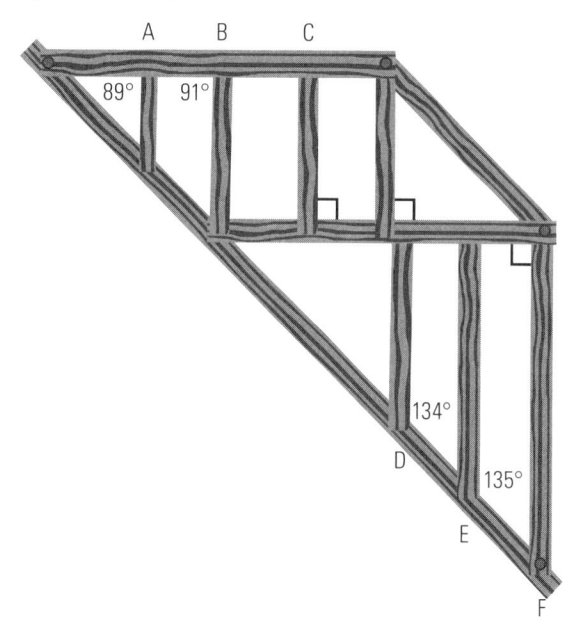

CHAPTER TEST

1. Classify each of the following as acute, right, obtuse, straight, or reflex angles.

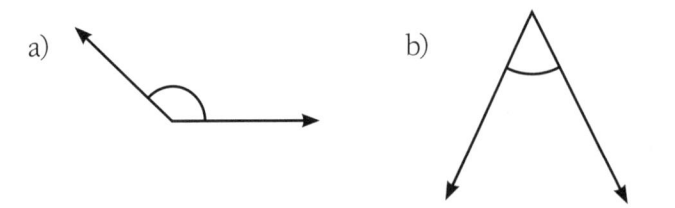

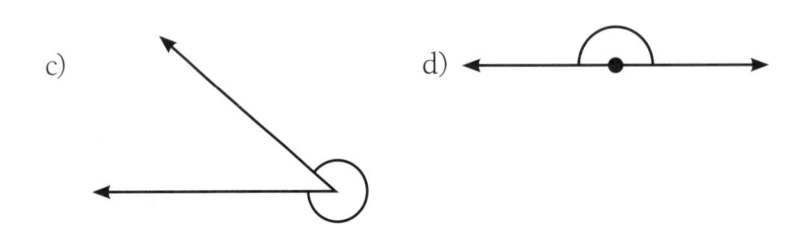

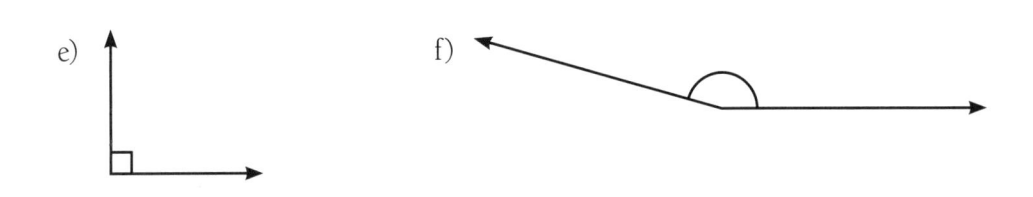

   a)

   b)

   c)

   d)

   e)

   f)

2. Fill in the missing parts in the table. If no such angle exists, explain why.

ANGLE CALCULATIONS			
Angle	Complement	Supplement	Resulting angle measure after the angle is bisected
58°			
			47°
		93°	
153°			
	25°		

3. Name the relationship between the indicated pairs of angles.

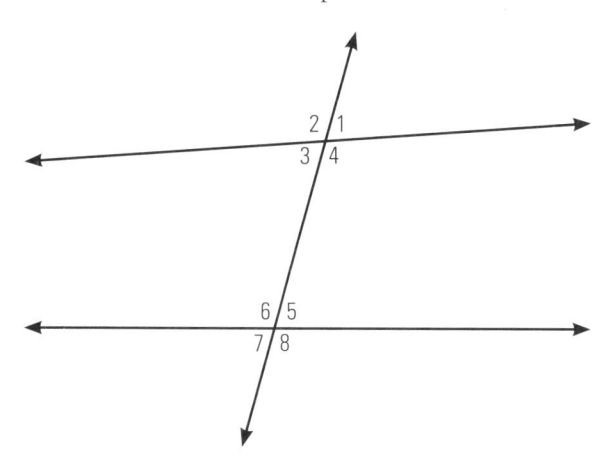

   a) ∠3 and ∠5

   b) ∠4 and ∠5

   c) ∠1 and ∠3

   d) ∠2 and ∠6

4. In the diagram below, ℓ_1 is parallel to ℓ_2. Determine the measures of the indicated angles and explain your reasons. Write the answers in the order that you calculated them.

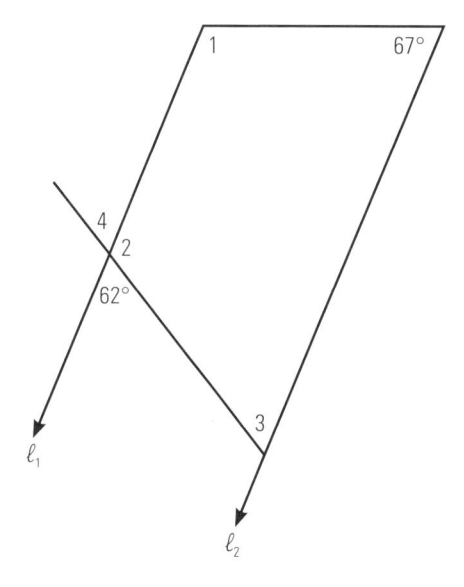

5. Given the following diagram, what must be the measures of ∠1 and ∠2 if BE is parallel to CD? State your reasons.

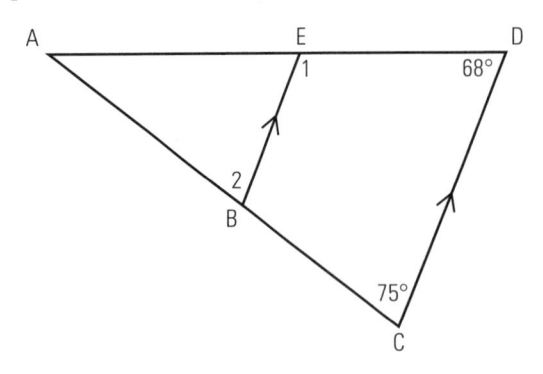

6. In trapezoid PQRS, PS is parallel to QR. What are the measures of ∠1 and ∠2?

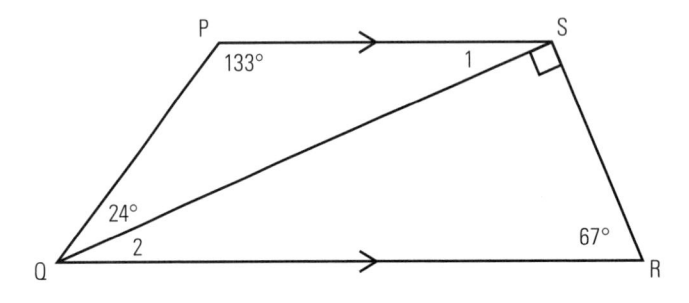

7. If ℓ_1 is parallel to ℓ_2, and ℓ_3 is parallel to ℓ_5, what are the following angle measures?

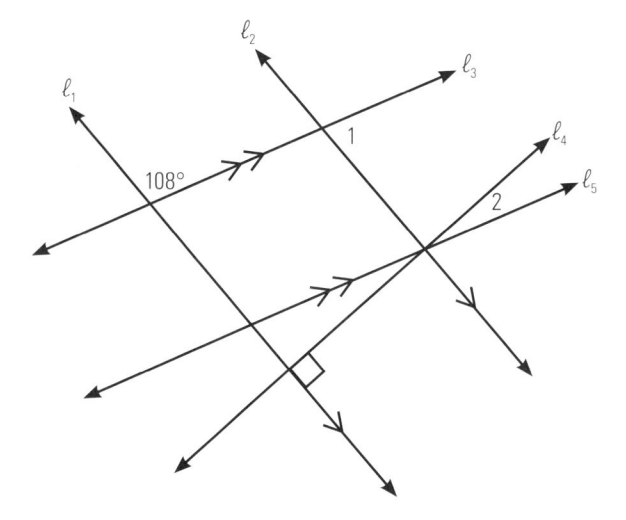

   a) the value of ∠1

   b) the value of ∠2 that will make ℓ_4 perpendicular to ℓ_2

8. On the map below, what is the true bearing from the following points?

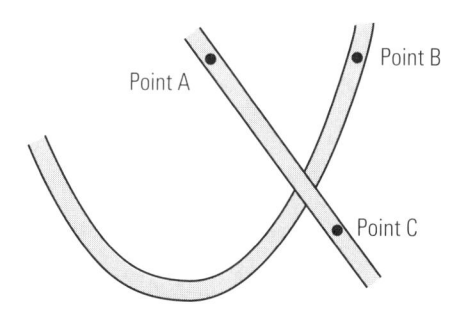

   a) A to B

   b) B to C

9. Fred states that if ℓ_1 is parallel to ℓ_2, and ℓ_2 is parallel to ℓ_3, then it follows that ℓ_1 is parallel to ℓ_3. Is Fred right? Show your answer using a diagram.

10. In the diagram below, ℓ_1 is parallel to ℓ_2, and ℓ_2 is parallel to ℓ_3. State two angles whose measures are the same as $\angle 7$. Explain your reasoning.

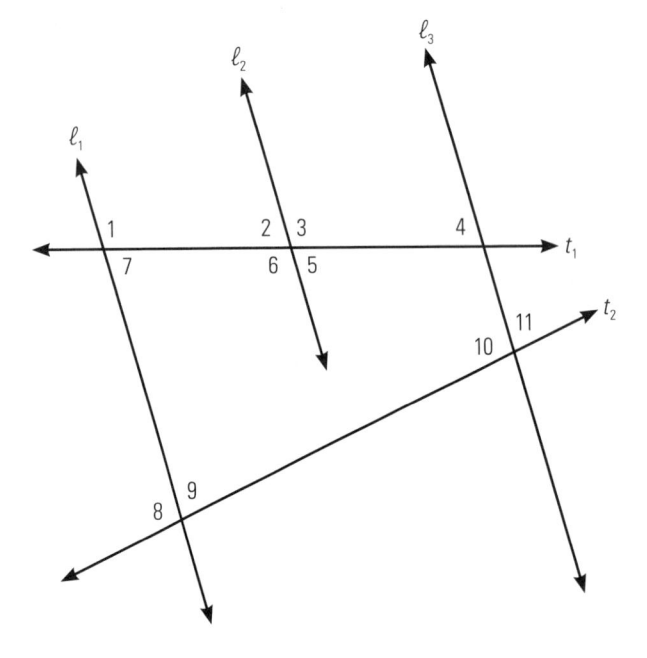

Chapter 6
Similarity of Figures

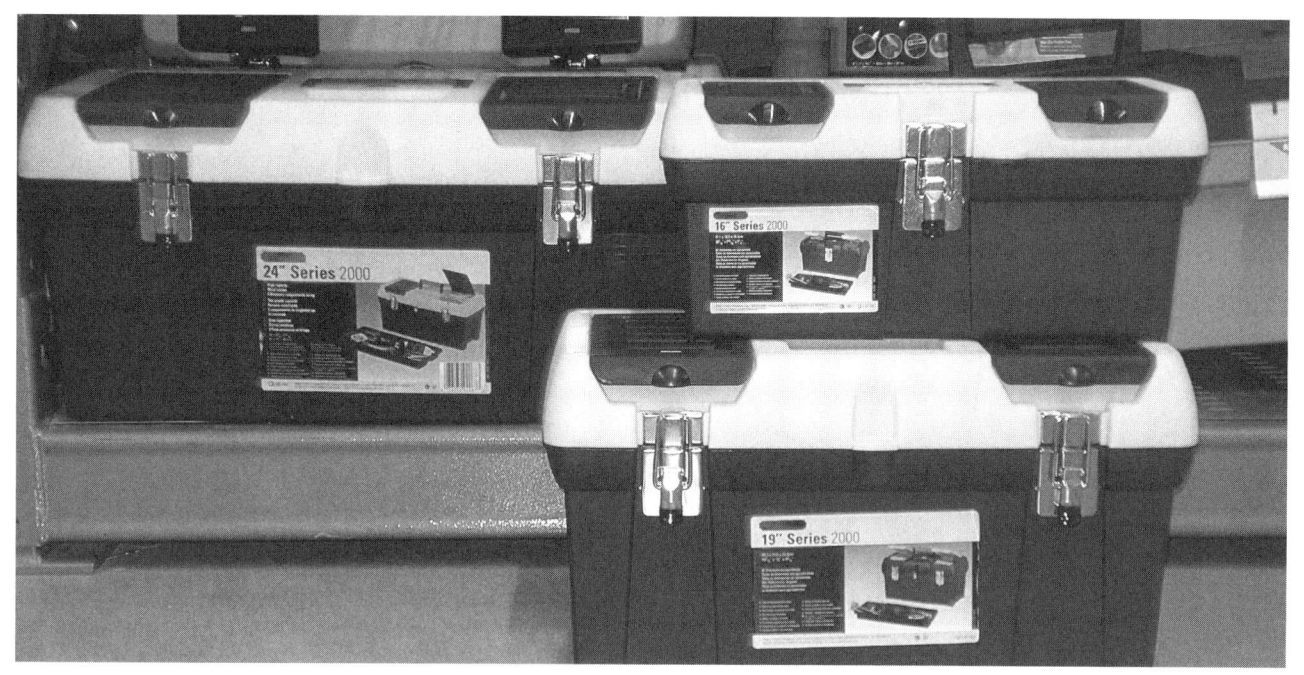

These nesting toolboxes were designed to be similar figures.

Similar Polygons 6.1

REVIEW: WORKING WITH RATIO, RATE, AND PROPORTIONAL REASONING

In this chapter, you will apply ratio, rate, and proportional reasoning.

See chapter 1 of this workbook for a review of these concepts.

NEW SKILLS: WORKING WITH SIMILAR FIGURES

Two figures are similar if they have the same shape but are different sizes. A diagram drawn to scale to another diagram creates a similar figure. Likewise, an enlargement of a photograph, when reproduced to scale, yields a similar figure.

For two figures to be similar:

corresponding sides:
two sides that occupy the same relative position in similar figures

- corresponding angles must be the same size; and
- **corresponding sides** must be in the same proportion.

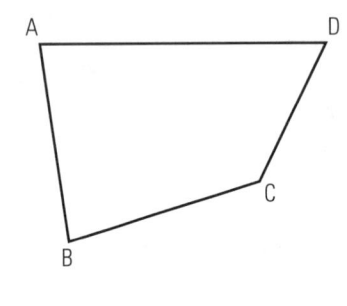

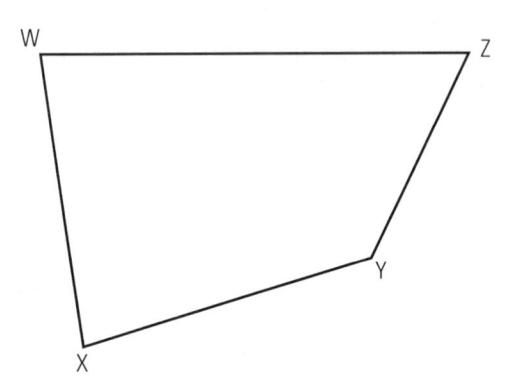

In quadrilateral ABCD and quadrilateral WXYZ, the following equivalencies are true.

$\angle A = \angle W$

$\angle B = \angle X$

$\angle C = \angle Y$

$\angle D = \angle Z$

$$\frac{AB}{WX} = \frac{BC}{XY} = \frac{YZ}{DC} = \frac{DA}{ZW}$$

The two quadrilaterals are similar. This can be written as ABCD ~ WXYZ.

For more details, see page 227 of *MathWorks 10*.

If two figures have the same size and shape, they are said to be congruent, or similar. Similarity is shown by the symbol ~.

Example 1

Tara has drawn a scale diagram of her bedroom so that she can sketch different arrangements of her furniture. On her diagram, the walls have the following lengths:

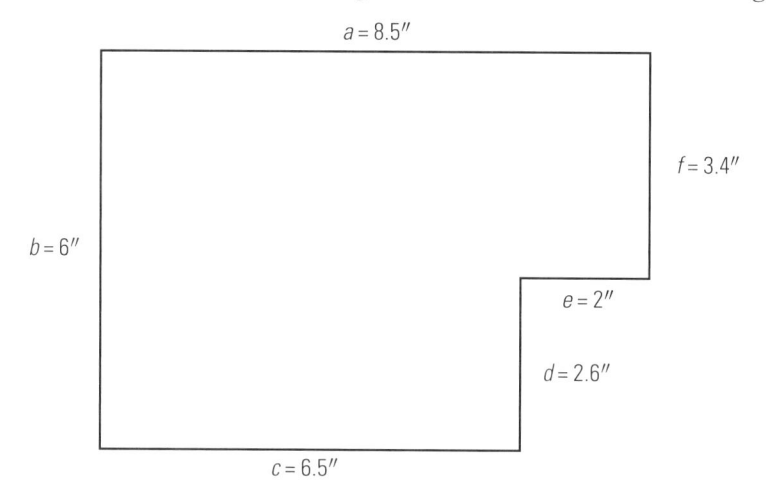

a = 8.5″
f = 3.4″
b = 6″
e = 2″
d = 2.6″
c = 6.5″

If the longest wall in her room is actually 12.75′, how long are the other walls?

SOLUTION

Set up proportions between the longest wall and each of the other walls. Label the walls of the actual room with the same letters as those in the scale drawing, but use upper case letters. (For example, wall *a* is 8.5″ on the drawing, and wall *A* is 12.75′ in the actual room.)

Start with wall *b*.

$$\frac{a}{A} = \frac{b}{B}$$

$$\frac{8.5}{12.75} = \frac{6}{B} \qquad \text{Substitute the known values.}$$

$$\frac{8.5}{12.75} = \frac{6}{B} \qquad \text{Work without units of measurement.}$$

$$\cancel{12.75} \times B \times \frac{8.5}{\cancel{12.75}} = \frac{6}{\cancel{B}} \times \cancel{B} \times 12.75 \qquad \text{Multiply by 12.75B.}$$

$$8.5B = 6 \times 12.75$$

$$8.5B = 76.5$$

$$\frac{8.5B}{8.5} = \frac{76.5}{8.5} \qquad \text{Divide to isolate B.}$$

$$B = 9$$

Use the same method to solve the following proportions:

$$\frac{a}{A} = \frac{c}{C}$$

$$\frac{8.5}{12.75} = \frac{6.5}{C}$$

$$\frac{a}{A} = \frac{d}{D}$$

$$\frac{8.5}{12.75} = \frac{2.6}{D}$$

$$\frac{a}{A} = \frac{e}{E}$$

$$\frac{8.5}{12.75} = \frac{2}{E}$$

$$\frac{a}{A} = \frac{f}{F}$$

$$\frac{8.5}{12.75} = \frac{3.4}{F}$$

The lengths of the walls in Tara's bedroom are:

$B = 9.0'$

$C = 9.75'$

$D = 3.9'$

$E = 3'$

$F = 5.1'$

ALTERNATIVE SOLUTION

Determine the unit scale. If 8.5" represents 12.75', then calculate how many feet 1 inch represents.

$12.75' \div 8.5 = 1.5'$

The remaining side lengths can be calculated by multiplying each scaled unit by 1.5 ft per inch.

$B = 6 \times 1.5$
$B = 9'$

$C = 6.5 \times 1.5$

$C = 9.75'$

$D = 2.6 \times 1.5$

$D = 3.9'$

$E = 2 \times 1.5$

$E = 3'$

$F = 3.4 \times 1.5$

$F = 5.1'$

BUILD YOUR SKILLS

1. The two figures shown below are similar. Find the lengths of the sides of the smaller figure. (The diagrams are not drawn to scale.)

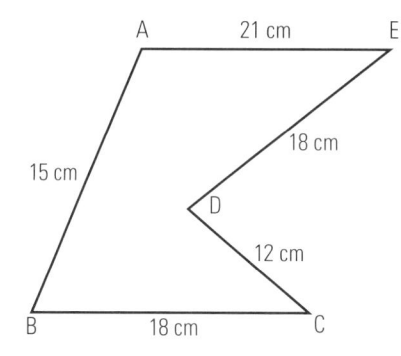

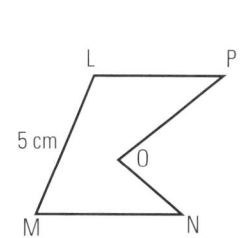

2. On a blueprint, a room measures 2.75 inches by 1.5 inches. If 1 inch represents 8 feet, what will be the dimensions of the room?

3. Identify the pairs of similar polygons below.

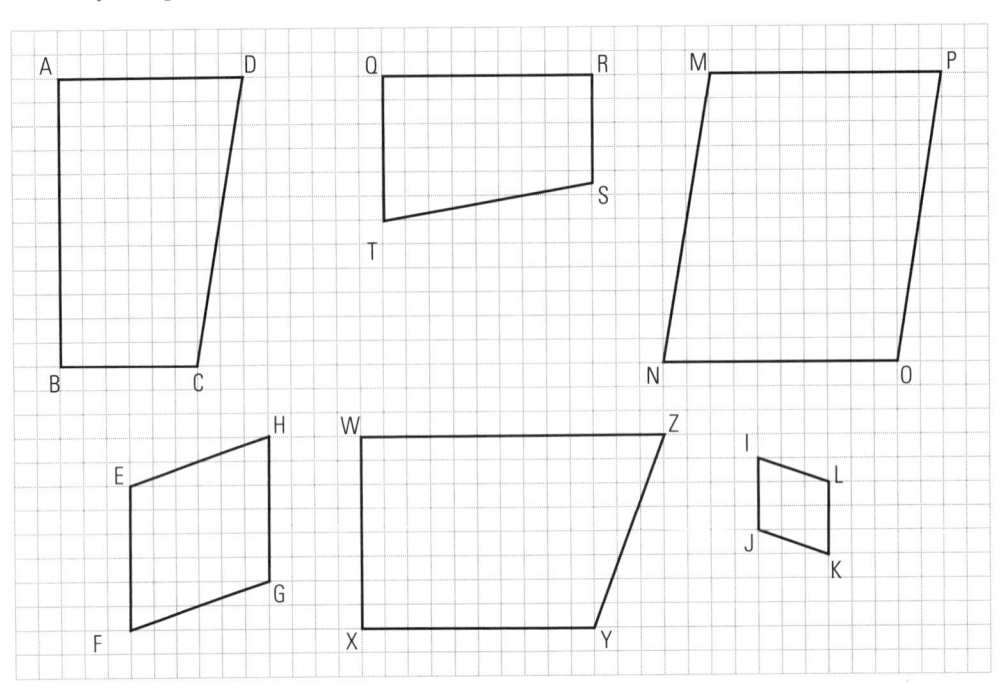

Example 2

If △RST is similar to △LMN and angle measures of △LMN are as follows, what are the angle measures of △RST?

∠L = 85°

∠M = 78°

∠N = 17°

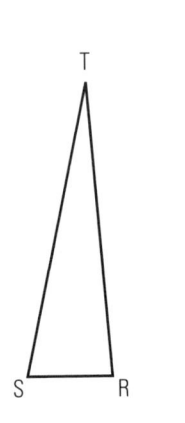

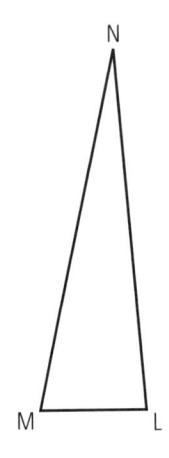

SOLUTION

Since the triangles are similar, corresponding angles must be equal.

∠R = ∠L
∠R = 85°

∠S = ∠M
∠S = 78°

∠T = ∠N
∠T = 17°

Could you have answered this question without being given ∠N? Explain your reasoning.

BUILD YOUR SKILLS

4. If two polygons ABCDEF and GHIJKL are similar, and the following angle measures are given, state the corresponding angles and their measures.

    ∠J = 73°

    ∠B = 21°

    ∠K = 40°

5. If △ABC is similar to △XYZ and the following angle measures are known, what are the values of the remaining angles?

    ∠A = 32°

    ∠C = 48°

    ∠Y = 100°

6. If trapezoid PQRS is similar to trapezoid LMNO, what are the values of *w*, *x*, *y*, and *z*?

Example 3

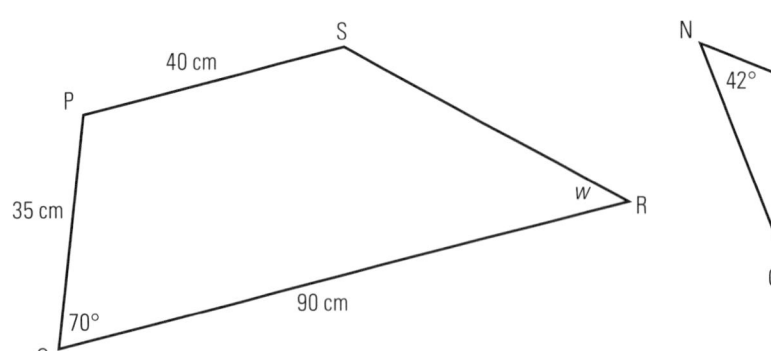

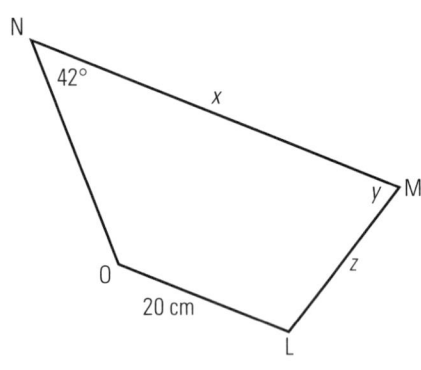

A true model must be mathematically similar in shape to the original.

Jason wants to build a model of his house. He will build the model using a scale where 5 cm represents 2 m. If one room is 6.5 m long, 4.8 m wide, and 2.8 m tall, what will its dimensions be in the model?

SOLUTION

Similarity can be applied to three-dimensional objects.

The ratio of the model to the actual room is 5 cm:2 m. Write this ratio without units as the fraction $\frac{5}{2}$.

Represent length, width, and height with ℓ, *w*, and *h*, respectively, and set up proportions to calculate their measures.

$$\frac{5}{2} = \frac{\ell}{6.5}$$

$$\frac{5}{2} = \frac{w}{4.8}$$

$$\frac{5}{2} = \frac{h}{2.8}$$

Solve for ℓ.

$$\frac{5}{2} = \frac{\ell}{6.5} \qquad \text{Substitute the known values.}$$

$$\cancel{2} \times 6.5 \times \frac{5}{\cancel{2}} = \frac{\ell}{\cancel{6.5}} \times \cancel{6.5} \times 2 \qquad \text{Multiply by the two denominators.}$$

$$6.5 \times 5 = 2\ell$$

$$32.5 = 2\ell \qquad \text{Divide to isolate } \ell.$$

$$\frac{32.5}{2} = \ell$$

$$16.25 = \ell$$

The length of the room in the model will be 16.25 cm.

Use the same method to solve for w and h.

$$\frac{5}{2} = \frac{w}{4.8}$$

$$12 = w$$

$$\frac{5}{2} = \frac{h}{2.8}$$

$$7 = h$$

The width in the model is 12 cm and the height is 7 cm.

BUILD YOUR SKILLS

7. Redo Example 3 by first determining a unit scale (the number of centimetres that represent 1 metre), then calculating length, width, and height for the model.

8. If a house is 40 feet long, 35 feet wide, and the top of the roof is 27 feet above ground level, what will the corresponding dimensions be of a model built so that 1 foot is represented by $\frac{1}{2}$ inch?

9. Theresa folds origami paper to make stacked boxes. The outer box is 12 cm by 8 cm by 4 cm. Theresa would like to make three smaller, similar boxes, each scaled down by $\frac{1}{4}$ of the previous box. What are the dimensions of the three smaller boxes?

PRACTISE YOUR NEW SKILLS

1. The scale of a model airplane to the actual airplane is 2:45. If the model is 38 centimetres long, how long is the actual airplane?

$$\frac{2 \cdot 45}{38} = 2.36$$

2. Two triangles are similar. One has sides of 8 m, 5 m, and 6 m. If the longest side of the second triangle is 5 m, what are the lengths of the other two sides?

3. A pentagon has interior angles of 108°, 204°, 63°, 120°, and 45°. Rudy wants to draw a similar pentagon with sides twice as long as the original. What size will the angles be?

4. Michaela has a microscope that enlarges images between 40 and 1600 times. How large will an object that is 1.2 mm by 0.5 mm appear to be at each of these extremes?

5. Marie-Claude has a series of four nested funnels in her kitchen that are similar to the one shown in the diagram. If the other three funnels have top diameters of 10 cm, 8 cm, and 6 cm, find the measures of the remaining parts for all three funnels.

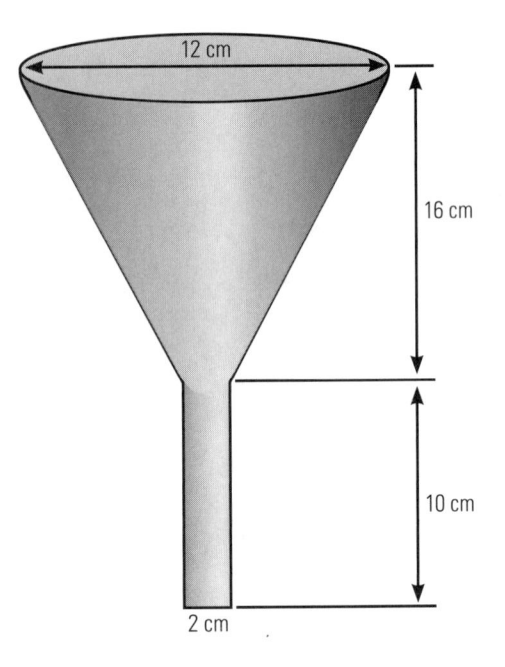

Determining if Two Polygons Are Similar   6.2

NEW SKILLS: WORKING WITH SIMILAR POLYGONS

In the last section, you considered two or more figures that were similar and found their corresponding sides and angles. How do you determine if two figures are similar, and what changes can you make to a given shape and keep it similar to the original?

> Figures are similar if corresponding angles are equal and corresponding sides are proportional.

Example 1

Are the two pentagons shown below similar? If so, explain how you know. If not, explain what you would need to know. (Angles marked with the same symbol are equal.)

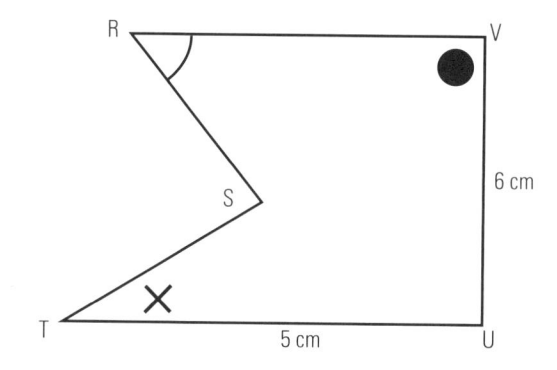

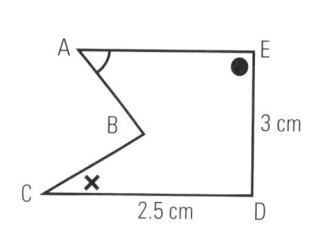

SOLUTION

You know that three angles of one pentagon are equal to the three corresponding angles of the second pentagon.

$\angle R = \angle A$

$\angle T = \angle C$

$\angle V = \angle E$

However, you cannot determine if the other two pairs of corresponding angles ($\angle S$ and $\angle B$, $\angle U$ and $\angle D$) are equal. Therefore, you cannot state for certain that the two pentagons are similar.

For more information, see page 239 of *MathWorks 10*.

BUILD YOUR SKILLS

1. Pierre drew two regular hexagons (6-sided figures with all sides equal in length). Are the two hexagons similar? Why or why not?

2. Frank enlarges a photo to poster size. The original photo is 4 inches by 6 inches. If Frank enlarges it to 1 m by 1.5 m, will it be similar in shape to the original?

3. Zora says that the two rectangles below are not similar because $\frac{60}{50}$ does not equal $\frac{100}{30}$. Is Zora right? Explain.

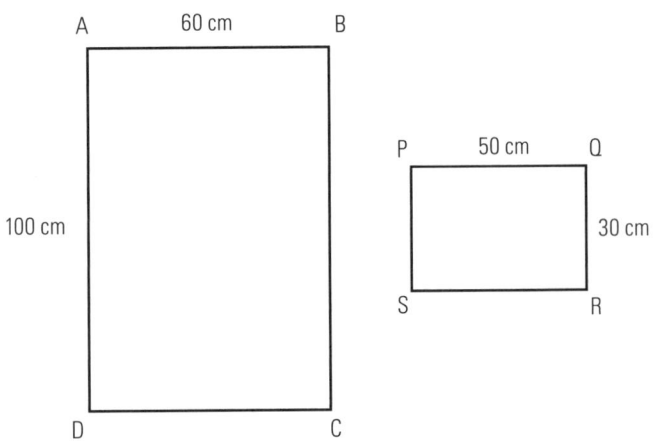

Example 2

Determine if the two given parallelograms, ABCD and WXYZ, are similar.

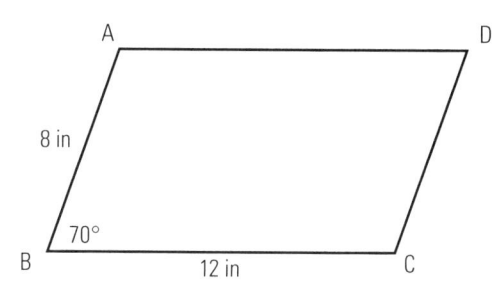

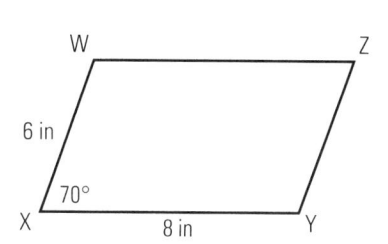

SOLUTION

In a parallelogram, opposite angles are always equal in measure.

$\angle A = \angle C$

$\angle B = \angle D = 70°$

$\angle X = \angle Z$

$\angle X = \angle Z = 70°$

Also, interior angles in a parallelogram always add up to 360°. Because the 70° angles in the two parallelograms correspond, the other angles must also correspond.

$\angle A = \angle C = \angle W = \angle Y$

Therefore, all corresponding angles are equal.

For the parallelograms to be similar, the sides would have to be proportional and the following would have to be true.

$$\frac{AB}{BC} = \frac{WX}{XY}$$

Calculate to determine if this is true.

$$\frac{AB}{BC} = \frac{8}{12}$$

$$\frac{AB}{BC} = \frac{8 \div 4}{12 \div 4}$$

$$\frac{AB}{BC} = \frac{2}{3}$$

$$\frac{WX}{XY} = \frac{6}{8}$$

$$\frac{WX}{XY} = \frac{6 \div 2}{8 \div 2}$$

$$\frac{WX}{XY} = \frac{3}{4}$$

$$\frac{2}{3} \neq \frac{3}{4}$$

The sides are not proportional, so the parallelograms are not similar.

BUILD YOUR SKILLS

4. Janelle stated that increasing or decreasing the sides of a given figure by the same factor will always produce a figure similar to the original. Is this true? Give one example that illustrates your answer.

5. Aidan frames a 24-inch by 36-inch picture with a 4-inch frame. Is the framed picture similar in shape to the unframed picture? Show your calculations.

6. One cylinder has a radius of 25 cm and a height of 35 cm. Another cylinder has a radius of 30 cm and a height of 40 cm. Are the cylinders similar? Show your calculations.

PRACTISE YOUR NEW SKILLS

1. The scale on a map is 2.5 cm:500 m.

   a) What distance is represented by a 12.5-cm segment on the map?

   b) How long would a segment on the map be if it represented 1.5 km?

2. Show whether a rectangular prism that is 6 m by 10 m by 8 m is similar to one that is 4 m by 7 m by 5 m.

3. Colin states that the following two figures are similar, but Tai disagrees, saying that they don't have enough information. Who is right? Show your calculations.

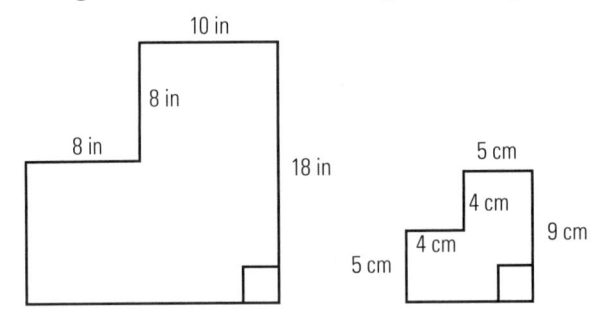

4. While he was at the pet food store, Jeremy saw three different sized dog mats. They measured 36 inches by 28 inches, 27 inches by 21 inches, and 24 inches by 18 inches. Are all the mats similar? Show your calculations.

5. Using two similar rectangles, show whether their areas are in the same proportion as the sides.

Drawing Similar Polygons 6.3

NEW SKILLS: WORKING WITH SCALE DIAGRAMS

Artists, architects, and planners use scale diagrams or models in their work. The diagrams or models should be in proportion to the actual objects so that others can visualize what the real objects look like.

In this section, you will practise drawing scale diagrams.

Example 1

Use graph paper to construct a figure similar to the one given, with sides that are $1\frac{1}{2}$ times the length of the original. Explain how you know that the corresponding angles are equal.

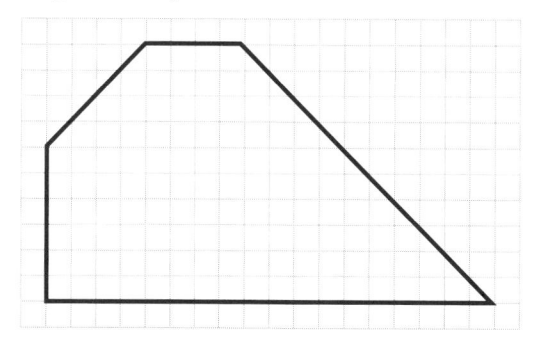

SOLUTION

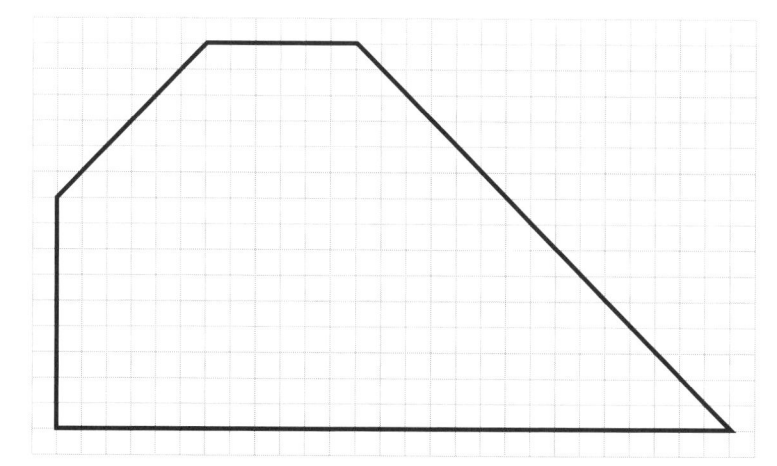

The sizes of the angles will not change by increasing the lengths of the sides, so the corresponding angles must be equal.

For more information, see pages 248–250 of *MathWorks 10*.

BUILD YOUR SKILLS

1. Draw and label the lengths of the sides of a rectangle that has a length of 8 cm and is similar to a rectangle that has a width of 10 cm and a length of 20 cm.

2. Maurice has drawn the plan below for his backyard. However, he finds that the diagram is too small to fit in all the details. Redraw the diagram at 2.5 times the size of the original.

3. Barnie's house is 55 ft wide and 40 ft deep. A drawing of his property shows the house is 10 in wide and 7.3 in deep. What scale was used on the drawing?

Example 2

Xavier is building a staircase using scale drawings. On the drawing, the height of one stair is 0.5 cm and the depth is 0.9 cm. Xavier will use a scale factor of 40 to build the stairs. Calculate the height and depth of the stairs he will build.

SOLUTION

A scale factor of 40 means that the actual measure is 40 times the measure on the drawing. This can be written as a ratio of 1:40 or $\frac{1}{40}$.

To calculate the height of one stair, set up a proportion.

$$\frac{0.5}{x} = \frac{1}{40}$$

$$40 \times \cancel{x} \times \frac{0.5}{\cancel{x}} = \frac{1}{\cancel{40}} \times x \times \cancel{40}$$

$$40 \times 0.5 = x$$

$$20 = x$$

The height of the stair will be 20 cm.

Use the same method to calculate the depth of the stair.

$$\frac{0.9}{x} = \frac{1}{40}$$

$$40 \times \cancel{x} \times \frac{0.9}{\cancel{x}} = \frac{1}{\cancel{40}} \times x \times \cancel{40}$$

$$40 \times 0.9 = x$$

$$36 = x$$

The depth of the stair will be 36 cm.

BUILD YOUR SKILLS

4. Simrin has built two end tables. The second table is a slightly larger version of the first. Given the dimensions below, calculate what scale factor Simrin used to make the larger table.

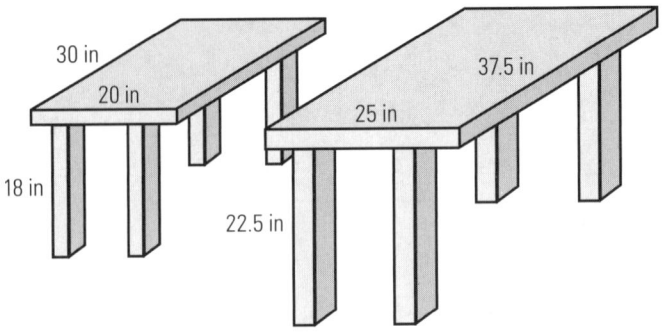

   Dimensions of first table: 30 in, 20 in, 18 in
   Dimensions of second table: 37.5 in, 25 in, 22.5 in

5. A craft store uses small gift boxes to wrap purchases. They have one box that is 20 cm by 12 cm by 5 cm. Another box is larger by a scale factor of 1.3. What are the dimensions of the larger box?

6. Hazuki made a kite with the dimensions shown below. She decided it would work better if it were bigger. If her new kite tail has a length of 49 cm, what scale factor did she use, and what are the kite's other dimensions?

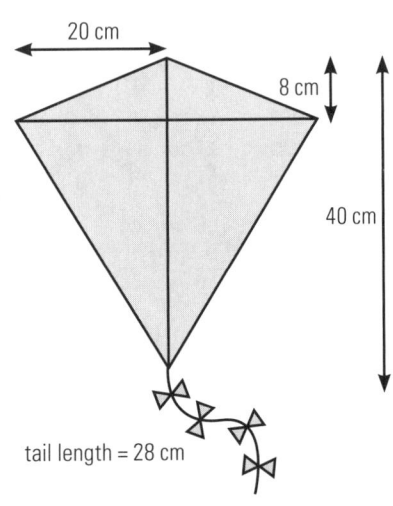

   Kite dimensions: 20 cm, 8 cm, 40 cm
   tail length = 28 cm

PRACTISE YOUR NEW SKILLS

1. The scale ratio (model:original) between two diagrams is 3:5. If one measure on the model is 45 mm, what was the measure on the original?

2. Draw a square with sides of 2 cm, and a second square with sides that are 3 cm.

   a) Is the second square similar to the first? Explain your reasoning.

   b) If you draw a rectangle whose sides are 5 cm and 8 cm, and a second rectangle with sides that are 3 cm longer, will the two be similar? Explain your reasoning.

3. Draw a rectangular prism similar to the one shown below with sides that are $\frac{1}{2}$ the length of the original.

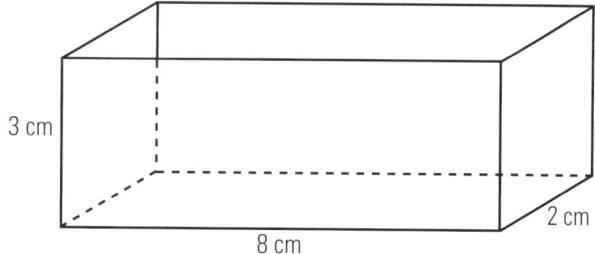

4. A poster shows a photograph of a cruise ship. The actual ship is 310 metres long. In the photograph, the cruise ship is 1.2 m long.

   a) What is the scale factor (to 4 decimal places)?

   b) A person 1.8 m tall was standing on the deck of the cruise ship when the photo was taken. How tall is the person on the photo (to the nearest tenth of a centimetre)?

5. A sporting goods store has miniature versions of tents on display. A six-person tent is 12′ long by 10′ wide. The miniature version has a length of $1\frac{1}{2}'$.

   a) What is the width of the miniature version?

   b) What is the scale ratio (miniature:actual)?

Similar Triangles 6.4

NEW SKILLS: WORKING WITH SIMILAR TRIANGLES

Similar triangles are very useful in making calculations and determining measurements.

The sum of the angles of a triangle is always 180°. If two corresponding angles in two triangles are equal, the third angles will also be equal.

Two triangles are similar if any two of the three corresponding angles are congruent, or one pair of corresponding angles is congruent and the corresponding sides adjacent to the angles are proportional.

Two right triangles are similar if one pair of corresponding acute angles is congruent.

Example 1

Given the two triangles below, find the length of n.

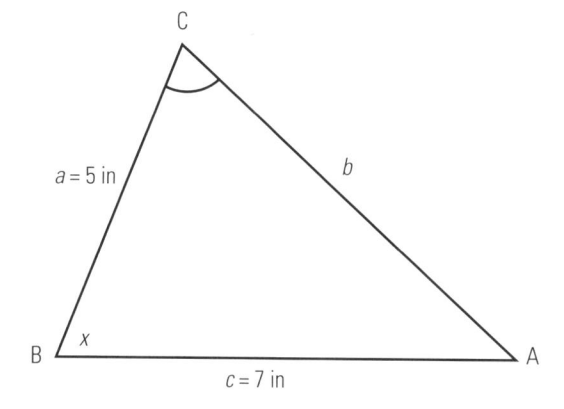

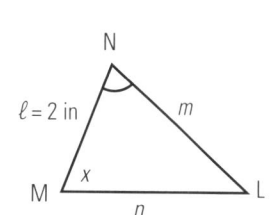

SOLUTION

You know that two of the three corresponding angles are congruent.

$\angle C = \angle N$

$\angle B = \angle M$

This means that $\triangle ABC$ is similar to $\triangle LMN$.

To solve for *n*, set up a proportion.

$$\frac{n}{c} = \frac{\ell}{a}$$

$$\frac{n}{7} = \frac{2}{5}$$

$$5 \times 7 \times \frac{n}{7} = \frac{2}{5} \times 7 \times 5$$

$$5n = 7 \times 2$$

$$5n = 14$$

$$n = \frac{14}{5}$$

$$n = 2.8$$

Side *n* is 2.8 in long.

For more information, see pages 257–258 of *MathWorks 10*.

BUILD YOUR SKILLS

1. In each of the diagrams below, $\triangle ABC$ is similar to $\triangle XYZ$. Find the length of the indicated side (to one decimal place).

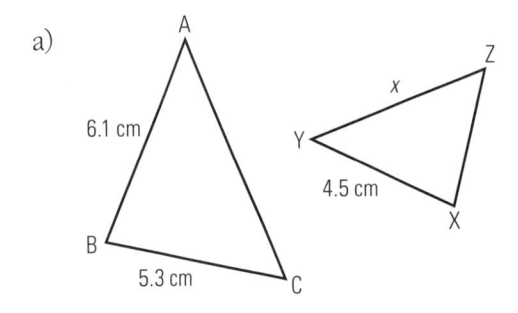

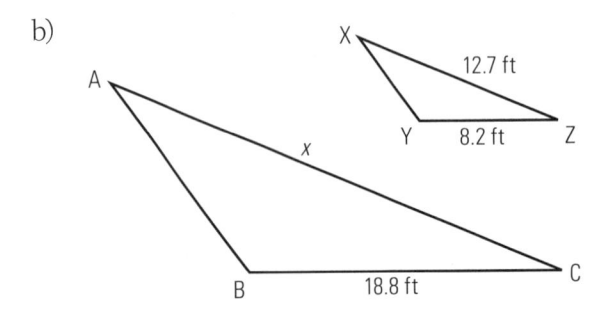

a)

- Triangle ABC: AB = 6.1 cm, BC = 5.3 cm
- Triangle XYZ: YZ = x, YX = 4.5 cm

b)

- Triangle XYZ: XZ = 12.7 ft, YZ = 8.2 ft
- Triangle ABC: AC = x, BC = 18.8 ft

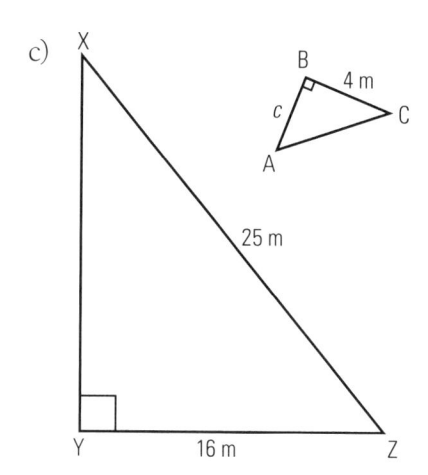

c)

2. Given that △ABC in similar to △RST, AB is 6 cm long, BC is 5 cm long, and RS is 8 cm long, find the length of a second side in △RST. Can you find the length of the third side? Explin your answer.

3. Carmen thinks that any two isosceles triangles will be similar. Use examples to prove or disprove her belief.

An isosceles triangle has two sides equal in length, and two angles of equal measure.

Example 2

Ravi notices that a 2-m pole casts a shadow of 5 m, and a second pole casts a shadow of 9.4 m. How tall is the second pole?

SOLUTION

Sketch the situation.

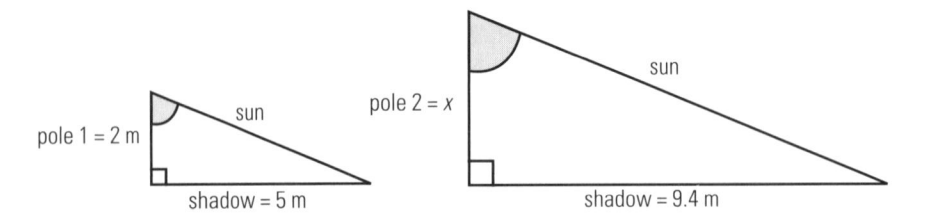

The angle between the rays of the sun and the pole is the same in both cases, so the two triangles are similar.

Set up a proportion to solve for the height of the second pole.

$$\frac{\text{height of pole 1}}{\text{shadow 1}} = \frac{\text{height of pole 2}}{\text{shadow 2}}$$

$$\frac{2}{5} = \frac{x}{9.4}$$

$$\cancel{5} \times 9.4 \times \frac{2}{\cancel{5}} = \frac{x}{\cancel{9.4}} \times \cancel{9.4} \times 5$$

$$9.4 \times 2 = 5x$$

$$18.8 = 5x$$

$$3.8 \approx x$$

The second pole is approximately 3.8 m tall.

BUILD YOUR SKILLS

4. Assuming that the slope of a hill is constant, and that a point 100 metres along the surface of the hill is 4.2 metres higher than the starting point, how high will you be if you walk 250 metres along the slope of the hill?

5. Maryam is sewing a patchwork quilt. The sketch she has drawn is to a scale of 1:8. Part of the design consists of right triangles that have legs that are 2.2 cm and 4.6 cm long. What will the lengths of the legs of the triangles in the finished quilt be?

6. Which of the following triangles are similar?

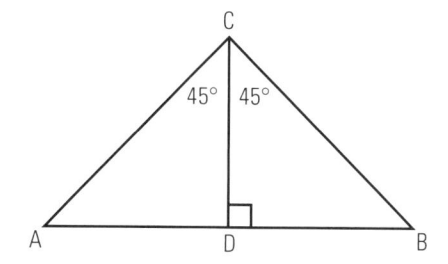

PRACTISE YOUR NEW SKILLS

1. In the following diagram, AB is parallel to ED, AB is 8 m, AC is 12 m, and CE is 7 m. Calculate ED to one decimal place.

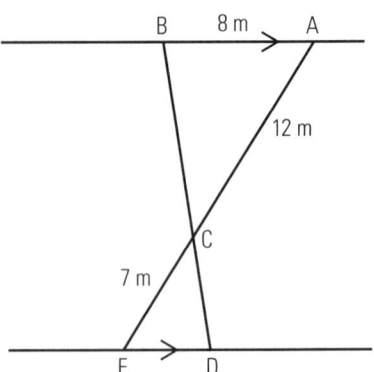

2. Madge has cut out two triangular shapes from a block of wood, as shown below. She says that the two shapes are similar. Is she correct? Show your calculations.

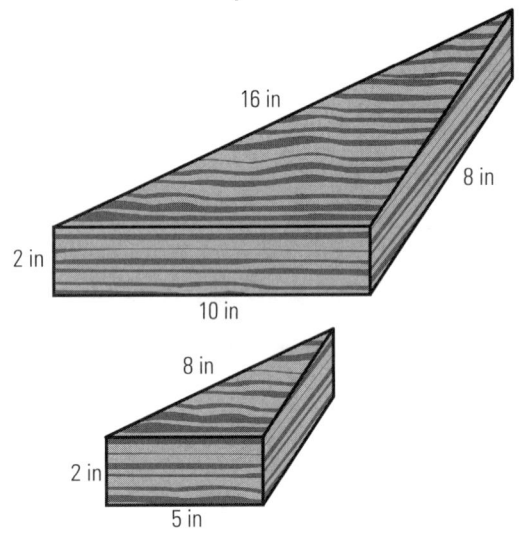

3. Given that $\triangle FGH \sim \triangle XYZ$, state which angles are equal and which sides are proportional.

4. Julian is visiting the Manitoba Legislative Building in Winnipeg, where he sees the statue of Louis Riel. Use the information in the diagram to find the height of the statue. Round your answer to a whole number.

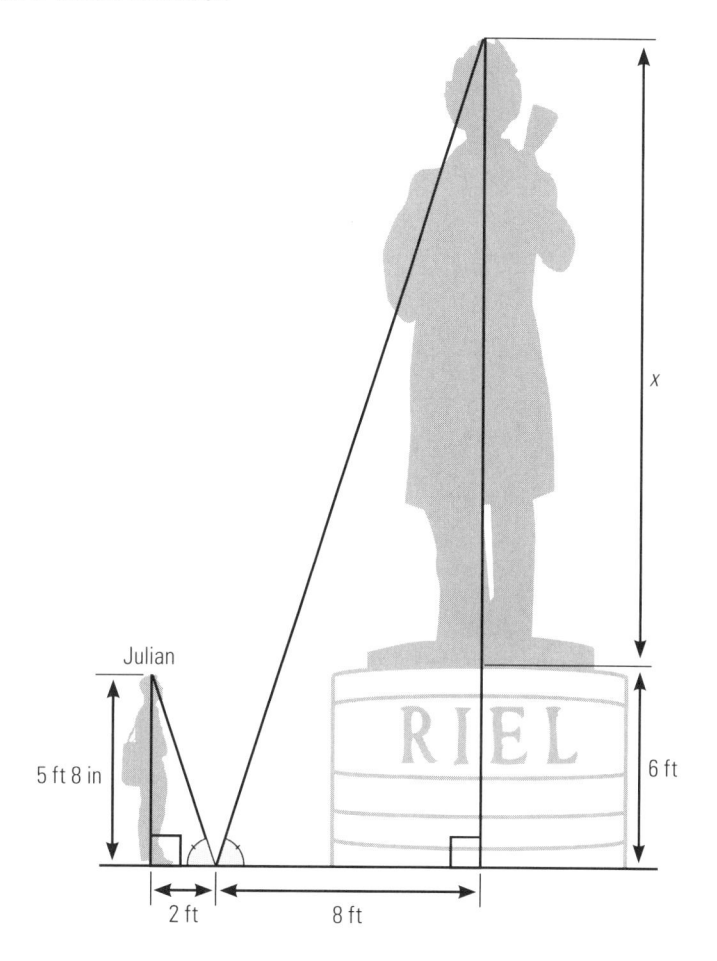

CHAPTER TEST

1. The lengths of the sides of a pentagon are 2″, 6″, 10″, 14″, and 24″. Calculate the lengths of the sides of a similar pentagon if the shortest side is 5″.

2. Given that the two figures shown are similar, determine the values of x and y.

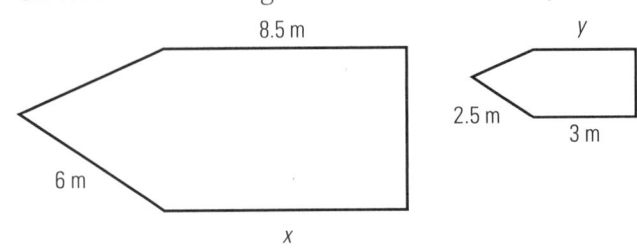

3. To determine the distance across a river (distance AB), Lila took the following measurements. Assuming the two triangles in the diagram are similar, how wide is the river?

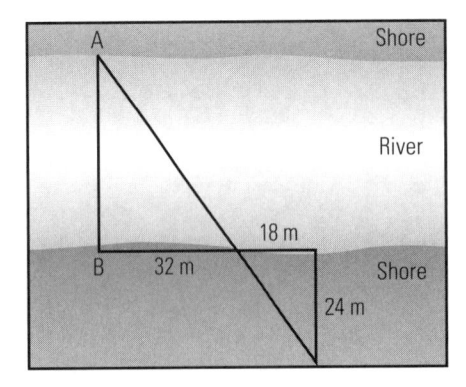

4. If a man casts a shadow that is 3.8 m long at the same time that an 8-m flagpole casts a shadow that is 15 m long, how tall is the man?

5. How does doubling the lengths of the sides of a rectangle to form a similar rectangle affect the area?

6. Amin cut out two blocks of wood as indicated. Are the two blocks similar in shape? Round your final calculations to two decimal places.

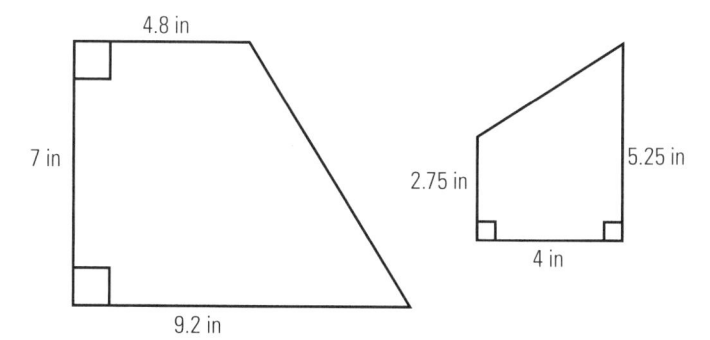

7. Determine if the following statements are true or false and explain your reasoning.

   a) All equilateral triangles are similar.

   b) All isosceles triangles are similar.

   c) Any pair of congruent triangles is similar.

8. A science teacher uses an overhead projector to display a diagram of a pulley system. The actual diagram is 6″ by 7.2″. The image projected onto the wall is 4′2″ by 5′. What is the scale factor of the projection?

9. Young-Mee draws a sketch of her new office space to envision different furniture and equipment placements. On her drawing, the main area is 6″ wide. What are the other dimensions of the drawing, given the measurements of the actual space shown in the diagram?

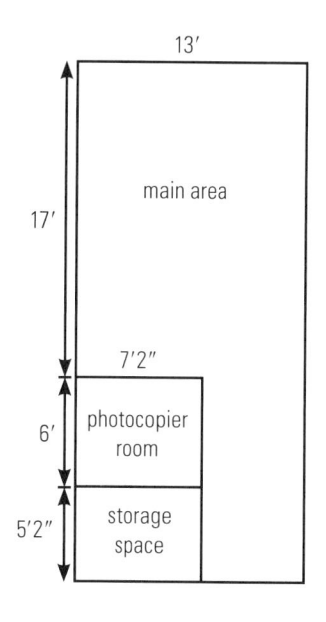

10. François is commissioned to paint a portrait based on a photograph. The photograph is 5″ by 7″, and the painting must be enlarged by a factor of 6.25. What are the dimensions of the painting?

11. Joanne knitted a blanket that measures 174 cm by 230 cm. Her sister asked Joanne to make a matching one for her son. If Joanne wants to make a similar blanket using a scale factor of 0.55, what will its dimensions be?

Chapter 7

Trigonometry of Right Triangles

This man is installing an angle brace. By incorporating right triangles, angle braces provide support and strength to bookshelves, building roofs, and beyond.

7.1 The Pythagorean Theorem

REVIEW: WORKING WITH TRIANGLES

Each vertex of a triangle is labelled with an upper case letter, and each side is labelled either with the lower case letter corresponding to the opposite vertex or with the upper case letters of the vertices it connects.

Example 1

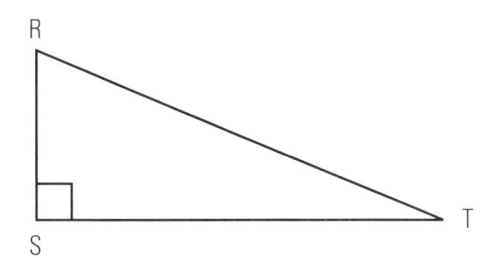

Consider △RST.

a) Label the sides with the appropriate lower case letter.

b) Name the sides using the upper case letters of the vertices they connect.

SOLUTION

a) Each side is labelled with the lower case letter corresponding to the opposite vertex.

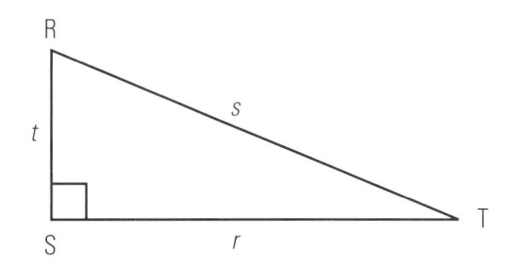

b) The sides can also be named according to the upper case letters of the vertices they connect.

Side r can be called side ST.

Side s can be called side TR.

Side t can be called side RS.

BUILD YOUR SKILLS

1. Label each side of the triangles below using a single lower case letter corresponding to the opposite vertex.

   a) 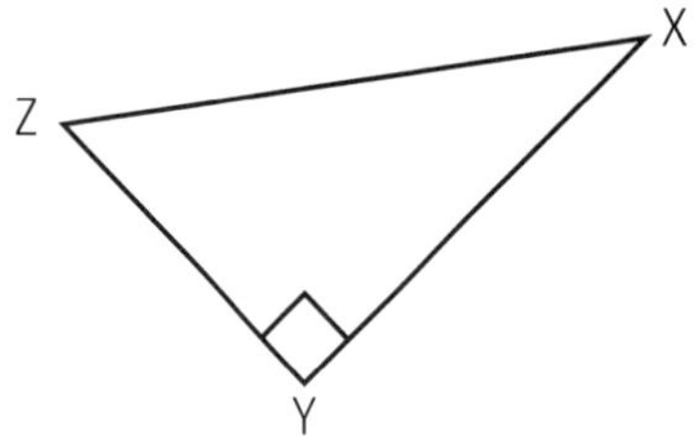 [Triangle with vertices Z, X, Y (right angle at Y)]

   b) 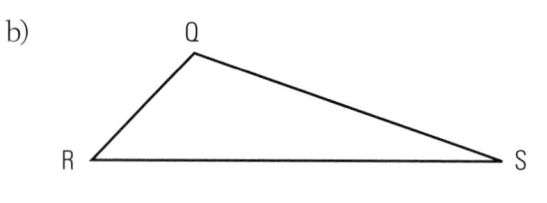 [Triangle with vertices Q, R, S]

   c) 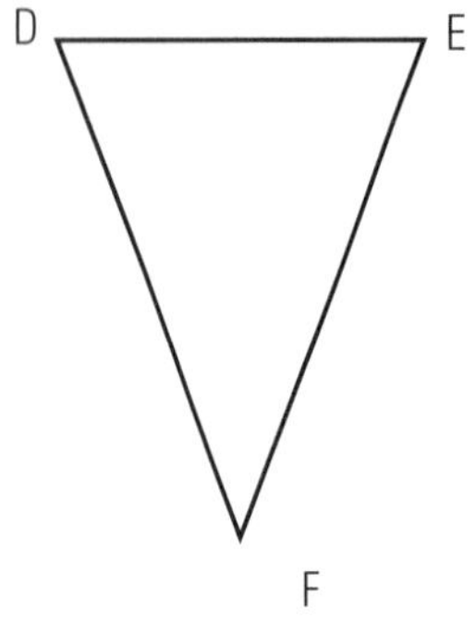 [Triangle with vertices D, E, F]

   d) [Triangle with vertices S, T, R]

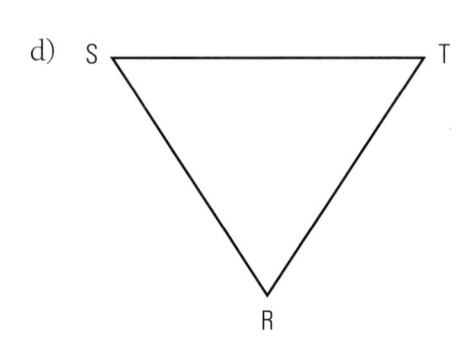

2. Label each vertex of the triangles below using a single upper case letter corresponding to the opposite side.

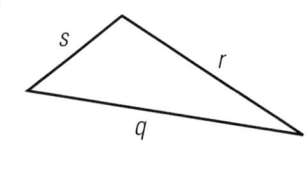

   a) 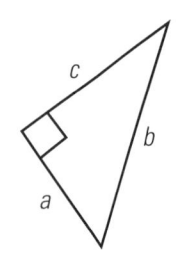 [Triangle with sides a, b, c]

   b) [Triangle with sides q, r, s]

   c) [Triangle with sides w, x, y]

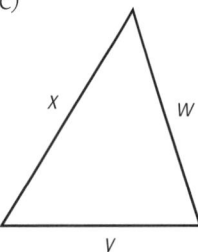

   d) 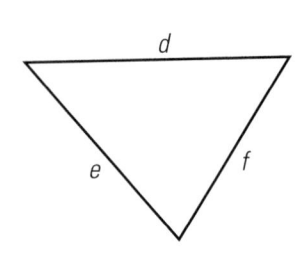 [Triangle with sides d, e, f]

NEW SKILLS: WORKING WITH THE PYTHAGOREAN THEOREM

A right triangle is a triangle with one right angle. The side opposite the right angle is the longest side and is called the **hypotenuse**. The other two sides are called legs (or, in some cases, arms).

The **Pythagorean theorem** states the relationship among the sides of a right triangle. Given a right triangle ABC with right angle C, the Pythagorean theorem states the following.

$a^2 + b^2 = c^2$

For more details, see page 272 of *MathWorks 10*.

hypotenuse: the longest side of a right triangle, opposite the 90° angle

Pythagorean theorem: in a right triangle, the sum of the squares of the lengths of the legs is equal to the square of the length of the hypotenuse

Example 2

Label the sides of the triangles and state the Pythagorean theorem as it applies to them.

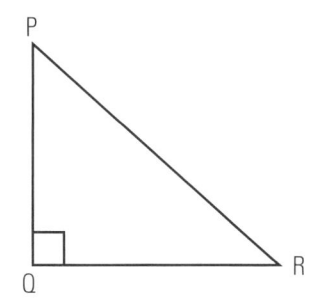

SOLUTION

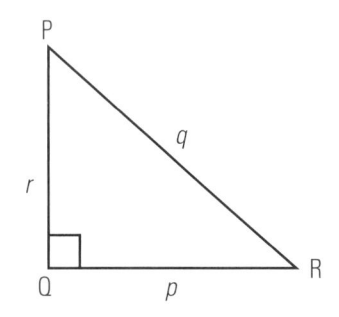

Since q is the hypotenuse, the Pythagorean theorem is written as follows.

$p^2 + r^2 = q^2$

BUILD YOUR SKILLS

3. Given the following diagram, use the lettering provided to state three Pythagorean relations that apply.

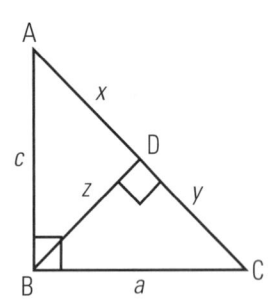

4. A ladder, ℓ, is placed against the side of a house, h. The foot of the ladder is a distance d from the base of the house. Draw a diagram and express the relationship that exists between ℓ, h, and d.

5. Rearrange the Pythagorean theorem to solve first for x and then for y.

$x^2 + y^2 = z^2$

Example 3

Use the Pythagorean theorem to find the lengths of the missing sides of the triangles to the nearest tenth of a unit.

a)

b)

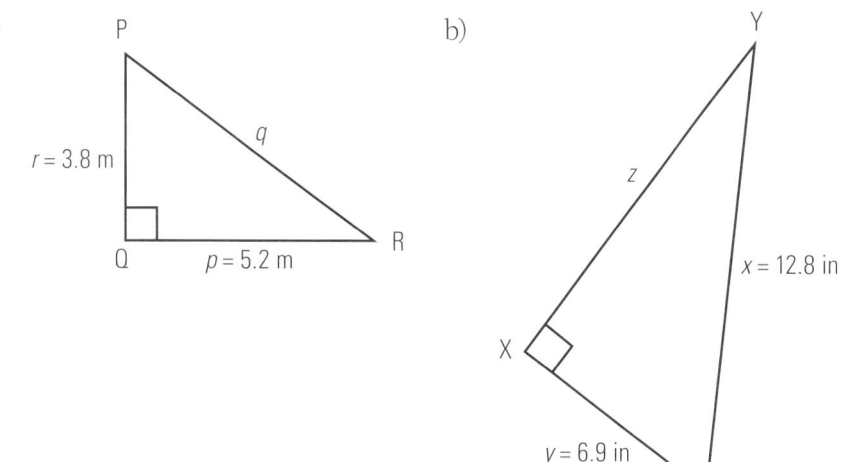

SOLUTION

a) Write the Pythagorean theorem using the labels on the given triangle.

$$p^2 + r^2 = q^2$$
$$5.2^2 + 3.8^2 = q^2 \quad \text{Substitute the known values.}$$
$$27.04 + 14.44 = q^2$$
$$41.48 = q^2$$
$$\sqrt{41.48} = q \quad \text{Take the square root of both sides.}$$
$$6.44 \approx q$$

Side q is approximately 6.4 m.

b) Write the Pythagorean theorem using the labels on the given triangle.

$$y^2 + z^2 = x^2$$
$$6.9^2 + z^2 = 12.8^2 \quad \text{Substitute the known values.}$$
$$47.61 + z^2 = 163.84$$
$$z^2 = 163.84 - 47.61 \quad \text{Subtract 47.61 from both sides to isolate } z.$$
$$z^2 = 116.23$$
$$z = \sqrt{116.23} \quad \text{Take the square root of both sides.}$$
$$z \approx 10.78$$

Side z is approximately 10.8 inches.

BUILD YOUR SKILLS

6. Calculate the values of x and y.

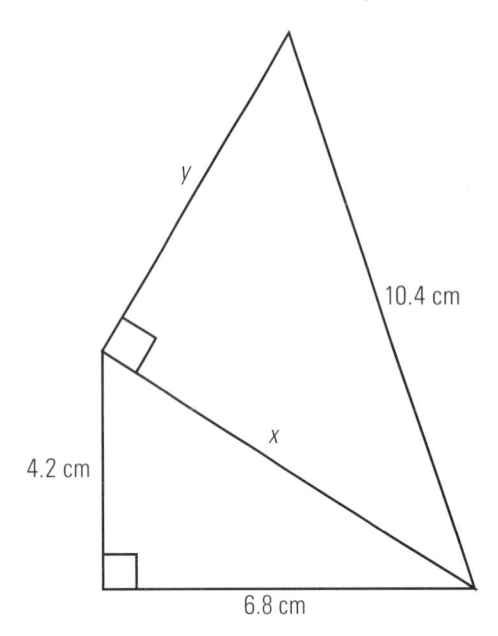

7. A 40-foot ladder reaches 38 feet up the side of a house. How far from the base of the house is the foot of the ladder?

8. A field is 120 m by 180 m. How much shorter is your route if you walk diagonally across the field rather than walking around the edge to the opposite corner?

PRACTISE YOUR NEW SKILLS

1. A stairway rises 6 feet 4 inches over a horizontal distance of 8 feet 6 inches. What is the diagonal length of the stairway?

2. A 28-metre long guy wire is attached to a point 24 m up the side of a tower. How far from the base of the tower is the guy wire attached?

3. The construction plans for a ramp show that it rises 3.5 metres over a horizontal distance of 10.5 metres. How long will the ramp surface be?

4. The advertised size of a TV screen is the distance between opposite corners. Sally bought a 52-inch TV. If the height of the TV is 32 inches, how wide is it?

5. A boat sailed due north at a rate of 12 km/h for 3 hours, then due east at a rate of 18 km/h for 2 hours. How far was it from its starting point, measuring the shortest distance?

The Sine Ratio 7.2

NEW SKILLS: WORKING WITH THE SINE RATIO TO SOLVE TRIANGLES

In chapter 6, you worked with similar triangles to discover that, in triangles with congruent angles, the ratio between the corresponding sides of the similar triangles is the same.

The following diagram shows similar triangles. $\triangle ABC \sim \triangle XYZ$.

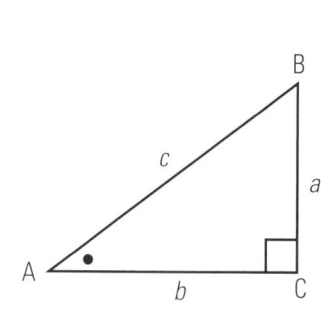

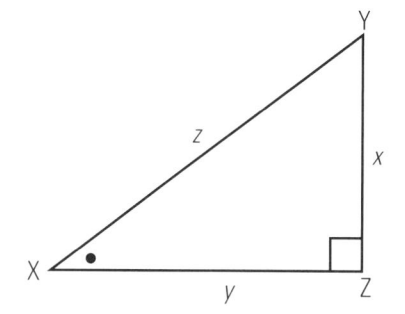

> Angles marked with the same symbol are equal.

The ratios between corresponding sides are equal, so we know that the following is true.

$$\frac{a}{x} = \frac{c}{z}$$

This proportion can be rearranged so that each side of the equation represents a ratio of sides from the same triangle.

$\cancel{x} \times z \times \dfrac{a}{\cancel{x}} = \dfrac{c}{\cancel{z}} \times \cancel{z} \times x$ Multiply both sides by the product of the denominators and simplify.

$za = cx$

$\dfrac{\cancel{z}a}{c\cancel{z}} = \dfrac{\cancel{c}x}{\cancel{c}z}$ Divide both sides by the same number and simplify.

$\dfrac{a}{c} = \dfrac{x}{z}$

When triangles are similar, the ratio of the length of the side opposite a given angle to the length of the hypotenuse is always the same. This ratio is referred to as the **sine ratio**.

Given any right triangle with acute angle A, the sine ratio can be written as follows.

$$\text{sine } \angle A = \frac{\text{length of side opposite } \angle A}{\text{length of hypotenuse}}$$

The ratio is abbreviated as follows.

$$\sin A = \frac{\text{opp}}{\text{hyp}}$$

For more details, see page 283 of *MathWorks 10*.

> **sine ratio:** in a right triangle, the ratio of the length of the side opposite a given angle to the length of the hypotenuse (abbreviated as sin)

> Use your scientific calculator to calculate the values of the sines of angles.

Example 1

Use your calculator to determine the following sine ratios. Round to four decimal places.

a) sin 15°

b) sin 30°

c) sin 60°

d) sin 80°

What do you notice about these values?

SOLUTION

a) sin 15° = 0.2588

b) sin 30° = 0.5000

c) sin 60° = 0.8660

d) sin 80° = 0.9848

The sine ratio determines that if you have a right triangle with an acute angle given, regardless of the size of the triangle, the ratio of the side opposite that angle to the hypotenuse will always be the same.

The value of the sine ratio increases as the angle gets bigger.

BUILD YOUR SKILLS

1. Calculate the value of sin A to two decimal places.

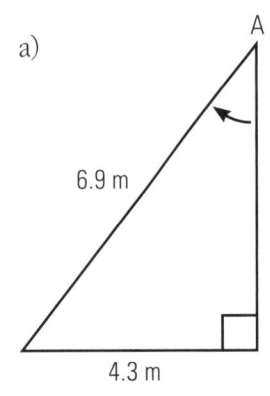

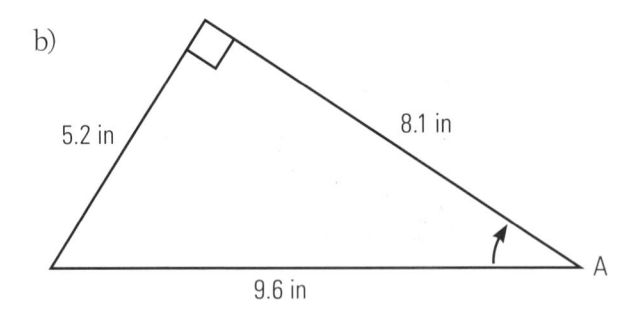

   a) [triangle with hypotenuse 6.9 m, base 4.3 m, angle A at top]

   b) [right triangle with sides 5.2 in, 8.1 in, and 9.6 in, angle A at right]

2. Use your calculator to determine the value of each of the following sine ratios to four decimal places.

   a) sin 10°

   b) sin 48°

   c) sin 62°

   d) sin 77°

3. Use your calculator to determine the value of sin 90°. Suggest a reason why this is so.

Example 2

The sine ratio can be used to help you find missing parts of a right triangle.

A ladder 8.5 metres long makes an angle of 72° with the ground. How far up the side of a building will it reach?

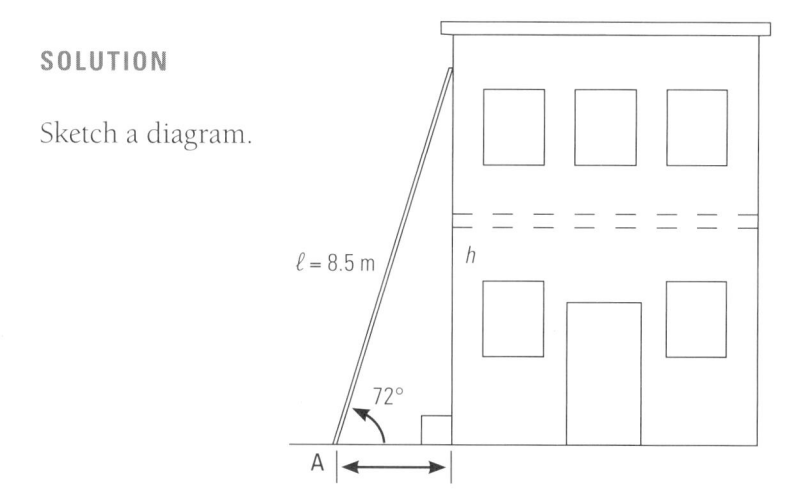

SOLUTION

Sketch a diagram.

The height, h, is opposite the 72° angle, and the ladder, ℓ, forms the hypotenuse of the triangle. A right triangle is formed, with h as the side opposite the 72° angle, and ℓ as the hypotenuse.

Use the sine ratio to calculate h.

$$\sin A = \frac{\text{opp}}{\text{hyp}}$$

$$\sin 72° = \frac{h}{8.5} \quad \text{Substitute the known values.}$$

$$8.5 \times \sin 72° = \frac{h}{8.5} \times 8.5 \quad \text{Multiply both sides by 8.5.}$$

$$8.5 \times \sin 72° = h$$

$$8.1 \approx h$$

The ladder reaches approximately 8.1 metres up the side of the building.

BUILD YOUR SKILLS

4. Calculate the length of the side opposite the indicated angle in the following diagrams.

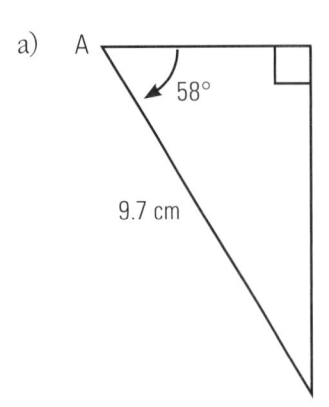

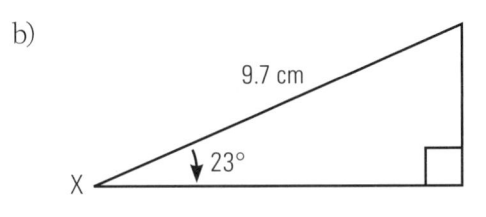

   a) [Right triangle with angle 58° at A and hypotenuse 9.7 cm]

   b) [Right triangle with angle 23° at X and hypotenuse 9.7 cm]

5. A rafter makes an angle of 28° with the horizontal. If the rafter is 15 feet long, what is the height at the rafter's peak?

6. How high is a weather balloon tied to the ground if it is attached to a 15-metre string and the angle between the string and the ground is 35°?

Example 3

Brad is building a ramp. The ramp must form an angle of 22° with the level ground and reach a point that is 1.5 metres above the ground. How long will the ramp be?

Wait until you have isolated the unknown variable before doing the calculation. This will minimize errors due to rounding.

SOLUTION

Sketch a diagram.

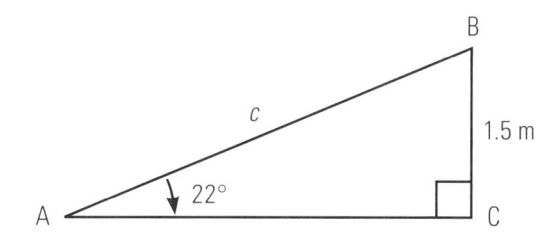

Let c represent the length of the ramp. On the diagram, 1.5 metres is opposite the 22° angle.

Use the sine ratio to solve for c.

$$\sin A = \frac{\text{opp}}{\text{hyp}}$$

$$\sin 22° = \frac{1.5}{c} \qquad \text{Substitute the known values.}$$

$$c \times \sin 22° = \frac{1.5}{c} \times c \qquad \text{Multiply both sides by } c.$$

$$c \times \sin 22° = 1.5 \qquad \text{Simplify.}$$

$$\frac{c \times \sin 22°}{\sin 22°} = \frac{1.5}{\sin 22°} \qquad \text{Divide both sides by } \sin 22° \text{ to isolate } c.$$

$$c = \frac{1.5}{\sin 22°}$$

$$c \approx 4.004$$

The ramp is approximately 4 metres long.

BUILD YOUR SKILLS

7. Find the length of the hypotenuse in the following diagrams.

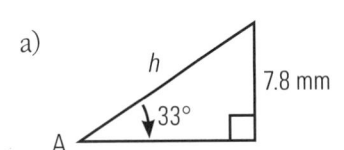

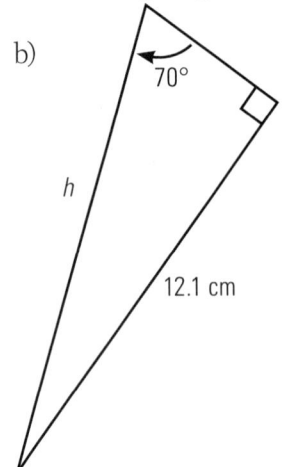

   a) [Triangle with angle 33° at A, side 7.8 mm opposite, hypotenuse h]

   b) [Triangle with angle 70°, side 12.1 cm, hypotenuse h]

8. How long is a guy wire that is attached 4.2 metres up a pole if it makes an angle of 52° with the ground?

9. A boat is carried with the current at an angle of 43° to the shore. If the river is approximately 15 metres wide, how far does the boat travel before reaching the opposite shore?

NEW SKILLS: WORKING WITH ANGLE OF ELEVATION AND DEPRESSION

When you look up at an airplane flying overhead, the angle between the horizontal and your line of sight is called an **angle of elevation.** When you look down from a cliff to a boat passing by, the angle between the horizontal and your line of sight is called an **angle of depression**.

For more details, see pages 288–289 of *MathWorks 10*.

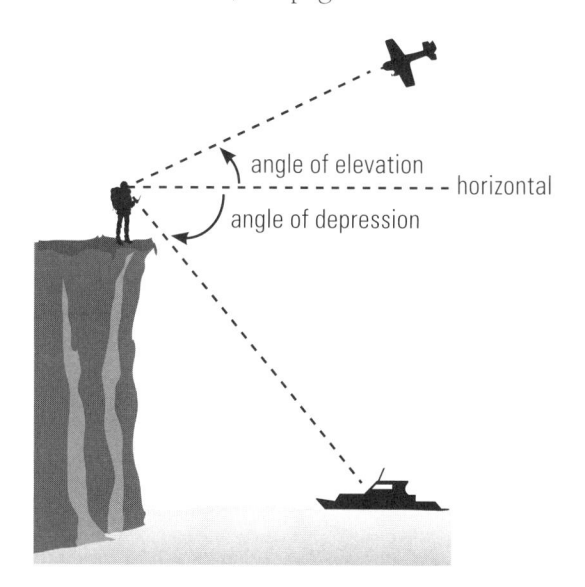

angle of elevation: the angle formed between the horizontal and the line of sight while looking upward; sometimes referred to as the angle of inclination

angle of depression: the angle formed between the horizontal and the line of sight when looking downward

Example 4

The angle of elevation of Sandra's kite string is 70°. If she has let out 55 feet of string, and is holding the string 6 feet above the ground, how high is the kite?

SOLUTION

Sketch and label a diagram.

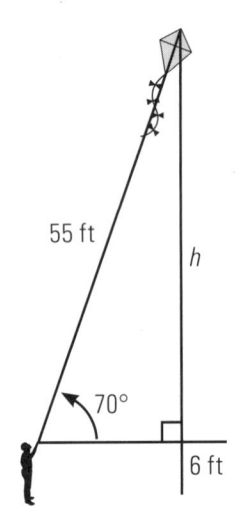

Use the sine ratio to solve for the height of the kite.

$$\sin H = \frac{opp}{hyp}$$

$$\sin 70° = \frac{h}{55} \quad \text{Substitute the known values.}$$

$$55 \times \sin 70° = \frac{h}{55} \times 55 \quad \text{Multiply both sides by 55.}$$

$$55 \times \sin 70° = h$$

$$51.7 \approx h$$

The kite is approximately 52 feet above where Sandra is holding it. Add 6 feet for the distance between the ground and the start of the string. The kite is about 58 feet above the ground.

BUILD YOUR SKILLS

10. George is in a hot air balloon that is 125 metres high. The angle of elevation from a house below, to the balloon, is 18°. How far is George from the house?

11. The angle of elevation of a road is 4.5°. What is the length of the section of road if it rises 16 metres?

12. The angle of elevation of a slide that is 3.6 metres long is 32°. How high above the ground is the top of the slide?

PRACTISE YOUR NEW SKILLS

1. Calculate the sine of the indicated angle.

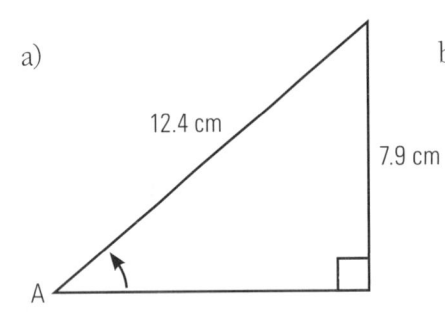

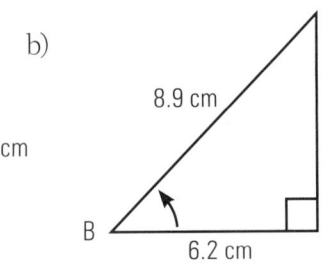

   a) [triangle with hypotenuse 12.4 cm, opposite side 7.9 cm, angle at A]

   b) [triangle with hypotenuse 8.9 cm, adjacent side 6.2 cm, angle at B]

2. Calculate the length of the indicated side.

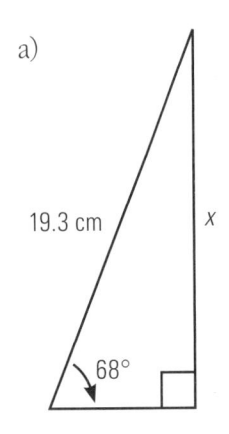

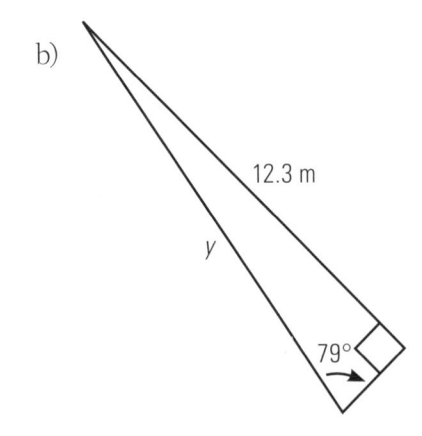

   a) [triangle with hypotenuse 19.3 cm, side x, angle 68°]

   b) [triangle with hypotenuse 12.3 m, side y, angle 79°]

3. A ramp with a length of 21.2 metres has an angle of elevation of 15°. How high up does it reach?

4. The angle of elevation from the bottom of a waterslide to the platform above is 20°. If the waterslide is 25 metres long, how high is the platform?

5. A man walks at an angle of 68° north of east for 45 metres. How far north of his starting point is he?

7.3 The Cosine Ratio

NEW SKILLS: WORKING WITH THE COSINE RATIO TO SOLVE TRIANGLES

cosine ratio: in a right triangle, the ratio of the length of the side adjacent a given angle to the length of the hypotenuse (abbreviated as cos)

Another important trigonometric ratio of right triangles is the ratio of the side adjacent to the given acute angle to the hypotenuse. This is called the **cosine ratio.**

For a given angle A, the cosine ratio can be stated as follows.

$$\text{cosine } \angle A = \frac{\text{length of side adjacent to } \angle A}{\text{length of hypotenuse}}$$

This ratio can be abbreviated as follows.

$$\cos A = \frac{\text{adj}}{\text{hyp}}$$

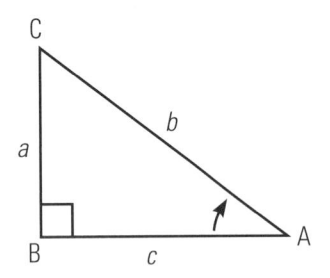

For triangle ABC, the cosine of $\angle A$ can be stated as the following.

$$\cos A = \frac{c}{b}$$

For more details, see page 293 of *MathWorks 10*.

Example 1

Given the triangles below, find the indicated side.

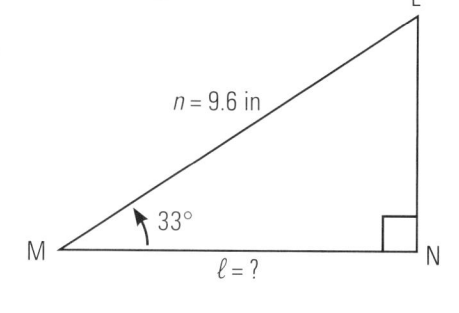

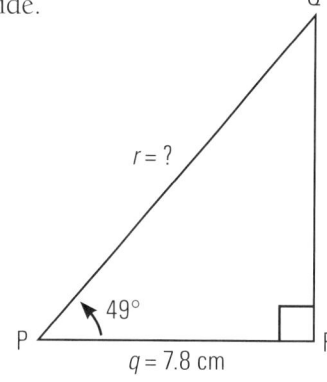

a) [Triangle LMN with n = 9.6 in, angle M = 33°, right angle at N, ℓ = ?]

b) [Triangle PQR with r = ?, angle P = 49°, right angle at R, q = 7.8 cm]

SOLUTION

a) Use the cosine ratio to solve for ℓ.

$$\cos M = \frac{\text{adj}}{\text{hyp}}$$

$$\cos 33° = \frac{\ell}{9.6}$$ Substitute the known values.

$$9.6 \times \cos 33° = \frac{\ell}{9.6} \times 9.6$$ Multiply both sides by 9.6 to isolate ℓ.

$$9.6 \cos 33° = \ell$$ Simplify.

$$8.05 \approx \ell$$

The missing side is approximately 8.1 inches long.

ALTERNATIVE SOLUTION

a) Since you know that the sum of the angles of a triangle is 180°, you can calculate angle L and then use the sine ratio to solve for ℓ.

$$180° - 90° - 33° = 57°$$

$$\sin L = \frac{\text{opp}}{\text{hyp}}$$

$$\sin 57° = \frac{\ell}{9.6}$$ Substitute the known values.

$$9.6 \sin 57° = \frac{\ell}{9.6} \times 9.6$$ Multiply both sides by 9.6 to isolate ℓ.

$$9.6 \sin 57° = \ell$$

$$8.05 \approx \ell$$

Side ℓ is approximately 8.1 inches long.

> The notation 9.6 cos 33°, without the multiplication symbol, can be used to mean 9.6 × cos 33°.

b) Use the cosine ratio to solve for r.

$$\cos P = \frac{\text{adj}}{\text{hyp}}$$

$$\cos 49° = \frac{7.8}{r} \qquad \text{Substitute the known values.}$$

$$r \cos 49° = \frac{7.8}{r} \times r \qquad \text{Multiply both sides by } r.$$

$$r \cos 49° = 7.8 \qquad \text{Simplify.}$$

$$\frac{r \cos 49°}{\cos 49°} = \frac{7.8}{\cos 49°} \qquad \text{Divide both sides by } \cos 49° \text{ to isolate } r.$$

$$r \approx 11.89$$

Side r is approximately 11.9 cm long.

BUILD YOUR SKILLS

1. Use your calculator to find the following pairs of ratios to four decimal places.

   a) $\cos 23° =$

   $\sin 67° =$

   b) $\cos 83° =$

   $\sin 7° =$

   c) $\cos 45° =$

   $\sin 45° =$

   d) $\cos 37° =$

   $\sin 53° =$

2. Find the measure of the indicated side in each triangle.

   a) 8.4 cm, 12°, x

   b) 8.4 cm, 78°, x

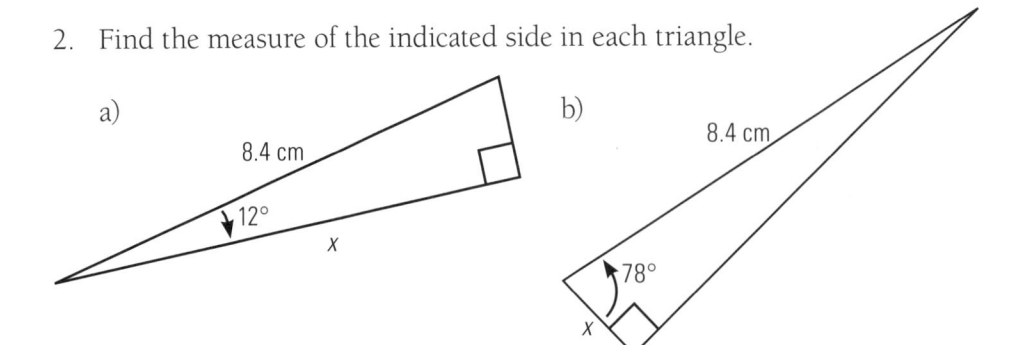

c)

d)

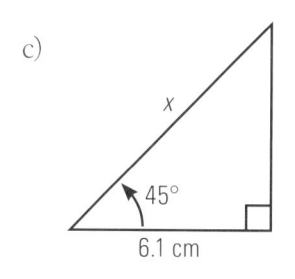

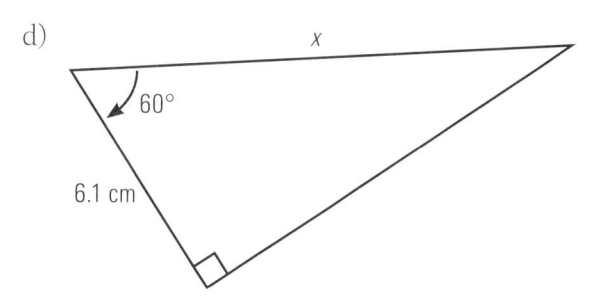

Example 2

How far from the base of a house is a 40-foot ladder if the angle of elevation is 72°?

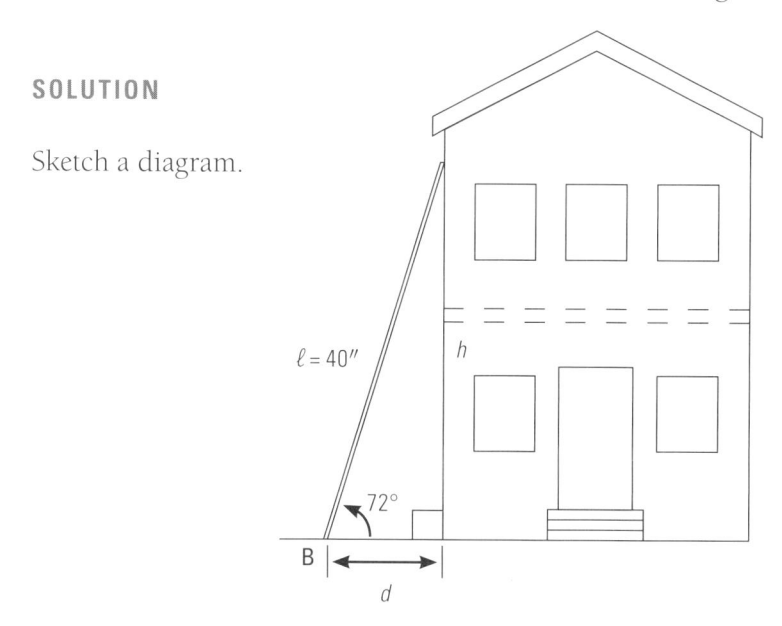

SOLUTION

Sketch a diagram.

Use the cosine ratio to solve for d.

$$\cos B = \frac{\text{adj}}{\text{hyp}}$$

$$\cos B = \frac{d}{\ell}$$

$$\cos 72° = \frac{d}{40} \qquad \text{Substitute the known values.}$$

$$40 \cos 72° = \frac{d}{40} \times 40 \qquad \text{Multiply both sides by 40.}$$

$$40 \cos 72° = d \qquad \text{Simplify.}$$

$$12.36 \approx d$$

The ladder rests about 12.4 feet from the house.

BUILD YOUR SKILLS

3. How far from the base of a flagpole must a guy wire be fixed if the wire is 12 metres long and it makes an angle of 63° with the ground?

4. Reba walks 25 yards across the diagonal of a rectangular field. If the angle between the width and the diagonal is 67°, how wide is the field?

5. A square pyramid has a slant height of 9 metres. The slant height makes an angle of 70° with the ground. What is the length of a side of the pyramid?

Example 3

The angle of a cable from a point 12.5 metres from its base is 52°. How long is the cable?

SOLUTION

Sketch a diagram.

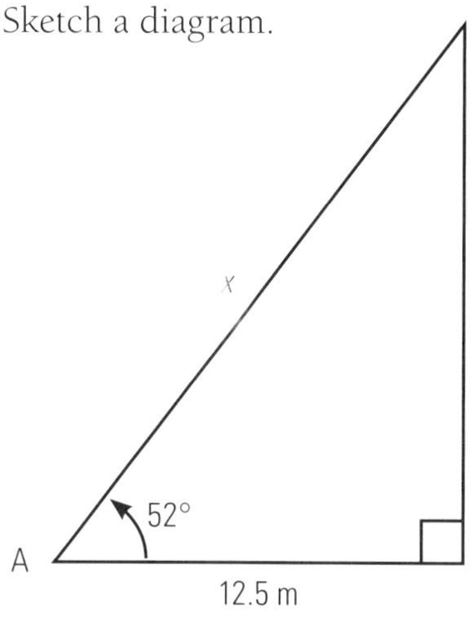

Use the cosine ratio to solve for x, the length of the cable.

$$\cos A = \frac{\text{adj}}{\text{hyp}}$$

$$\cos 52^\circ = \frac{12.5}{x}$$ Substitute the known values.

$$x \cos 52^\circ = \frac{12.5}{x} \times x$$ Multiply both sides by x.

$$x \cos 52^\circ = 12.5$$ Simplify.

$$\frac{x \cos 52^\circ}{\cos 52^\circ} = \frac{12.5}{\cos 52^\circ}$$ Divide both sides by cos 52° to isolate x.

$$x = \frac{12.5}{\cos 52^\circ}$$

$$x \approx 20.30$$

The cable is approximately 20.3 metres long.

BUILD YOUR SKILLS

6. Arul needs to string a bridge line across the river from A to B. What must the length of the bridge line be, given his measurements?

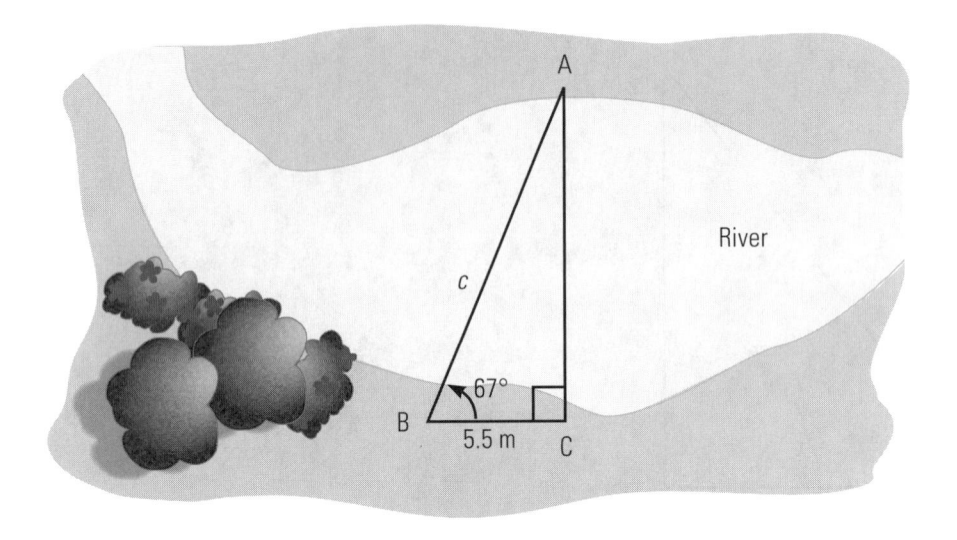

7. What is the length of a rafter that makes an angle of 35° with the floor of an attic whose centre is 9.5 metres from the edge?

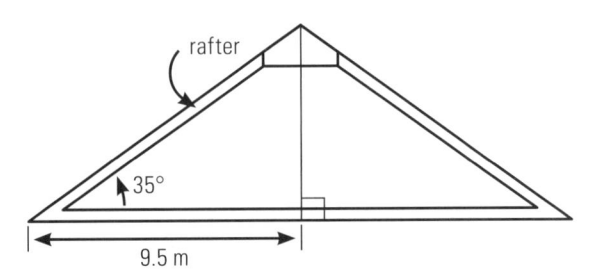

8. An airplane starts descending at an angle of depression of 5°. If the horizontal distance to its destination is 500 kilometres, what is the actual distance the airplane will travel before it lands?

PRACTISE YOUR NEW SKILLS

1. Find the lengths of the indicated sides.

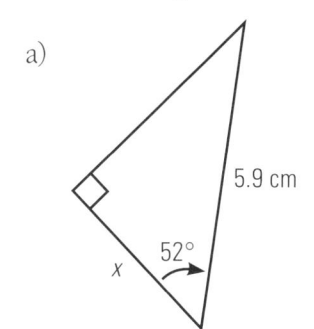

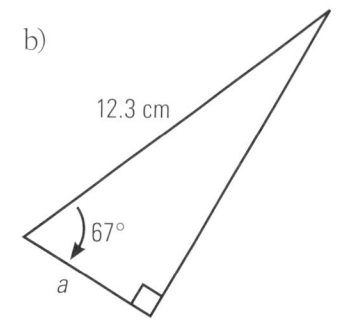

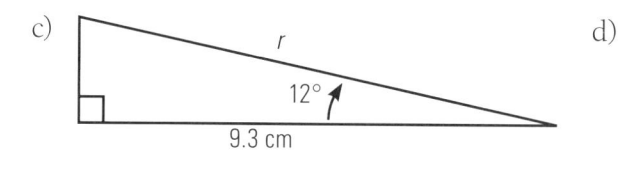

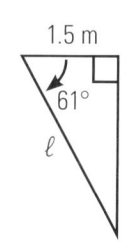

a) 5.9 cm, 52°, x

b) 12.3 cm, 67°, a

c) r, 12°, 9.3 cm

d) 1.5 m, 61°, ℓ

2. A screw conveyor is sometimes used to move grains and other materials up an incline. How far from the base of a barn must a 20-metre screw conveyor be placed if the angle of elevation to the loft is to be 30°?

3. What is the slant height of a cone if the diameter is 20 centimetres and the angle made with it is 65°?

4. A hot air balloon travels 1.2 kilometres horizontally from its take-off point. The angle of elevation from the take-off point to the balloon is 15°. How far did the balloon travel?

5. What horizontal distance has a car travelled if the incline of the road averages 3.2° and the car's odometer reads 8.5 kilometres?

6. The horizontal distance between two clothesline poles is 3.4 metres. When wet clothes are hung in the middle of the line, it sags at an angle of depression of 6°. How long is the clothesline?

7.4 The Tangent Ratio

NEW SKILLS: WORKING WITH THE TANGENT RATIO TO SOLVE TRIANGLES

tangent ratio: in a right triangle, the ratio of the length of the side opposite a given angle to the length of the side adjacent to the angle (abbreviated as tan)

You have studied two trigonometric ratios, the sine ratio and the cosine ratio. The third trigonometric ratio is the **tangent ratio.**

The tangent ratio is defined as the ratio of the side opposite an acute angle of a right triangle to the side adjacent the angle. For angle A, the ratio can be stated as follows.

$$\text{tangent } \angle A = \frac{\text{length of side opposite } \angle A}{\text{length of side adjacent to } \angle A}$$

This can be abbreviated as the following ratio.

$$\tan A = \frac{\text{opp}}{\text{adj}}$$

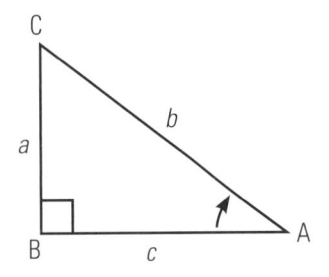

For triangle ABC, the tangent of angle A can be stated as follows.

$$\tan A = \frac{a}{c}$$

For more details, see page 301 of *MathWorks 10*.

Example 1

Find the indicated side of each triangle.

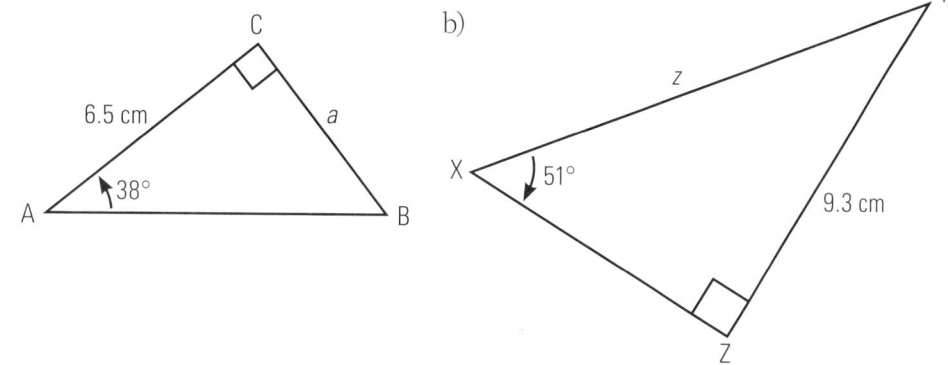

a) Triangle ABC with right angle at C, angle A = 38°, AC = 6.5 cm, side a = BC.

b) Triangle XYZ with right angle at Z, angle X = 51°, YZ = 9.3 cm, side z = XY.

SOLUTION

a) Use the tangent ratio to solve for a.

$$\tan A = \frac{\text{opp}}{\text{adj}}$$

$\tan 38° = \dfrac{a}{6.5}$ Substitute the known values.

$6.5 \tan 38° = \dfrac{a}{6.5} \times 6.5$ Multiply both sides by tan 6.5 to isolate a.

$6.5 \tan 38° = a$

$5.08 \approx a$

Side a is approximately 5.1 centimetres long.

b) Use the tangent ratio to solve for z.

$$\tan X = \frac{\text{opp}}{\text{adj}}$$

$\tan 51° = \dfrac{9.3}{z}$ Substitute the known values.

$z \tan 51° = 9.3$ Multiply both sides by z.

$\dfrac{z \tan 51°}{\tan 51°} = \dfrac{9.3}{\tan 51°}$ Divide both sides by tan 51° to isolate z.

$z = \dfrac{9.3}{\tan 51°}$

$z \approx 7.53$

Side z is approximately 7.5 centimetres long.

BUILD YOUR SKILLS

1. Find the length of the indicated sides of the triangles.

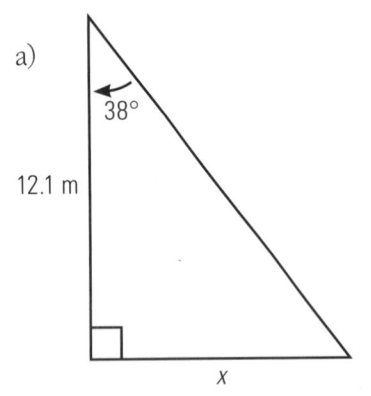

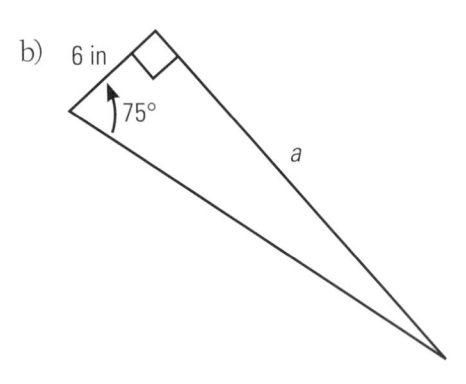

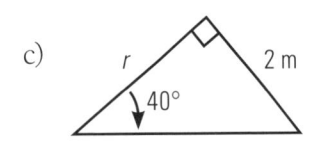

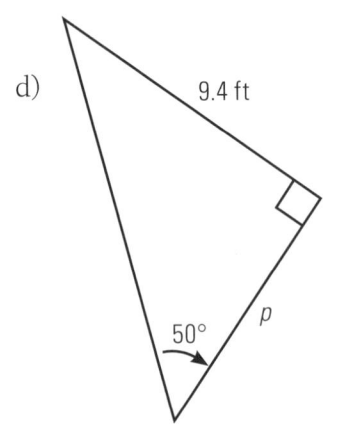

   a) 38°, 12.1 m, x

   b) 6 in, 75°, a

   c) r, 2 m, 40°

   d) 9.4 ft, 50°, p

2. The angle of depression to a boat from the top of a 150-metre cliff is 20°. How far is the boat from the base of the cliff?

3. When sand is piled onto a flat surface, it forms a cone. If the pile is 8 m wide, and the angle between the ground and the slope of the pile is 28°, what is the height of the pile?

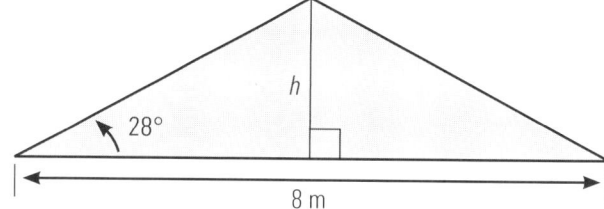

PRACTISE YOUR NEW SKILLS

1. A 1.7-metre tall man stands 12 m from the base of a tree. He views the top of the tree at an angle of elevation of 58°. How tall is the tree?

2. Two buildings are 18.5 metres apart. The angle of elevation from the top of one building to the top of the other is 18°. If the taller building is 15 metres tall, how tall is the shorter building?

3. How far from the base of the house is the foot of a ladder if the angle of elevation is 70° and it reaches 15 feet up the side of the house?

4. About how tall is a tower if the angle of depression from its top to a point 75 metres from the base is 62°?

5. A rafter's angle of elevation with the horizontal is 25°. How far from the corner could a 6-foot man stand up straight?

6. Determine the distance, AB, across the river, given the following measurements.

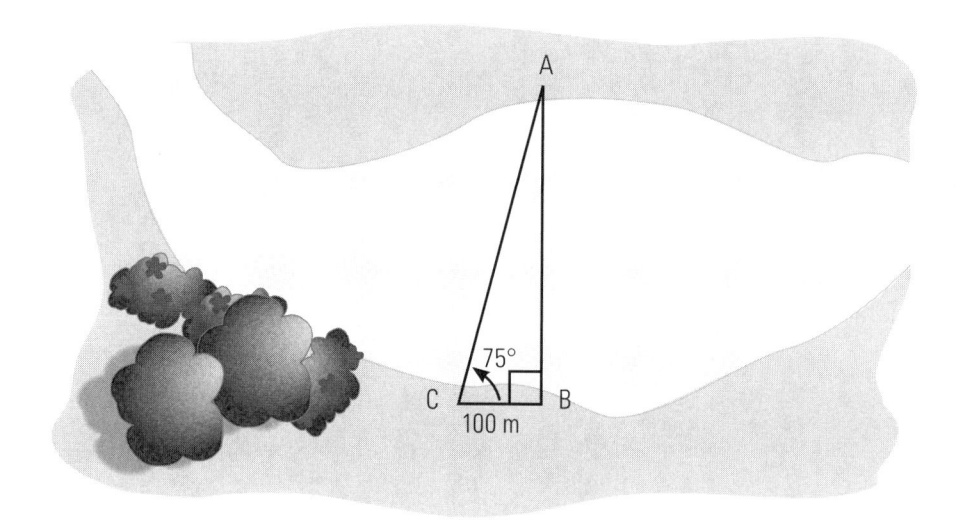

7.5 Finding Angles and Solving Right Triangles

NEW SKILLS: WORKING WITH INVERSE TRIGONOMETRIC RATIOS

The trigonometric ratios discussed in this chapter are unaffected by the size of the triangle, provided that the acute angle remains the same.

If you know the trigonometric ratio, you can calculate the size of the angle. This requires an "inverse" operation. You can use your calculator to find the opposite of the usual ratio calculation. You can think of the inverse in terms of subtraction and addition: subtraction is the inverse, or opposite, of addition because it "undoes" the operation.

For more details, see page 307 of *MathWorks 10*.

Example 1

Calculate each angle to the nearest degree.

a) sin A = 0.2546

b) cos B = 0.1598

c) tan C = 3.2785

SOLUTION

Use the inverse function on your calculator.

a) sin A = 0.2546

$A = \sin^{-1}(0.2546)$

A ≈ 14.7

∠A is approximately 15°.

b) cos B = 0.1598

$B = \cos^{-1}(0.1598)$

B ≈ 80.8

∠B is approximately 81°.

c) $\tan C = 3.2785$

   $C = \tan^{-1}(3.2785)$

   $C \approx 73.0$

∠C is approximately 73°.

BUILD YOUR SKILLS

1. Calculate the angle to the nearest degree.

   a) $\sin D = 0.5491$

   b) $\cos F = 0.8964$

   c) $\tan G = 2.3548$

   d) $\sin H = 0.9998$

2. In right triangle △XYZ, the ratio of the side opposite ∠X to the hypotenuse is $\frac{7}{8}$. What is the approximate size of ∠X?

   When solving this problem on your calculator, put brackets around $\frac{7}{8}$.

3. What is the approximate size of an angle in a right triangle if the ratio of the side opposite the angle to the side adjacent to the angle is $\frac{15}{8}$?

Example 2

Determine the angle of elevation to the top of a 5-metre tree at a point 3 metres from the base of the tree.

SOLUTION

Sketch a diagram.

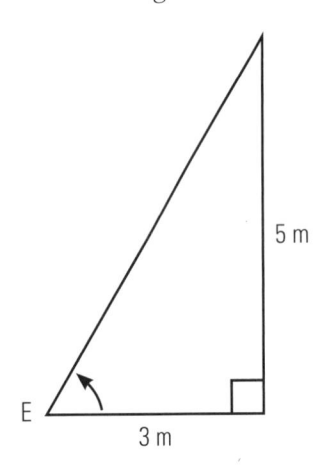

When solving this problem on your calculator, put brackets around $\frac{5}{3}$.

You are given the height (h, 5 metres) and the length (ℓ, 3 metres) of the triangle, and you need to solve for the angle of elevation. Use the tangent ratio.

$\tan E = \dfrac{\text{opp}}{\text{adj}}$

$\tan E = \dfrac{5}{3}$ Substitute the known values.

$E = \tan^{-1}\left(\dfrac{5}{3}\right)$ Use the inverse function to solve for E.

$E \approx 59.0362$

The angle of elevation is approximately 59°.

BUILD YOUR SKILLS

4. What is the angle of depression from the top of a 65-metre cliff to an object 48 metres from its base?

5. At what angle to the ground must you place a support if it is 6.8 metres long and must reach 4.2 metres up the side of a tower?

6. At what angle to the ground is an 8-metre long conveyor belt if it is fastened 5 metres from the base of a loading ramp?

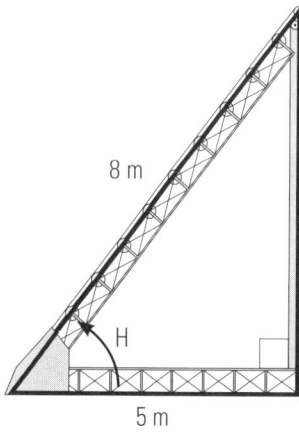

NEW SKILLS: WORKING WITH RATIOS TO SOLVE TRIANGLES

Solving a triangle means finding the values of all the unknown sides and angles. In a right triangle, you already know that one angle is 90°, so there are only five other parts to consider: the three sides, and the two other angles. If you are given any two sides, or any one side and one angle, you can use trigonometry to find the other values.

Example 3

Solve the right triangle. Give lengths to the nearest tenth.

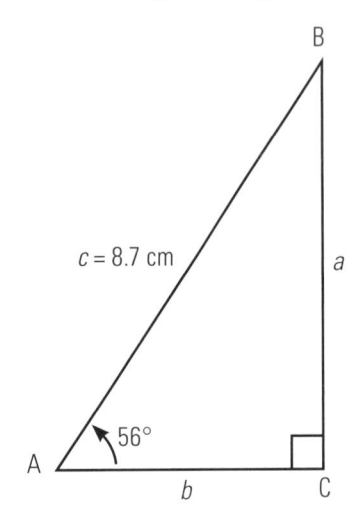

SOLUTION

You are given two of the three angles, so you can solve for the third angle.

$\angle B = 180° - 90° - 56°$

$\angle B = 34°$

To solve for side a, you can use the sine ratio. Use $\angle A$, and the length of the hypotenuse, c.

$\sin A = \dfrac{\text{opp}}{\text{hyp}}$

$\sin A = \dfrac{a}{c}$

$\sin 56° = \dfrac{a}{8.7}$ Substitute the known values.

$8.7 \sin 56° = \dfrac{a}{8.7} \times 8.7$ Multiply both sides by 8.7 to isolate a.

$7.2126 \approx a$

Side a is approximately 7.2 cm long.

To solve for *b*, use the cosine ratio.

$$\cos A = \frac{\text{adj}}{\text{hyp}}$$

$$\cos A = \frac{b}{c}$$

$$\cos 56° = \frac{b}{8.7} \quad \text{Substitute the known values.}$$

$$8.7 \cos 56° = \frac{b}{8.7} \times 8.7 \quad \text{Multiply both sides by 8.7 to isolate } b.$$

$$8.7 \cos 56° = b \quad \text{Simplify.}$$

$$4.8650 \approx b$$

Side *b* is approximately 4.9 cm long.

> You could have used the Pythagorean theorem to find side *b*, but this would have been less accurate because you would have used an approximation for side *a*. It is always better to use the numbers given, if possible, rather than one you calculated.

BUILD YOUR SKILLS

7. Solve the given triangle without using the Pythagorean theorem.

[Triangle PQR with right angle at R, angle P = 48°, side QR = 5.4 m, hypotenuse PQ = r, side PR = q]

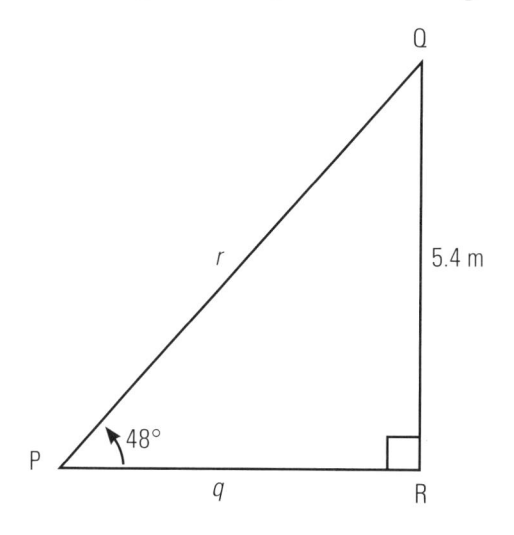

8. The two equal angles of an isosceles triangle are each 70°. Determine the measures of the rest of the triangle if it has a height of 16 cm.

9. The length of the rafter is 5.5 yards, and the side height of the building is 3.5 yards. Determine the width of the building and its total height.

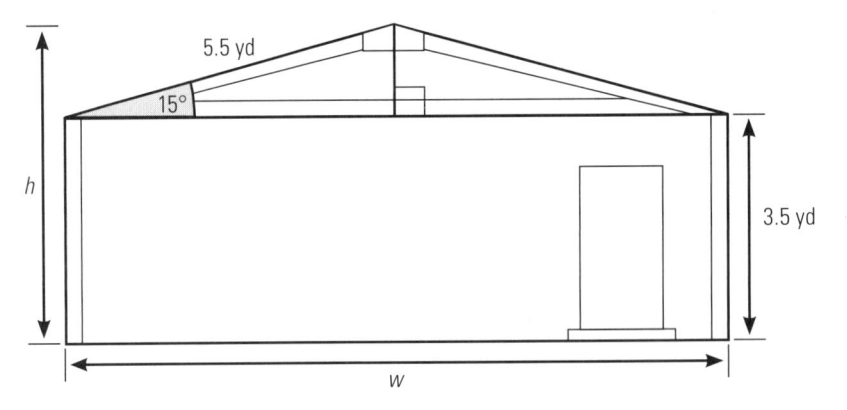

Example 4

Solve the given triangle.

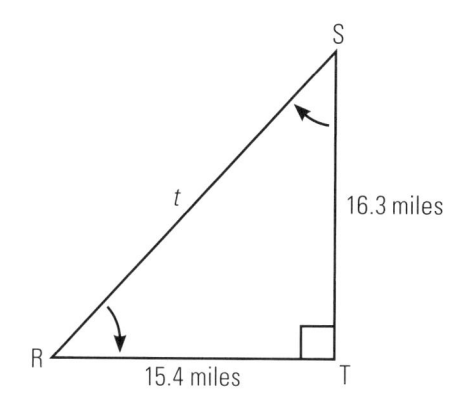

SOLUTION

Calculate ∠R using the tangent ratio.

$\tan R = \dfrac{\text{opp}}{\text{adj}}$

$\tan R = \dfrac{ST}{TR}$

$\tan R = \dfrac{16.3}{15.4}$ Substitute the known values.

$\angle R = \tan^{-1}\left(\dfrac{16.3}{15.4}\right)$ Use the inverse function to solve for ∠R.

$\angle R \approx 46.6263$

∠R is approximately 47°.

Calculate ∠S using the measures of the angles in the triangle.

$\angle S = 180° - 90° - 47°$

$\angle S = 43°$

Calculate the length of side t using the Pythagorean theorem.

$r^2 + s^2 = t^2$

$16.3^2 + 15.4^2 = t^2$

$\sqrt{16.3^2 + 15.4^2} = t$

$\sqrt{265.69 + 237.16} = t$

$\sqrt{502.85} = t$

$22.42 \approx t$

Side t is approximately 22.4 miles long.

> You could have found ∠S first using the tangent ratio.

> You could have solved for side t using the sine or cosine functions, but this would have involved rounding errors.

BUILD YOUR SKILLS

10. Solve the following triangles.

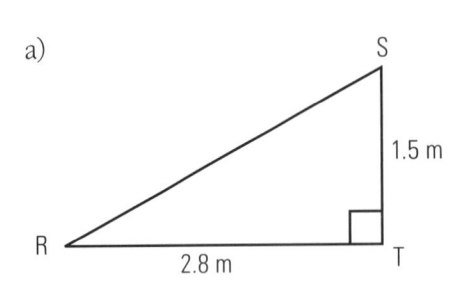

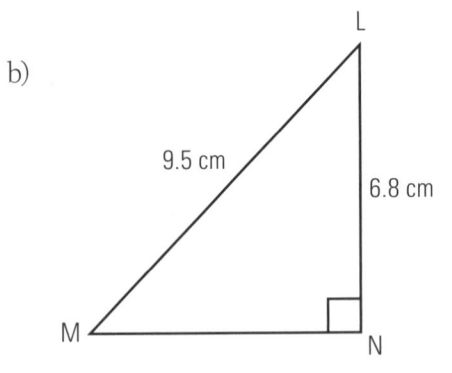

    a) Triangle RST with right angle at T, ST = 1.5 m, RT = 2.8 m.

    b) Triangle LMN with right angle at N, LM = 9.5 cm, LN = 6.8 cm.

11. What height is a pole, and how far away from it is a cable attached to the ground, if the angle of elevation is 25° and the cable is 18 m long?

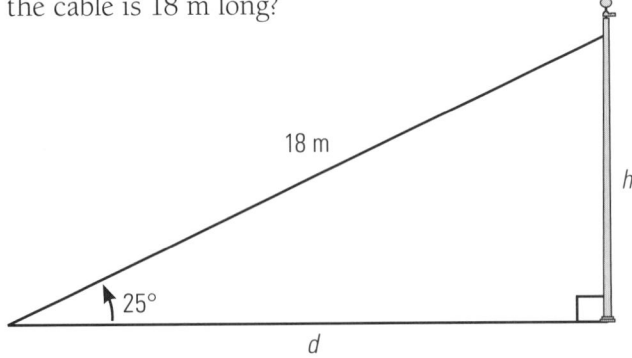

12. Find the values of a, b, c, and d.

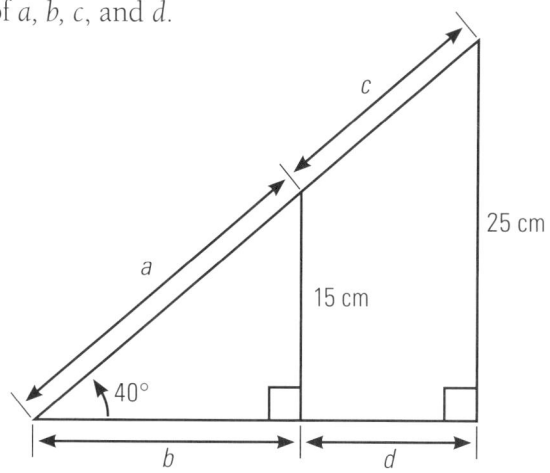

PRACTISE YOUR NEW SKILLS

1. Find the indicated angle in each of the following diagrams.

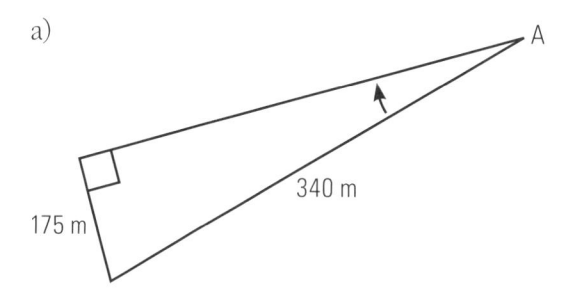

   a)

b)

135 cm
200 cm
B

2. In a right triangle, one acute angle is 22° and the hypotenuse is 70 cm. Find the lengths of the legs and the other angle measure.

3. What is the angle of elevation if a ramp with a height of 1 metre and a horizontal length of 3 metres?

4. A grain auger is 25 feet long. The largest angle of elevation at which it can safely be used is 75°. What is the maximum height to which it can reach and how far from the base of the granary will it be, assuming that it dumps right at the edge?

5. Maura's driveway has an angle of depression of 40° from the flat roadway. If it levels off to the garage floor, which is 3 metres below the roadway, how long is the driveway and how far into the lot is the garage entrance?

6. If a boat is 150 metres from the base of a cliff that is 90 metres high, what is the angle of elevation from the boat to the cliff top?

CHAPTER TEST

1. What is the length of a diagonal brace used to support a table that is 120 cm wide by 50 cm tall?

2. The Pyramid of Khufu is approximately 140 metres tall. If the base is a square with sides measuring 230 metres, what is the slant height from the centre of one of the sides of the pyramid? (Hint the slant height is the hypotenuse of a right triangle.)

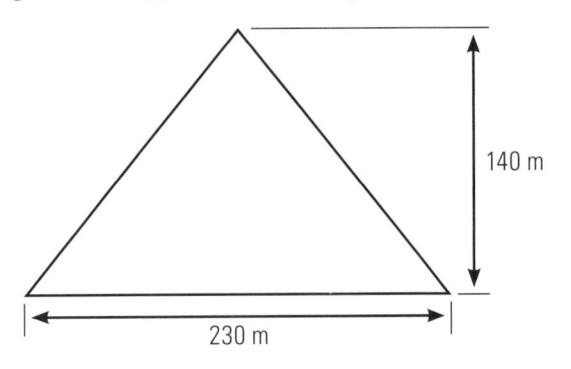

3. A plane travels 12 km along its flight path while climbing at a constant rate of 8°. What is the vertical change in height during this time?

4. A ramp 12 metres long makes an angle of 15° with the ground. What is the height of the ramp? If the ramp is doubled in length, what will the total height be?

5. A chute from an open window to the ground makes an angle of 52° with the side of a building. If the window is 18 metres from the ground, how long is the chute?

6. A tree casts a shadow that is 10 metres long. If the angle of elevation to the top of the tree from the ground at the end of the shadow is 60°, how high is the tree?

7. The angle of elevation from the bottom of one building to the top of another building is 78°. The angle of elevation from the bottom of the second building to the top of the first is 62°. If the distance between them is 150 metres, how much taller is the higher building than the shorter one?

8. In an A-frame building, the angle of elevation of the roof is 50° and the building is 12 metres wide.

   a) How high is the building at the centre?

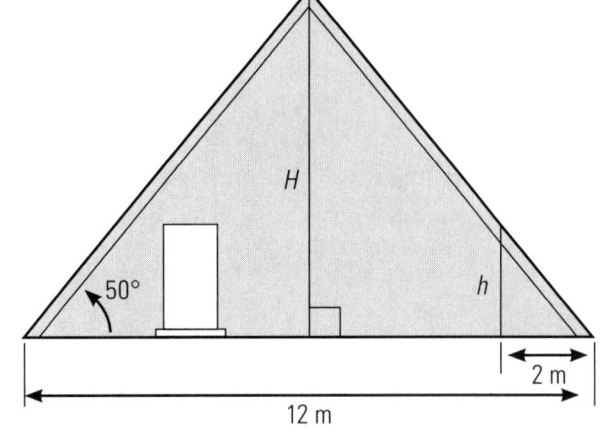

   b) How high is it 2 metres in from an edge?

9. A box is 1.5 m long, 1.0 m deep, and 8.0 m tall. What is the length of the longest object that can fit in the box?

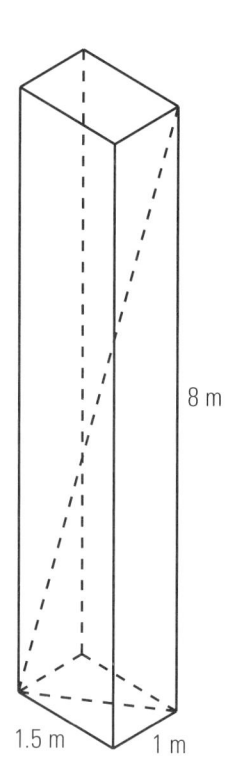

10. A lifeguard sits in a chair that is 2.5 metres high. He spots a child in trouble in the water at an angle of depression of 23°. How far out from the chair is the child?

11. What is the angle of elevation of a playground slide that is 1.2 m high and has a horizontal length of 2.6 m?

Glossary

alternate exterior angles: angles in opposite positions outside two lines intersected by a transversal

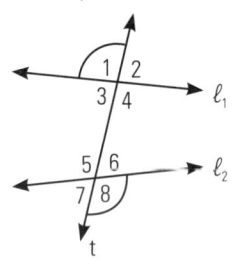

alternate interior angles: angles in opposite positions between two lines intersected by a transversal and also on alternate sides of the same transversal

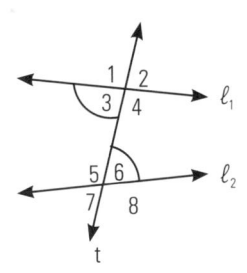

angle bisector: a segment, ray, or line that separates two halves of a bisected angle

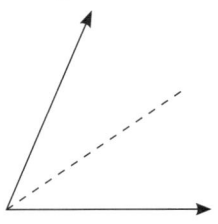

angle of depression: the angle formed between the horizontal and the line of sight while looking downward

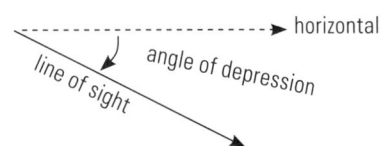

angle of elevation: the angle formed between the horizontal and the line of sight when looking upward; sometimes referred to as the angle of inclination

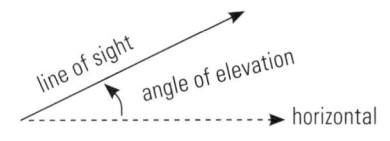

capacity: the maximum amount that a container can hold

circumference: the measure of the perimeter of a circle

complementary angles: two angles that have measures that add up to 90°

corresponding angles: two angles that occupy the same relative position at two different intersections

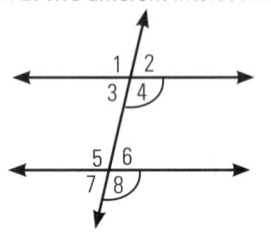

corresponding sides: two sides that occupy the same relative position in similar figures

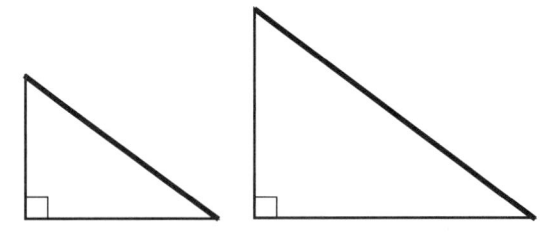

cosine ratio: in a right triangle, the ratio of the length of the side adjacent to a given angle to the length of the hypotenuse (abbreviated as cos)

deduction: money taken off your paycheque to pay taxes, union fees, and for other benefits and programs

divisor: in a division operation, the number by which another number is divided; in $a \div b = c$, b is the divisor

exchange rate: the price of one country's currency in terms of another country's currency

factor: one of two or more numbers that, when multiplied together, form a product. For example, 1, 2, 3, and 6 are factors of the product 6 because:

1 x 6 = 6
2 x 3 = 6
3 x 2 = 6
6 x 1 = 6

gross pay: the total amount of money earned before deductions; also called gross earnings or gross income

hypotenuse: the longest side of a triangle, opposite the 90° angle

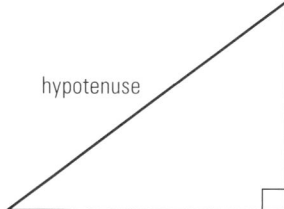

imperial system: the system most commonly used in the United States; the standard unit of measurement for length is the foot

kilogram: the mass of one litre of water at 4°C

markup: the difference between the amount a dealer sells a product for (retail price) and the amount he or she paid for it (wholesale price)

mass: a measure of the quantity of matter in an object

multiple: the product of a number and any other number. For example, 2, 4, 6, and 8 are some multiples of 2 because:

2 x 1 = 2
2 x 2 = 4
2 x 3 = 6
2 x 4 = 8

net: a two-dimensional pattern used to construct three-dimensional shapes

net income: income after all taxes and other deductions have been applied; also called take-home pay

percentage: a ratio with a denominator of 100; percent (%) means "out of 100"

perimeter: the sum of the lengths of all the sides of a polygon

promotion: an activity that increases awareness of a product or attracts customers

proportion: a fractional statement of equality between two ratios or rates

Pythagorean theorem: in a right triangle, the sum of the squares of the lengths of the legs is equal to the square of the length of the hypotenuse

quotient: the result of a division; in $a \div b = c$, c is the quotient

rate: a comparison between two numbers measured with different units

ratio: a comparison between two numbers measured in the same units

sine ratio: in a right triangle, the ratio of the length of the side opposite a given angle to the length of the hypotenuse (abbreviated as sin)

supplementary angles: two angles that have measures that add up to 180°

surface area: the total area of all the faces, or surfaces, of a three-dimensional object; measured in square units

Système International (SI): the modern version of the metric system; uses the metre as the basic unit of length

tangent ratio: in a right triangle, the ratio of the length of the side opposite a given angle to the length of the side adjacent to the angle (abbreviated as tan)

taxable income: income after before-tax deductions have been applied, on which federal and provincial taxes are paid

transversal: a line that intersects two or more lines

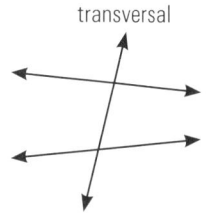

true bearing: the angle measured clockwise between true north and an intended path or direction, expressed in degrees

unit price: the cost of one unit; a rate expressed as a fraction in which the denominator is 1

vertically opposite angles: angles created by intersecting lines that share only a vertex

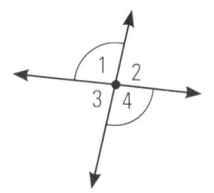

volume: the amount of space an object occupies

weight: a measure of the force of gravity on an object

Answer Key

**CHAPTER 1
UNIT PRICING AND CURRENCY EXCHANGE
1.1 PROPORTIONAL REASONING**

BUILD YOUR SKILLS, P. 11

1. a) $\frac{1}{4}$ b) $\frac{1}{4}$
   c) $\frac{1}{3}$ d) $\frac{5}{7}$
   e) $\frac{4}{9}$ f) $\frac{9}{20}$
   g) $\frac{2}{5}$ h) $\frac{1}{7}$
   i) $\frac{1}{8}$

2. a) $x = 8$ b) $x = 24$
   c) $x = 7$ d) $x = 54$
   e) $x = 1542$ f) $x = 60$
   g) $x = 276$ h) $x = 125$

3. a) 1500 mL b) 500 mL

4. 3:1

5. 4:9

6. 1:1.13

7. 1:4

8. 1:32

9. 20 cups of flour and 10 cups of shortening

10. 10.4 L of the first chemical and 34.6 L of the second chemical

11. Cheryl will use 15 L of paint and 9 L of thinner

12. $65.00:3 months, $65.00/3 months, or $\frac{\$65.00}{3 \text{ months}}$

13. $74.00:8-hour day, $74.00/8-hour day, or $\frac{\$74.00}{8\text{-hour day}}$

14. 1 cm:2500 km

15. $5.57/350 g

16. 75 g

17. approximately 6.9 kg

PRACTISE YOUR NEW SKILLS, P. 21

1. a) $x = 16$ b) $x \approx 6.5$
   c) $x = 42$ d) $x = 63$
   e) $x = 29$ f) $x \approx 52.1$
   g) $x \approx 0.5$ h) $x = 60$

2. a) $\frac{20}{3}$ b) $\frac{1}{5}$
   c) $\frac{2}{1}$ d) $\frac{4.8}{1}$

3. 8 drops of yellow pigment

4. 30 cm

5. 5 cans of paint

6. The smaller gear has 24 teeth.

7. It will take Stephie approximately 11 minutes; this is a rate problem.

8. 2.25 cups or $2\frac{1}{4}$ cups of flour

9. 1020 parts

1.2 UNIT PRICE

BUILD YOUR SKILLS, P. 27

1. $0.85

2. $0.095 or about 10 cents

3. a) approximately $1.70
   b) $3.80

4. The first package is the better deal.

5. A dozen muffins for $14.99 is a better buy.

6. Buying pieces of 6-foot lumber is a better deal.

7. a) The first roll is less expensive per foot.
   b) The difference in price is $0.01 per foot.

8. $23.10

9. $52.32

PRACTISE YOUR NEW SKILLS, P. 32

1. a) approximately $0.71
   b) $10.10

2. a) at least 84 m² (the area of the room)
   b) $684.60

3. a) $160.00
   b) $5.00/sq ft

4. a) $10.44
   b) 3 cases cost $84.48; each brush costs $4.69

5. 8 oz of Brie cheese for $4.95 is a better buy.

6. a) 54 loaves
   b) $270.00

7. You would save $0.0014/mL.

8. A carton of 18 is a better buy, by $0.14 per unit.

1.3 SETTING A PRICE

BUILD YOUR SKILLS, P. 37

1. a) 0.78   b) 0.93
   c) 1.25   d) 3.24
   e) 0.005   f) 0.0038
   g) 0.012   h) 1

2. a) 45   b) 675
   c) 98   d) 42
   e) 3.9   f) 0.525
   g) 112   h) 33.75

3. a) 20%   b) 33.3%
   c) 162%   d) 20%
   e) 8.3%   f) 1250%

4. $562.50

5. $1.81

6. $187.92

7. $15.75

8. $104.95

9. $1048.93

10. $44.64

11. GST: $2.30; PST: $2.75

12. $74.26

13. $26.65

PRACTISE YOUR NEW SKILLS, P. 46

1. a) 3.6 b) 22
   c) 304 d) 47.25
2. a) $50.75 b) $304.50
3. 135%
4. $495.49
5. $20.10
6. $21.56
7. Harry will save $1.11 by buying the MP3 player in Alberta.

1.4 ON SALE!

BUILD YOUR SKILLS, P. 50

1. $296.99
2. $1.79
3. $249.99
4. $17.46
5. $37.85
6. $255.00
7. about 14%
8. 20%
9. 17%
10. $109.52
11. $206.21
12. a) $112.97 b) 40%

PRACTISE YOUR NEW SKILLS, P. 56

1. $1481.85
2. a) $14.99 b) $34.99
3. $6.59
4. $59.95
5. a) $669.75 b) $2679.02
6. approximately 30%
7. a) $87.45 b) $96.20
   c) $34.98 d) $38.48
   e) $57.72 f) 60%

1.5 CURRENCY EXCHANGE RATES

BUILD YOUR SKILLS, P. 60

1. 90 038.95 Ft
2. £118.22
3. 535.41 kr
4. €215.40
5. 421.68 SFr
6. 1236.10 Trinidad and Tobago dollars
7. a) approximately 345.81 Brazilian reals
   b) approximately 1742.27 Moroccan dirhams
   c) approximately 1544.55 Ukrainian hryvnia
   d) approximately 639.78 Polish zloty
8. $339.69 CAD
9. $176.21 CAD

10. $88.48 CAD

11. You will get more units of the currency than of Canadian dollars.

12. $384.48 CAD

13. $32.57

PRACTISE YOUR NEW SKILLS, P. 67

1. a) 47 746 Japanese yen
   b) 705 Turkish Lira
   c) 340 euros
   d) 3215 Chinese yuan
   e) 3659 Hong Kong dollars

2. a) 6112 Mexican pesos
   b) 5322 Estonian kroon
   c) 374 British pounds
   d) 54 213 South Korean won
   e) 21 784 Indian rupees
   f) 14 178 Russian rubles

3. a) $91.63 CAD
   b) $638.09 CAD
   c) $367.52 CAD
   d) $466.54 CAD

4. a) $552.21 CAD
   b) $193.95 CAD
   c) $344.29 CAD
   d) $26.45 CAD

5. $47.74 CAD

6. $5.30 CAD

7. $28.84

CHAPTER TEST, P. 70

1. 42 L

2. a) 5.5 L/100 km, 5.5 L:100 km, or $\dfrac{5.5 \text{ L}}{100 \text{ km}}$
   b) 22 L

3. 296 km

4. $3.25

5. $14.43

6. $2.87/dozen

7. a) $1105.97
   b) No. The original price is reduced by 35%, and then the sale price is reduced by 20%.

8. 9%

9. 62%

10. $103.80

11. $177.00 CAD

12. a) €306.10
    b) $183.76 CAD

CHAPTER 2
EARNING AN INCOME
2.1 WAGES AND SALARIES

BUILD YOUR SKILLS, P. 76

1. a) $4\frac{1}{7}$ b) $54\frac{7}{9}$
   c) $34\frac{19}{29}$ d) $7\frac{1}{2}$
   e) $24\frac{7}{8}$ f) $66\frac{2}{3}$

2. a) $\frac{61}{11}$ b) $\frac{43}{9}$
   c) $\frac{263}{17}$ d) $\frac{61}{8}$
   e) $\frac{64}{5}$ f) $\frac{127}{12}$

3. $83.60

4. $834.80

5. $1215.50

6. a) $3765.28
   b) $868.91

7. $13.82/h

8. $9.88/h

9. **TIME CARD: MONTY**

Day	IN	OUT	Total Hours
Monday	3:30	6:45	3.25 h
Tuesday			
Wednesday	5:00	9:30	4.5 h
Thursday	5:00	9:30	4.5 h
Friday	3:30	7:00	3.5 h

Monty earned $148.84.

10. **TIME CARD: HAE-RIN**

Day	Morning IN	Morning OUT	Afternoon IN	Afternoon OUT	Total Hours
Monday	7:45	9:00	5:00	7:45	1.25 h + 2.75 h
Tuesday			4:00	8:00	4 h
Wednesday	9:00	11:00			2 h
Thursday	9:00	11:00	3:00	5:00	2 h + 2 h
Friday			3:00	6:00	3 h
Saturday	9:00	12:00			3 h

Hae-rin earned $255.20.

11. Pete will earn $971.68 for the week.

12. Ingrid will earn $537.81 per week.

13. Nathalie will earn $5436.24 during the summer.

PRACTISE YOUR NEW SKILLS, P. 85

1. $107.50

2. $92.70

3. Juanita would earn more per week at the second job, even though she would be working fewer hours, so she should take the second job.

4. $129.96

5. $300.16

6. $381.70

2.2 ALTERNATIVE WAYS TO EARN MONEY

BUILD YOUR SKILLS, P. 87

1. $366.00

2. $51.75

3. $51.00

Answer Key **347**

4. $254.00/job

5. $3.75/quart

6. 550 words

7. $94.31

8. $15 018.00

9. $701.05

10. 7%

11. 5%

12. $2128.89

13. $479.52

14. $414.63

15. about 11%

PRACTISE YOUR NEW SKILLS, P. 95

1. a) $231.00   b) $189.00

2. $160.00

3. $6250.00

4. $12.63/h

5. a) The other contractor's bid is $14 382.00. Jeff could lower his bid to that amount; he would make a profit of $1683.90.

   b) $33.68/h

2.3 ADDITIONAL EARNINGS

BUILD YOUR SKILLS, P. 98

1. $175.00

2. Since $275.00/month is more than 12% of his regular pay, he should take that offer.

3. Darren: $198.40; Sean: $123.04

4. $527.75

5. $481.25

6. The bonus of 28% of his regular pay is more than $1250.00, so Chen should take the 28% bonus.

7. $208.10/day

8. about 12%

9. $121.30

PRACTISE YOUR NEW SKILLS, P. 104

1. $51 890.00

2. $795.63

3. a) Each waiter would receive $2028.40 in tips for the month.

   b) Each waiter would make $1521.30.

4. $840.29

5. $4887.62

2.4 DEDUCTIONS AND NET PAY

BUILD YOUR SKILLS, P. 107

1. $112.50

2. $1.50

3. $78.11

4. about 23%

5. a) about 15% b) 5.9%

6. about 1.7%

7. $687.62

8. $2301.43

9. a) $575.00/week b) $470.27/week

   c) 8.3%

PRACTISE YOUR NEW SKILLS, P. 113

1. a) $1098.84 b) $2211.96

2. about 23%

3. $790.21

CHAPTER TEST, P. 114

4. $12.54/h

5. $19 500.00

6. $42 816.00

7. The second job would pay $40.00 more per year.

8. 3%

9. $281.20

10. $186.30

11. $873.75

12. $75.87

13. $3274.16

14. $38.73

15. a) $985.80 b) $24.65/h

CHAPTER 3
LENGTH, AREA, AND VOLUME
3.1 SYSTEMS OF MEASUREMENT

BUILD YOUR SKILLS, P. 120

1. a) 53.6 cm b) 43.6 cm

   c) 7.6 m

2. 780 cm

3. 240 m

4. 122 ft

5. about 33.3 m

6. 104 m

7. 1099.5 cm

8. Bernard needs $13\frac{1}{2}$ ft of 2 by 4 lumber and $52\frac{1}{2}$ ft of 2 by 2 lumber.

9. 12 ft

10. 740 boards

11. The cages will not fit along a 30′ wall. They are 2″ too wide.

12. The garden circumference is about 20 feet, so Gordon will need 20 geraniums.

13. The height of the pipe is 6′7″. Craig is 6′6″ tall, so he will be able to walk under the finished pipe.

PRACTISE YOUR NEW SKILLS, P. 129

1. a) $3\frac{1}{2}$ feet b) 1 ft 4 in

   c) $2\frac{2}{3}$ yards d) 8800 yards

2. 34'4"

3. 65'2"

4. 64 packages

5. 11.4 blocks

3.2 CONVERTING MEASUREMENTS

BUILD YOUR SKILLS, P. 132

1. 760 sq ft

2. The diameter of the rug is 2.4 m; this is less than the dimensions of the space Travis wants to cover, so the rug will fit into the space.

3. The label is 28.3 cm long.

4. 20.3 cm by 10.2 cm

5. $2227.14

6. a) $28.56/linear yard

   b) $31.73/linear metre

   c) $123.75

7. $554.82

8. a) 27 boxes   b) $511.65

9. $1072.85

PRACTISE YOUR NEW SKILLS, P. 139

1. a) 132 inches   b) 11 feet

   c) 3 yd 2 ft

2. 387.5 mi

3. 45 m by 25.5 m

4. The height of the semi-trailer is 10 ft 8.4 in. It will not fit through the tunnel.

5. $38.14

6. 10.5 lb

7. $643.72

3.3 SURFACE AREA

BUILD YOUR SKILLS, P. 145

1. 468 sq in

2. 66 sq ft

3. 11 305 sq in

4. a) 959 sq in   b) 6.7 sq ft

5. 149.2 sq in

6. 1.4 sq ft

7. 374 sq ft

8. 214.2 sq in

9. 112.7 sq ft

10. $1234.80

11. $1312.85

12. $179.70

PRACTISE YOUR NEW SKILLS, P. 155

1. 35.3 sq ft

2. 36 sq ft

3. 50 of the 39 cm by 39 cm tiles would be needed. 155 of the 18 cm by 27 cm tiles would be needed.

4. 47.3 sq in

5. 11.8 in by 7.5 in

6. 14.7 sq in

7. 922 320 sq ft

3.4 VOLUME

BUILD YOUR SKILLS, P. 159

1. a) 12 960 in^3 b) 7.5 ft^3

2. 11.25 ft^3

3. Volume of box: 72 in^3. Volume of cube: 64 in^3. The contents of the box will not fit in the cube.

4. 3 bags

5. 1875 cubic feet

6. 4446 in^3

7. a) 14.5 US gallons   b) $43.36
   c) $120.29

8. 2675 ft^3

9. 6.2 ft

PRACTISE YOUR NEW SKILLS, P. 166

1. a) 72 cubic feet   b) 2.7 cubic yards

2. 687.5 mL

3. 150 mL

4. 10.4 US gallons

5. Fav will need about 4.7 L of fertilizer, so he will need 2 bottles.

6. $366.12

CHAPTER TEST, P. 169

1. a) 6 ft 6.4 in

   b) Robert Pershing Wadlow: about 2.7 m; He Pingping: about 0.7 m.

   c) 2 m

2. Height of tunnel: 3.15 m. Franklin's truck is higher than that, so it will not fit through the tunnel.

3. 7 panels

4. a) 129 tiles   b) 47 geraniums

5. 2.3 gallons (likely rounded up to 3 gallons)

6. 354.8 sq ft

7. Soccer field dimensions: 118.8 yd by 79.6 yd. Yes, it does fit the league's specifications.

8. 158 400 cm^3

9. 2.7 cubic yards

10. 1 US gal = 3800 mL; 0.5 US gal = 1900 mL; 1 quart = 950 mL; 0.5 pint = 237.5 mL

11. a) $\frac{5}{8}$ cup or 0.625 cup

    b) 125 mL

Answer Key 351

CHAPTER 4
MASS, TEMPERATURE, AND VOLUME
4.1 TEMPERATURE CONVERSIONS

BUILD YOUR SKILLS, P. 177

1. 176.7°C
2. 114.4°C
3. 1198.9°C
4. Ashley's dog has a temperature of 104°F. This is outside (higher than) the normal range.
5. The temperature is 48°F. The paint can be safely applied.
6. a) 103°F
   b) Minimum temperature: −47.8°C; maximum temperature: 9.4°C
   c) 57.2°C

PRACTISE YOUR NEW SKILLS, P. 179

1. a) 95°F   b) 17.6°F
   c) 329°F   d) 69.8°F
   e) −40°F   f) 395.6°F
2. a) −28.9°C   b) 26.7°C
   c) 190.6°C   d) −16.7°C
   e) −17.8°C   f) −18.9°C
3. The blowtorch flame is 2372°F. The candle flame is 998.9°C. The blowtorch is hotter than the candle flame, by 542°F or 301.1°C.
4. a) between 93.3°C and 126.7°C
   b) between 18.3°C and 37.8°C
   c) between 71.1°C and 98.9°C

5. The temperature rose from −2.2°F to 71.6°F.
6. 5°C
7. −77°C
8. 1260°C

4.2 MASS IN THE IMPERIAL SYSTEM

BUILD YOUR SKILLS, P. 185

1. 12 lb 3 oz
2. 17 lb 8 oz
3. 5.3 baskets of raspberries, rounded up to 6
4. The weight of the load is about 1.6 tons, so it is unsafe and over the acceptable limit of 1.5 tons.
5. 28 slabs
6. 14.4 tons
7. The 2.5-lb jar is the best buy.
8. 5.3 skeins, rounded up to 6
9. approximately 4693 chocolate bars
10. $2.20/lb
11. $0.08/lb
12. $1.29/oz

PRACTISE YOUR NEW SKILLS, P. 192

1. a) 1.5 lb   b) 3.945 tn
   c) 3 lb 6 oz   d) 98 oz
   e) 9080 lb   f) 40 lb 14 oz
2. 6 lb
3. $6\frac{2}{3}$ oz

4. 3425 lb

5. The paint will weigh 13.5 lb, so Harinder can safely paint the structure.

6. a) $1.67/lb   b) $1.25/12 oz

7. $1.73/lb

4.3 MASS IN THE SYSTÈME INTERNATIONAL

BUILD YOUR SKILLS, P. 196

1. 5.75 tonnes

2. 414 g

3. a) $6.27   b) $17.90

4. about 6.3 oz

5. 3522.4 g

6. 149.6 lb

7. $4.43

8. 200 g at $3.85 is the better buy.

9. a) 4.2 mg   b) $8.19

PRACTISE YOUR NEW SKILLS, P. 200

1. a) 2500 kg   b) 2800 g
   c) 0.125 kg   d) 0.0024 kg
   e) 2200 lb   f) 3272.4 kg

2. 1 tonne (t) ≈ 1.1 tons (tn)

3. 3450 g

4. 2045 kg

5. 6.6 lb

6. $16.61/kg

7. 16 hamburgers

4.4 MAKING CONVERSIONS

BUILD YOUR SKILLS, P. 204

1. a) 67.9 kg   b) 149 lb

2. White beans weigh more per unit volume.

3. $5.33/bu

4. 187 bushels

5. 22.9 tonnes

6. Wheat is approximately twice as heavy as sunflower seeds, per unit volume.

7. about 2.8 kg

8. The sandstone weighs about 4.8 t, so the crane can be used.

9. The total weight of the package is 1.7 kg, so she will be able to send it at the cheaper rate.

PRACTISE YOUR NEW SKILLS, P. 207

1. about 199 bushels

2. Total weight: 5216 kg. This is over the limit, so the load cannot be safely carried.

3. approximately 909 kg

4. about 8 adults

5. 150 mL

6. 23.6 ha

CHAPTER TEST, P. 210

1. a) 77°F b) –3.9°C
   c) –40°C d) –31.7°C
   e) 207.2°C f) 113°F

2. 932°F to 36 032°F

3. a) 196 oz b) 4600 lb
   c) 2 tn 1284 lb d) 60 oz
   e) 10.3 lb f) approximately 1 lb

4. 140 318 trees

5. 1 lb 7 oz

6. 6.25 lb, or 6 lb 4 oz

7. 14 eggs

8. 1571 kg

9. approximately 1.2 tonnes

CHAPTER 5
ANGLES AND PARALLEL LINES
5.1 MEASURING, DRAWING, AND ESTIMATING ANGLES

BUILD YOUR SKILLS, P. 214

1. a) acute b) reflex
   c) obtuse d) acute
   e) straight f) obtuse
   g) reflex h) reflex

2. ∠A measures about 40°.

   ∠B measures about 75°.

   ∠C measures about 65°.

   ∠D measures about 10°.

3. The angle is about 20°.

4. ∠A measures about 140° or 150°.

   ∠B measures about 230° or 240°.

   ∠C measures about 170°.

   ∠D measures about 330°.

5. The angle is about 100°.

6.

| ANGLE COMPLEMENTS AND SUPPLEMENTS |||
Angle	Complement	Supplement
45°	90° – 45° = 45°	180° – 45° = 135°
78°	90° – 78° = 12°	180° – 78° = 102°
112°	Does not exist, because angle is greater than 90°.	180° – 112° = 68°
160°	Does not exist, because angle is greater than 90°.	180° – 160° = 20°
220°	Does not exist, because angle is greater than 90°.	Does not exist, because angle is greater than 180°.

7. a) 32°   b) 148°

8. a) 90°   b) 90°

9. 115°

10. 180°

11. 337.5°

PRACTISE YOUR NEW SKILLS, P. 222

1. a) acute   b) obtuse
   c) reflex   d) obtuse
   e) acute   f) reflex

2. a) The angle is slightly greater than 60°, about 65°.
   b) The angle is slightly greater than 45°, about 50°.
   c) The angle is about 45°.
   d) Angle x is about 120°, and angle y is about 60°.

3. 25°

4. ∠A is more than 90°; it is about 110°.

5. a) 175°   b) 220°

5.2 ANGLE BISECTORS AND PERPENDICULAR LINES

BUILD YOUR SKILLS, P. 226

1. 45°

2. a)

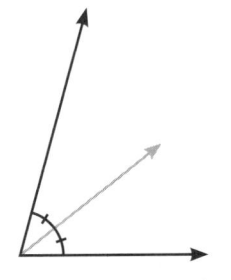

   b)

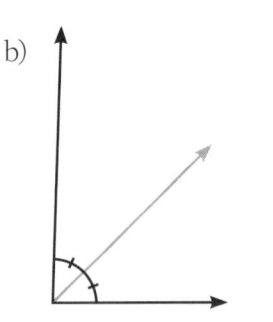

   c)

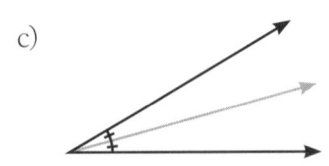

3. 156°

4. 120°

5. 3.3°

6. approximately 35°

7. a = 45°; b = 50°; c = 55°; d = 30°

PRACTISE YOUR NEW SKILLS, P. 229

1. a) Not perpendicular.
   b) Not perpendicular.
   c) Yes, the lines are perpendicular.
   d) Yes, the lines are perpendicular.

2.

| ANGLE CALCULATIONS ||||
Angle	Complement	Supplement	Resulting angle measures after angle is bisected
73°	17°	107°	36.5°
78°	12°	102°	39°
15°	75°	165°	7.5°
48°	42°	132°	24°
90°	0°	90°	45°
68°	22°	112°	34°
41°	49°	139°	20.5°
136°	n/a	44°	68°
80°	10°	100°	40°
254°	n/a	n/a	127°

3. $x = 67.5°$, $y = 22.5°$

4. a) $y = 110°$, $x = 70°$

   x and y are supplementary.

   b) $x = 72°$

   c) $x = 99°$

   x and the 81° angle are supplementary.

   d) $x = 245°$

5. 67.5°

5.3 NON-PARALLEL LINES AND TRANSVERSALS

BUILD YOUR SKILLS, P. 233

1. a) alternate interior angles

   b) corresponding angles

   c) exterior angles on the same side of the transversal

   d) interior angles on the same side of the transversal

2. a) ∠6   b) ∠3

   c) ∠3   d) ∠3

3. a) ∠7, using lines ℓ_3 and ℓ_4 with transversal ℓ_1.

   ∠3, using lines ℓ_1 and ℓ_2 with transversal ℓ_3.

   b) ∠4, using lines ℓ_3 and ℓ_4 with transversal ℓ_2.

   c) ∠10, using lines ℓ_3 and ℓ_4 with transversal ℓ_2.

   d) ∠5, using lines ℓ_3 and ℓ_4 with transversal ℓ_2.

   ∠7, using lines ℓ_1 and ℓ_2 with transversal ℓ_4.

4. CB and BD intersect AB and AD.

5. Line t cannot be a transversal because it does not pass through two distinct points. It is concurrent to ℓ_1 and ℓ_2 because they all pass through the same point.

6. t and ℓ_3 are intersected by ℓ_1 and ℓ_2.

PRACTISE YOUR NEW SKILLS, P. 236

1. a) ∠3 and ∠5; ∠2 and ∠8

   b) ∠1 and ∠5; ∠2 and ∠6; ∠3 and ∠7; ∠4 and ∠8

   c) ∠2 and ∠5; ∠3 and ∠8

2. ∠3 and ∠5; ∠4 and ∠6.

3. a) ℓ_3 is the transversal that makes ∠1 and ∠2 corresponding angles for ℓ_1 and ℓ_2.

   b) ℓ_4 is the transversal that makes ∠3 and ∠4 alternate interior angles for ℓ_1 and ℓ_2.

4. ∠3 = 95°

   ∠4 = 68°

   ∠5 = 112°

   ∠3 + ∠4 + ∠5 = 360°

5. ∠1 = 60°

   ∠2 = 120°

   ∠3 = 60°

   ∠4 = 110°

   ∠5 = 70°

   ∠6 = 110°

5.4 PARALLEL LINES AND TRANSVERSALS

BUILD YOUR SKILLS, P. 240

1. ∠1 and the 71° angle are interior angles on the same side of the transversal.

   ∠1 = 109°

   ∠2 is supplementary to the 118° angle.

   ∠2 = 62°

   ∠3 corresponds to the 118° angle.

   ∠3 = 118°

   ∠4 corresponds to ∠2, and is also supplementary to ∠3.

   ∠4 = 62°

2. ∠1 = 112°

   ∠2 = 68°

   ∠3 = 68°

   ∠4 = 112°

3. ∠A is 106°. It is supplementary to ∠B (74°) because they are interior angles on the same side of the transversal, given parallel lines BC and AD and transversal AB.

   ∠C is 106°. It is supplementary to ∠B (74°) because they are interior angles on the same side of the transversal, given parallel lines AB and CD and transversal BC.

   ∠D is 74°. It is supplementary to ∠A (106°) because they are interior angles on the same side of the transversal, given parallel lines AB and CD and transversal AD.

4. ℓ_1 and ℓ_3 are parallel.

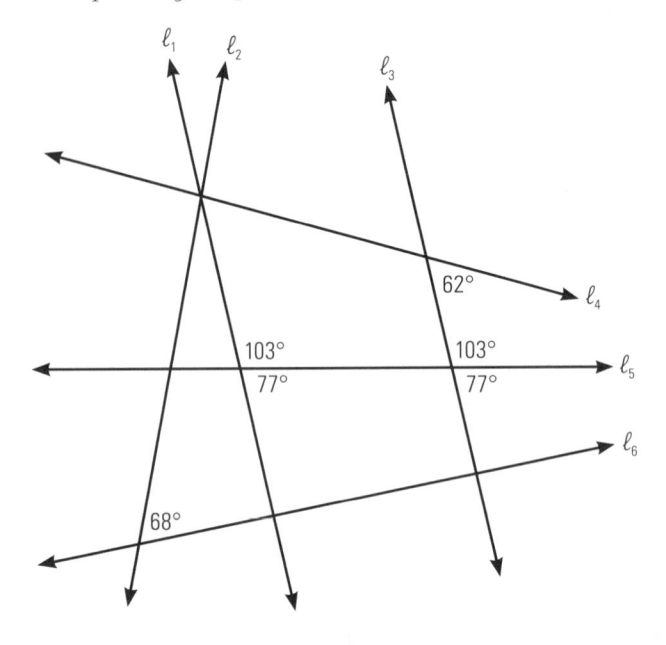

5. ∠1 = 57°

6. 4°

7.
SOLVING ANGLE MEASURES	
Angle measure	Reason
∠1 = 54°	It is vertically opposite the 54° angle.
∠2 = 54°	It is an alternate interior angle to ∠1.
∠3 = 97°	It is supplementary to the 83° angle.
∠4 = 83°	It is an interior angle on the same side of the transversal as ∠3, so is supplementary to it. Also, it is vertically opposite 83°.

8. ∠1 = 122°

   ∠2 = 90°

9. ∠2 = 127°

PRACTISE YOUR NEW SKILLS, P. 246

1. ∠1 is supplementary to the 112° angle.

   ∠1 = 68°

∠2 is supplementary to the 112° angle, and vertically opposite ∠1.

∠2 = 68°

∠3 is an interior angle on the same side of the transversal as 112°, and is an alternate interior angle to ∠2.

∠3 = 68°

∠4 is supplementary to the 60° angle.

∠4 = 120°

∠5 is vertically opposite ∠3.

∠5 = 68°

2. ∠1 = 57°

∠2 = 33°

3.

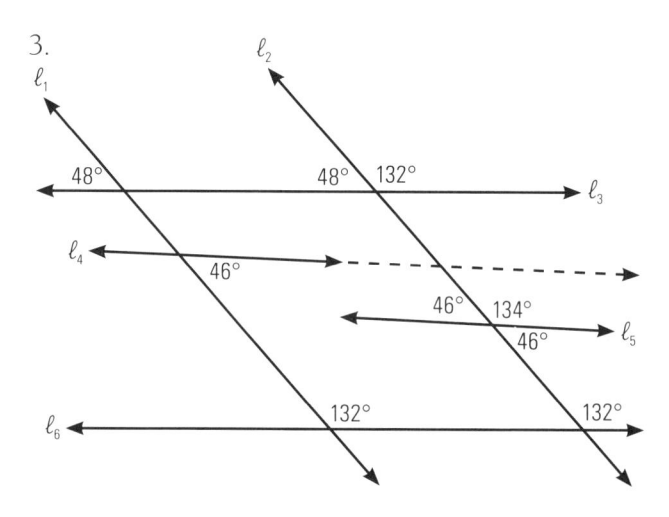

ℓ_1 is parallel to ℓ_2 because, with transversal ℓ_3, the corresponding angles are equal.

ℓ_3 is parallel to ℓ_6 because, with transversal ℓ_2, two corresponding angles are 132°.

ℓ_4 is parallel to ℓ_5 because, with transversals ℓ_1 and ℓ_2, the corresponding angles are equal.

4. The top of stud A must be moved 1° to the right, to change the 89° angle to 90°.

The top of stud B must be moved 1° to the left, to change the 91° angle to 90°.

The top of stud D must be moved 1° to the left, to change the 134° angle to 135°.

CHAPTER TEST, P. 248

1. a) obtuse   b) acute
   c) reflex   d) straight
   e) right   f) obtuse

2.

Angle	Complement	Supplement	Resulting angle measures after angle is bisected
58°	32°	122°	29°
94°	Does not exist, because angle is greater than 90°.	86°	47°
87°	Does not exist, because angle is greater than 90°.	93°	43.5°
153°	Does not exist, because angle is greater than 90°.	27°	76.5°
65°	25°	115°	32.5°

3. a) alternate interior angles
   b) interior angles on the same side of the transversal
   c) vertically opposite angles
   d) corresponding angles

4. ∠2 is supplementary to the 62° angle.

   ∠2 = 118°

   ∠4 is vertically opposite to the 62° angle or supplementary to ∠2.

   ∠4 = 62°

   ∠3 is the alternate interior angle to the 62° angle, and is an interior angle on the same side of the transversal as ∠2.

   ∠3 = 62°

   ∠1 is an interior angle on the same side of the transversal to the 67° angle.

   ∠1 = 113°

5. ∠1 is an interior angle on the same side of the transversal (line A) as ∠D (68°).

   ∠1 = 112°

   ∠2 is the corresponding angle to ∠C (75°), given transversal AC.

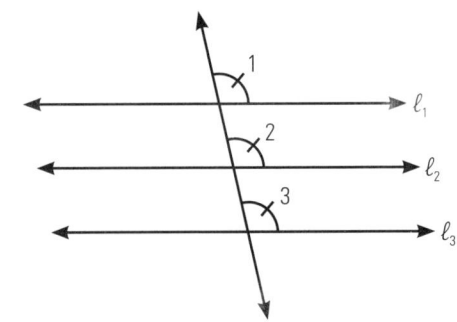

   ∠2 = 75°

6. ∠1 = 23°

   ∠2 = 23°

7. a) ∠1 = 72°   b) ∠2 = 18°

8. a) 90°   b) 185°

9. Fred is correct. ∠1 is equal to ∠3 and ℓ_1 is parallel to ℓ_3 since the corresponding angles are equal.

10. ∠2 = ∠7

    Using ℓ_1 and ℓ_2, and transversal t_1, ∠2 and ∠7 are alternate interior angles.

    ∠5 = ∠7

    Using ℓ_1 and ℓ_2, and transversal t_1, ∠5 and ∠7 are corresponding angles.

    ∠4 = ∠7

    Using ℓ_1 and ℓ_3, and transversal t_1, ∠4 and ∠7 are alternate interior angles.

CHAPTER 6
SIMILAR FIGURES
6.1 SIMILAR POLYGONS

BUILD YOUR SKILLS, P. 257

1. LP = 7 cm

   OP = 6 cm

   ON = 4 cm

   MN = 6 cm

2. 22 feet by 12 feet

3. ABCD~QRST and EFGH~LKJI

4. Corresponding angles:

   ∠A = ∠G

   ∠B = ∠H

   ∠C = ∠I

   ∠D = ∠J

   ∠E = ∠K

   ∠F = ∠L

   Angle measures:

   ∠D = 73°

   ∠H = 21°

   ∠E = 40°

5. ∠B = 100°

   ∠X = 32°

   ∠C = 48°

6. w = 42°

   x = 45 cm

   y = 70°

   z = 17.5 cm

7. length: 16.25 cm; width: 12 cm; height: 7 cm

8. length: 20 in; width: 17.5 in; height: 13.5 in

9. Box 1: 9 cm by 6 cm by 3 cm;
   Box 2: 6.75 cm by 4.5 cm by 2.25 cm;
   Box 3: 5.1 cm by 3.4 cm by 1.7 cm

PRACTISE YOUR NEW SKILLS, P. 262

1. 855 cm or 8.55 m

2. about 3.1 m and 3.75 m

3. 108°, 204°, 63°, 120°, and 45°

4. 48 mm by 20 mm; 1920 mm by 800 mm

5. Funnel 1: height about 13.3 cm, spout length about 8.3 cm, spout diameter about 1.7 cm

   Funnel 2: height about 10.7 cm, spout length about 6.7 cm, spout diameter about 1.3 cm

   Funnel 3: height 8 cm, spout length 5 cm, spout diameter 1 cm

6.2 DETERMINING IF TWO POLYGONS ARE SIMILAR

BUILD YOUR SKILLS, P. 266

1. Yes, the two hexagons are similar. If a hexagon is regular, all the angles are congruent and all sides are congruent. Therefore, the two hexagons Pierre drew will have congruent corresponding angles, and are similar.

2. Yes, the picture and poster are similar.

3. Zora is correct if she is comparing rectangle ABCD to rectangle PQRS. But if Zora compares the longer sides of the two rectangles, and the shorter sides of the two rectangles, she will find that they are similar. She can compare rectangle ABCD to rectangle QRSP. Since $\frac{100}{50}$ is equal to $\frac{60}{30}$, Zora can say that rectangle ABCD is similar to rectangle QRSP.

4. Yes, it is true that if you increase or decrease the side lengths of a figure by the same factor, the resulting figure will be similar to the original. If you multiply or divide by the same number, you are keeping the same proportion.

   Examples will vary.

5. The framed picture is not similar to the original.

6. The two cylinders are not similar.

PRACTISE YOUR NEW SKILLS, P. 269

1. a) 2500 m   b) 7.5 cm

2. The prisms are not similar.

3. Colin is correct as there is enough information given to determine that corresponding sides are proportional and all the angles are right angles.

4. Mats 1 and 2 are similar. Mat 3 is not similar to mat 1 or mat 2.

5. Consider two rectangles, one with sides ℓ and w, and the other with sides double the length, 2ℓ and $2w$. The area of the second rectangle is 4 times the area of the first; this is not the same proportion as the sides.

6.3 DRAWING SIMILAR POLYGONS

BUILD YOUR SKILLS, P. 272

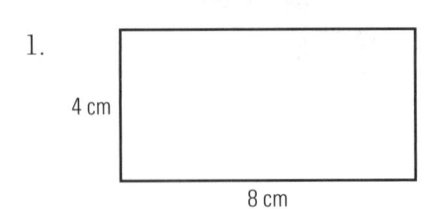

1.

2. See diagram on the next page

3. 1 in:5.5 ft

4. scale factor: 1.25

5. 26 cm by 15.6 cm by 6.5 cm

6. length: 70 cm; upper portion: 14 cm; half-width: 35 cm

PRACTISE YOUR NEW SKILLS, P. 275

1. 75 mm

2.

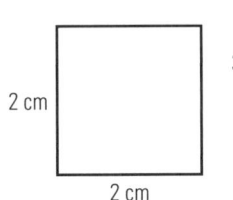

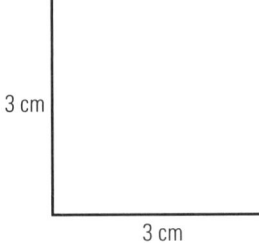

   a) Yes, the squares are similar because the sides are proportional.

   b) No, the rectangles will not be similar.

3.

4. a) scale factor: approximately 0.0039

   b) 0.7 cm

5. a) 1.25 feet   b) 1:8

6.3 Drawing Similar Polygons, Build Your Skills, Question 2.

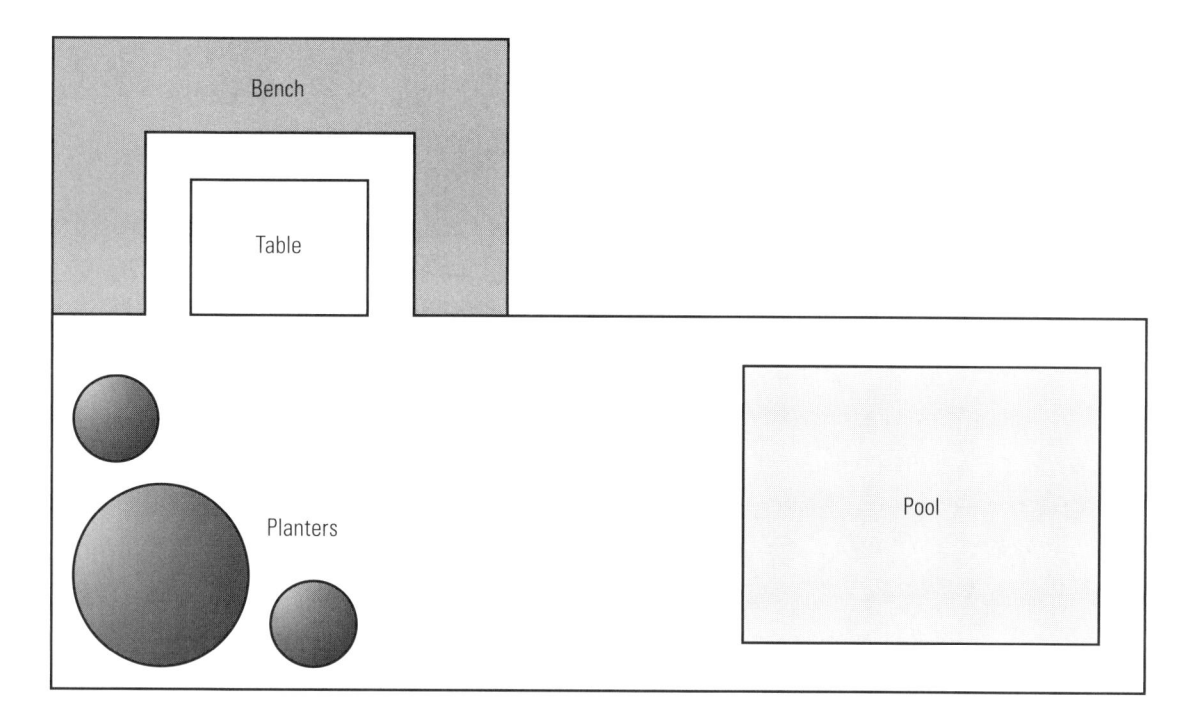

6.4 SIMILAR TRIANGLES

BUILD YOUR SKILLS, P. 278

1. a) $x \approx 3.9$ cm

    b) $x \approx 29.1$ ft

    c) $c \approx 4.8$ m

2. ST ≈ 6.7 cm; you are not given enough information to find the length of the third side, TR.

3. No, not all isosceles triangles are similar.

4. You will be 10.5 m higher.

5. 17.6 cm and 36.8 cm

6. $\triangle ABC \sim \triangle ACD \sim \triangle CBD$

PRACTISE YOUR NEW SKILLS, P. 282

1. ED ≈ 4.7 m

2. No, the triangular blocks of wood are not similar. While the triangular faces are similar, both blocks are 2 inches thick. In order for the blocks to be similar, their thicknesses would have to be proportional.

3. $\angle F = \angle X$

    $\angle G = \angle Y$

    $\angle H = \angle Z$

    FG ~ XY

    GH ~ YZ

    FH ~ XZ

4. about 17 ft

CHAPTER TEST, P. 284

1. 5 in, 15 in, 25 in, 35 in, and 60 in

2. $x = 7.2$ m

   $y \approx 3.5$ m

3. The river is approximately 42.7 m wide.

4. The man is approximately 2 m tall.

5. When the side lengths of a rectangle are doubled, the area is quadrupled.

6. When the ratios are rounded to 2 decimal places, the shapes are similar.

7. a) True, all equilateral triangles are similar. In equilateral triangles, the angles are always 60° and the ratios of the sides will always be equal.

   b) False, all isosceles triangles are not similar. The angles do not need to be equal, nor do the sides have to be proportional.

   c) True, congruent triangles are similar. The corresponding angles are equal and the ratios of sides will be 1:1.

8. The scale factor of the projection is about 8.3.

9. 17′ is represented by 7.8″.

   6′ is represented by 2.8″.

   5′2″ is represented by 2.4″.

   7′2″ is represented by 3.4″.

10. The painting will be 31.25 inches by 43.75 inches.

11. 95.7 cm by 126.5 cm

CHAPTER 7: TRIGONOMETRY OF RIGHT TRIANGLES
7.1 THE PYTHAGOREAN THEOREM

BUILD YOUR SKILLS, P. 290

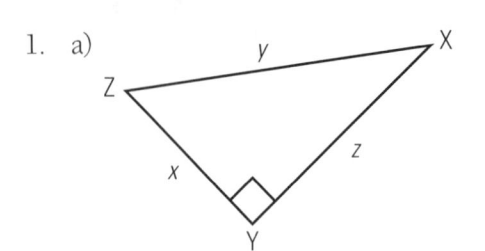

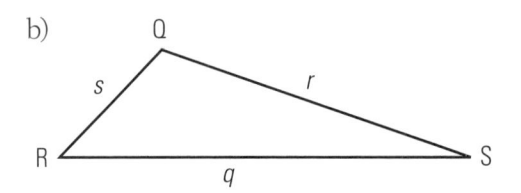

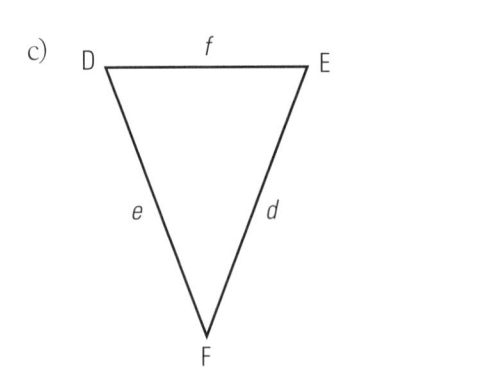

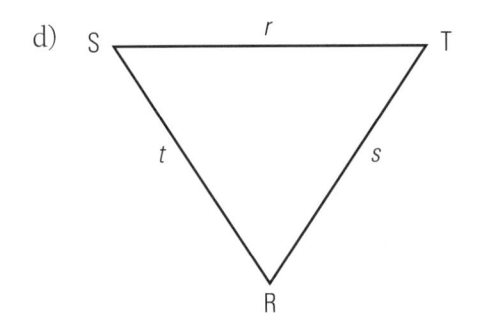

1. a)

   b)

   c)

   d)

2. a)

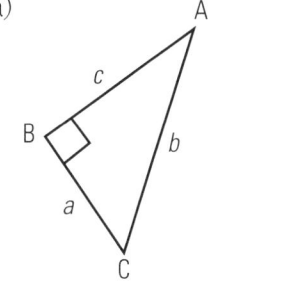

b)

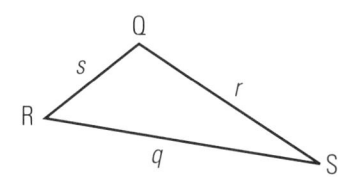

c)

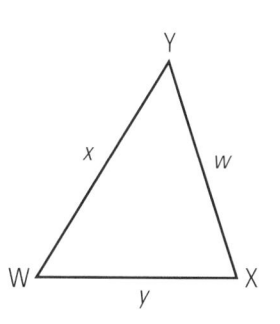

d)

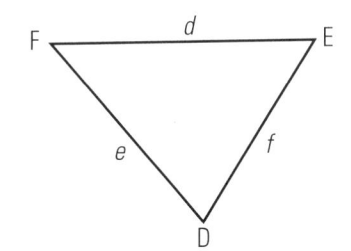

3. In △ABC:

$a^2 + c^2 = (x + y)^2$

In △ABD:

$x^2 + z^2 = c^2$

In △BDC:

$z^2 + y^2 = a^2$

4.

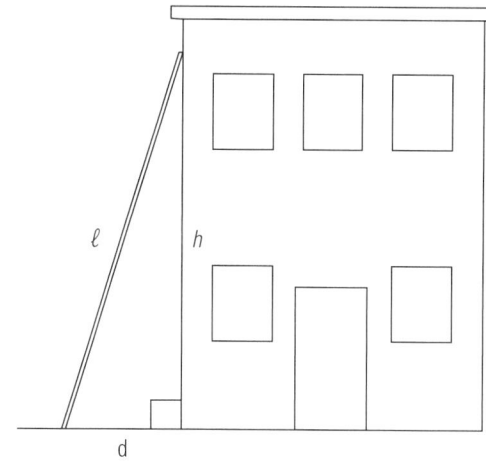

$h^2 + d^2 = \ell^2$

5. $x = \sqrt{z^2 - y^2}$

   $y = \sqrt{z^2 - x^2}$

6. $x \approx 8.0$ cm

   $y \approx 6.7$ cm

7. approximately 12.5 feet

8. Your route would be about 83.7 m shorter by walking diagonally across the field.

PRACTISE YOUR NEW SKILLS, P. 295

1. approximately 10 ft 7.2 in

2. approximately 14.4 m

3. approximately 11.1 m

4. approximately 41 in

5. approximately 50.9 km

7.2 THE SINE RATIO

BUILD YOUR SKILLS, P. 298

1. a) sin A ≈ 0.62   b) sin A ≈ 0.54

2. a) sin 10° = 0.1736   b) sin 48° = 0.7431
   c) sin 62° = 0.8829   d) sin 77° = 0.9744

3. sin 90° = 1

   Possible reasons will vary.

4. a) a ≈ 8.2 cm
   b) x ≈ 3.8 cm

5. about 7 ft

6. about 8.6 m

7. a) h ≈ 14.3 mm
   b) h ≈ 12.9 cm

8. approximately 5.3 m long

9. about 22 m

10. about 404.5 m

11. approximately 203.9 m

12. about 1.9 m

PRACTISE YOUR NEW SKILLS, P. 306

1. a) sin A ≈ 0.6371   b) sin B ≈ 0.7191

2. a) x ≈ 17.9 cm   b) y ≈ 12.5 cm

3. about 5.5 m

4. about 8.6 m

5. about 41.7 m

7.3 THE COSINE RATIO

BUILD YOUR SKILLS, P. 310

1. a) cos 23° = 0.9205

   sin 67° = 0.9205

   b) cos 83° = 0.1219

   sin 7° = 0.1219

   c) cos 45° = 0.7071

   sin 45° = 0.7071

   d) cos 37° = 0.7986

   sin 53° = 0.7986

2. a) x ≈ 8.2 cm   b) x ≈ 1.7 cm
   c) x ≈ 8.6 cm   d) x ≈ 12.2 cm

3. about 5.4 m

4. about 9.8 yards

5. about 6.2 m

6. about 14.1 m

7. about 11.6 m

8. about 502 km

PRACTISE YOUR NEW SKILLS, P. 315

1. a) x ≈ 3.6 cm   b) a ≈ 4.8 m
   c) r ≈ 9.5 cm   d) ℓ ≈ 3.1 m

2. approximately 17.3 m

3. approximately 23.7 m

4. about 1.24 km

5. about 8.49 km

6. about 3.42 m

7.4 THE TANGENT RATIO

BUILD YOUR SKILLS, P. 320

1. a) $x \approx 9.5$ m   b) $a \approx 22.4$ in
   c) $r \approx 2.4$ m   d) $p \approx 7.9$ in

2. about 412 m

3. about 2.1 m

PRACTISE YOUR NEW SKILLS, P. 321

1. about 21 m
2. about 9 m
3. about 5.5 ft
4. about 141.1 m
5. about 12.9 ft
6. about 373 m

7.5 FINDING ANGLES AND SOLVING RIGHT TRIANGLES

BUILD YOUR SKILLS, P. 325

1. a) $D \approx 33°$
   b) $F \approx 26°$
   c) $G \approx 67°$
   d) $H \approx 89°$

2. $\angle X \approx 61°$
3. about 62°
4. about 54°
5. about 38°
6. about 51°

7. $r \approx 7.3$ m
   $q \approx 4.9$ m
   $\angle Q = 42°$

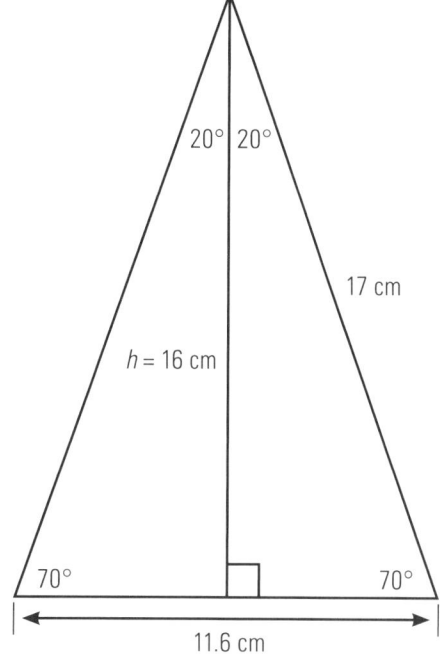

8. (triangle: 20°/20° at apex, 70°/70° at base, sides 17 cm, h = 16 cm, base 11.6 cm)

9. width: about 10.6 yards; total height of building: about 4.9 yards.

10. a) $\angle R \approx 28°$
    $\angle S \approx 62°$
    $t \approx 3.2$ m
    b) $\ell \approx 6.6$ cm
    $\angle M \approx 45°$
    $\angle L \approx 45°$

11. pole height: about 8 m; the cable is attached about 16 m away from the pole.

12. a) $a \approx 23$ cm   b) $b \approx 18$ cm
    c) $c \approx 16$ cm   d) $d \approx 12$ cm

PRACTISE YOUR NEW SKILLS, P. 333

1. a) ∠A ≈ 31°   b) ∠B ≈ 48°

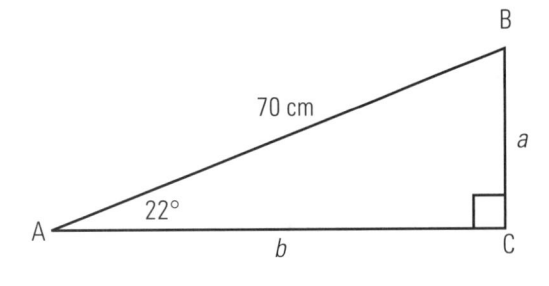

2.

∠B = 68°

a = 26 cm

b = 65 cm

3. about 18.4°

4. about 24.1 ft

5. The driveway is about 4.7 m long. The garage entrance is about 3.6 m into the lot.

6. about 31°

CHAPTER TEST, P. 336

1. 130 cm

2. about 181 m

3. about 1.67 km

4. The ramp rose about 3.1 m.

   Because of similarity of triangles, a 24-m ramp would rise double that of a 12-m ramp, or about 6.2 m.

5. about 29.2 m

6. about 17.3 m

7. about 423.6 m

8. a) about 7.2 m

   b) about 2.4 m

9. about 8.2 m

10. about 6 m

11. about 25°